D1261371

Religion and the Politics of Ethnic Identity in Bahia, Brazil

New World Diasporas

UNIVERSITY PRESS OF FLORIDA

Florida A&M University, Tallahassee
Florida Atlantic University, Boca Raton
Florida Gulf Coast University, Ft. Myers
Florida International University, Miami
Florida State University, Tallahassee
New College of Florida, Sarasota
University of Central Florida, Orlando
University of Florida, Gainesville
University of North Florida, Jacksonville
University of South Florida, Tampa
University of West Florida, Pensacola

New World Diasporas

Edited by Kevin A. Yelvington

This series seeks to stimulate critical perspectives on diaspora processes in the New World. Representations of "race" and ethnicity, the origins and consequences of nationalism, migratory streams and the advent of transnationalism, the dialectics of "homelands" and diasporas, trade networks, gender relations in immigrant communities, the politics of displacement and exile, and the utilization of the past to serve the present are among the phenomena addressed by original, provocative research in disciplines such as anthropology, history, political science, and sociology.

International Editorial Board

Herman L. Bennett, Rutgers University
Gayle K. Brunelle, California State University at Fullerton
Jorge Duany, Universidad de Puerto Rico
Sherri Grasmuck, Temple University
Daniel Mato, Universidad Central de Venezuela
Kyeyoung Park, University of California at Los Angeles
Richard Price, College of William and Mary
Sally Price, College of William and Mary
Vicki L. Ruiz, Arizona State University
John F. Stack, Jr., Florida International University
Mia Tuan, University of Oregon
Peter Wade, University of Manchester

More Than Black: Afro-Cubans in Tampa, by Susan D. Greenbaum (2002)
Carnival and the Formation of a Caribbean Transnation, by Philip W. Scher (2003)
Dominican Migration: Transnational Perspectives, edited by Ernesto Sagás and Sintia Molina (2004)
Salvadoran Migration to Southern California: Redefining El Hermano Lejano, by Beth Baker-Cristales (2004)
The Chrysanthemum and the Song: Music, Memory, and Identity in the South American Japanese Diaspora, by Dale A. Olsen (2004)
Andean Diaspora: The Tiwanaku Colonies and the Origins of South American Empire, by Paul S. Goldstein (2005)
Migration and Vodou, by Karen E. Richman (2005)
True-Born Maroons, by Kenneth Bilby (2006)
The Tears of Hispaniola: Haitian and Dominican Diaspora Memory, by Lucía M. Suárez (2006)
Dominican-Americans and the Politics of Empowerment, by Ana Aparicio (2006)
Nuer-American Passages: Global Migration in the Twentieth Century, by Dianna J. Shandy (2006)
Religion and the Politics of Ethnic Identity in Bahia, Brazil, by Stephen Selka (2007)

Religion and the Politics of Ethnic Identity in Bahia, Brazil

Stephen Selka

University Press of Florida
Gainesville
Tallahassee
Tampa
Boca Raton
Pensacola
Orlando
Miami
Jacksonville
Ft. Myers
Sarasota

Copyright 2007 by Stephen Selka
Printed in the United States of America on acid-free paper
All rights reserved

12 11 10 09 08 07   6 5 4 3 2 1

Library of Congress Cataloging-in-Publication Data
Selka, Stephen.
Religion and the politics of ethnic identity in Bahia, Brazil / Stephen Selka.
p. cm. — (New World diasporas)
Includes bibliographical references (p.) and index.
ISBN 978-0-8130-3171-2 (alk. paper)
1. Brazil—Religion. 2. Salvador (Brazil)—Religion. 3. Religion and politics—Brazil—Salvador.
4. Ethnicity—Brazil—Salvador. 5. Ethnicity—Religious aspects I. Title.
BL2590.B7S45 2007
305.800981'42--dc22
2007027405

The University Press of Florida is the scholarly publishing agency for the State University
System of Florida, comprising Florida A&M University, Florida Atlantic University, Florida
Gulf Coast University, Florida International University, Florida State University, New College
of Florida, University of Central Florida, University of Florida, University of North Florida,
University of South Florida, and University of West Florida.

University Press of Florida
15 Northwest 15th Street
Gainesville, FL 32611-2079
www.upf.com

All photographs are by the author unless otherwise noted.

BL2590
.B7
S45
2007

D 154704859

Those who say that religion has nothing to do with politics do not know what religion means.

Mahatma Gandhi

Contents

List of Figures   viii
Acknowledgments   ix

1. Introduction   1
2. Religion and Race in Brazil   9
3. Catholicism and Afro-Brazilian Identity   48
4. Candomblé, Afro-Brazilian Culture, and Anti-Racism   73
5. Alternative Identities, Emergent Politics   97
6. The Politics of Afro-Brazilian Identity   120

Notes   153
References   157
Index   170

figures

1. A view of Cachoeira   10
2. Cachoeiran women participating in a Candomblé ceremony   38
3. A Candomblé initiate making a public debut   39
4. The church of Our Lady of the Rosary of the Blacks in Salvador   52
5. Escrava Anastácia at the church of Our Lady of the Rosary of the Blacks   53
6. Statues of the orixás in Salvador   75
7. A banner featuring images of Africa in Salvador during Carnaval 2002   86
8. The Catedral da Fé of the Igreja Universal do Reino de Deus in Salvador   101

Acknowledgments

I would like to thank a number of people without whom this book would not have been possible. First and foremost, I thank my parents, whose dedication to scholarship and learning inspired my decision to become an anthropologist. Your moral and material support over these years will always be remembered. I could not have completed this book without the help of my wife, Kristen, who has been by my side ever since this project was just a vague idea in my head. She provided encouragement when I needed it, consolation when things were not going my way, and an occasional swift kick in the ass to get me going again when I faltered.

Early on in college and graduate school, Jake Early and Susan Brown encouraged my interest in the study of syncretism and religious complexity. Later, Jim Collins helped me refine the theoretical perspective from which this book is written; Liliana Goldín coached me as I wrote the grant proposals that funded my fieldwork; and Louise Burkhart provided candid feedback and close editing of the text (and corrected me on the finer points of Catholic doctrine that had apparently escaped me in catechism). In addition, I benefited greatly from John Burdick's encouragement and support over the years.

My initial visits to Brazil would not have been possible without financial support from the Department of Anthropology, Graduate Student Organization, and Benevolent Foundation at the University at Albany. In addition, I am very grateful to have been awarded a grant from the National Science Foundation to fund my extended fieldwork. In Brazil, my contacts at the Universidade Federal da Bahia (UFBA), especially Mark Cravalho and Miriam Rabelo, helped me get established in Brazil and have never hesitated to provide assistance whenever I needed it. Thanks are also due to Jeferson Bacelar and Livio Sansone at the Centro dos Estudos Afro-Oreintais (CEAO) in Salvador.

In Chicago, where I began working on my manuscript, I benefited from the encouragement and advice of a number of people, including Willie Hart of the

Friends of the Amistad Research Center and Michael Hanchard of Northwestern University. In 2004, I moved to New Orleans to teach at Tulane University and to continue working on my book. I am grateful to my colleagues at Tulane in the Department of Anthropology and Stone Center for Latin American Studies who provided support and votes of confidence, especially Vicki Bricker, Judie Maxwell, Chris Dunn, Martha Huggins, Adeline Masquelier, and Bob Hill.

Unfortunately, my time at Tulane was cut short by Hurricane Katrina. Back in Chicago, however, I was welcomed by so many people who went out of their way to accommodate a displaced colleague trying to finish a book. Special thanks to Jean Comaroff from the Department of Anthropology and Dain Borges from Latin American Studies at the University of Chicago; Bill Leonard from the Department of Anthropology, Richard Joseph from the Program of African Studies, and Brodwyn Fischer from the Latin American Studies Department at Northwestern University; and John Monaghan from the Department of Anthropology at the University of Illinois at Chicago.

Most importantly, I would like to thank everyone who participated in this study: the members of the Irmandade do Rosário, members of the Pastoral Afro and the Movimento Evangélico Progressista (MEP), activists in the Movimento Negro Unificado (MNU) and the Partido dos Trabalhadores (PT), and all of the *candomblecistas* and evangelicals who patiently and generously shared their time and insights with me. Finally, I give particular thanks to Kevin Yelvington, Eli Bortz, and Susan Albury for their editorial guidance on this project.

1

Introduction

Is a holy war raging in Brazil? By many accounts, evangelical Christians and practitioners of African-derived Candomblé are engaged in a battle for Brazilian souls. While I was living in Brazil between 2000 and 2002, for example, several reports of evangelical Christians attacking Candomblé *terreiros* (temples) circulated in the news. For some Afro-Brazilians, however, these attacks are more than just religious antagonisms. Many Candomblé practitioners equate evangelical attacks on their terreiros with racism. In fact, the symbolic connection between African-derived religion and Afro-Brazilian identity is close enough that images of Candomblé are often featured prominently in antiracist campaigns in Brazil. "Without Candomblé, there would be no black movement!" exclaimed a practitioner who lives in Salvador, the capital of the state of Bahia. Candomblé is deeply rooted in Bahia, and for my friend and many others like her, African-derived religion and the struggle against racism are intimately linked.

Yet in my time in Brazil, and contrary to much of what I had read about the topic, I found that the relationship between religion and racial consciousness is more complicated than a simple dichotomy between Candomblé antiracist activists and the evangelical race traitors. Later in our interview, for example, the Candomblé practitioner I quoted above admitted that none of the other members of her terreiro were involved with antiracist politics. Furthermore, while I was in Brazil I worked closely with evangelical Christians in Bahia who are passionately devoted to the struggle against racism. In fact, my research suggested that in general, involvement with one or another religious group was not significantly associated with more or less concern about racism. Nevertheless, Candomblé remains a potent emblem of racial consciousness. This book explores this puzzle by examining the role of religion in the politics of Afro-Brazilian identity.

The anthropological fieldwork upon which this book is based took place in the northeastern state of Bahia, known for its rich Afro-Brazilian traditions and as a center of racial consciousness in Brazil. Activists in Bahia today are confronting racism and racial inequalities that until recently many Brazilians refused to acknowledge. Many groups engaging these problems are religious, and ethnic affirmation based in African-derived religion is at the heart of the antiracism movement in Bahia. Christian organizations, however, vary widely in their views about such affirmations of Afro-Brazilian culture.

An estimated 15 percent of Brazil's population is Protestant, about two-thirds of which are Pentecostals, the fastest growing religious group in Brazil today (Freston 1994). While most Brazilians still identify themselves as Catholic, many people are at the same time involved with African-derived religions such as Candomblé. My fieldwork centered on the capital of Bahia, Salvador, considered "the Rome of Afro-Brazilian religion," and on a smaller town in the interior of Bahia called Cachoeira, widely known for its deeply rooted Afro-Brazilian traditions.

For many Bahians involved with the antiracism movement, activism goes hand in hand with affirming one's ethnic identity through the practice of Candomblé. While some groups in the Catholic Church encourage such cultural affirmations, involvement with Candomblé is forbidden for the growing number of Pentecostal Christians in Brazil. In fact, only a small percentage of Brazilians report being involved with Candomblé (Prandi 1995). Yet many of the images publicized by cultural organizations, international tourist agencies, and the media suggest a single, uncontested way of being "Afro-Brazilian" based in traditional Afro-Brazilian culture. Bahian communities are in fact divided largely along religious lines on questions of Afro-Brazilian identity.

Accordingly, J. Lorand Matory (2005, 81) argues that Afro-Brazilian identity politics provides a counterpoint to the emphasis on homogeneity in discussions of the construction of national and ethnic "imagined communities" (Anderson 1983). In other words, Afro-Brazilian identity is based on multiple and overlapping imagined communities that are themselves based on different religions (Catholicism, Protestantism, Candomblé) and national identities (Brazilian, Jejê, Nâgo, etc.). In fact, Protestant, Catholic, and Candomblé organizations assign radically different meanings to traditional Afro-Brazilian symbols and practices. This book explores the ways Bahians of African descent engage these religious meanings as they construct their identities and how these identities articulate with discourses about anti-racism and Afro-Brazilian culture.

In the following pages I advance three main arguments about the relationship between religion, Afro-Brazilian ethnicity, and identity politics in Bahia.

First, as I have already indicated, I stress the heterogeneity of Afro-Brazilian ethnoreligious identities. The focus on "Afro-Brazilian culture" among anthropologists, activists, the tourism industry, and others has implied that there is a well-bounded and stable set of traditions that people of African descent in Brazil share. By contrast, I focus on competing representations of what it means to be Afro-Brazilian. As I explore in this book, this multiplicity of identities complicates—and in a sense drives—mobilization efforts in the black consciousness movement.

Competing discourses about mixture and purity are central to debates about black identity in Brazil, particularly the opposition between discourses of *mestiçagem* (hybridity) and ethnic absolutism and, as I explore in this book, the parallel opposition between syncretism and anti-syncretism. My second argument is that although hybridity is at the center of representations of Brazilian identity, discourses of difference have long been a part of the landscape and have entered the realm of public discourse in Brazil in the past decade or so through discussions of racism and debates about affirmative action. This, along with the recognition that Brazilians regularly employ distinctions between white and nonwhite in their everyday speech (Sheriff 2001), should lead us to explore the complementary rather than mutually exclusive relationship between discourses of mixture and opposition.

Finally, I argue that we need approaches to understanding Brazil's black movement that directly engage, rather than attempt to explain away, the multitude of competing ways of being Afro-Brazilian. Much of what has been written about the black movement in Brazil has, on the one hand, relied on too sharp a distinction between culture and politics and, on the other, presented the movement as something more unified than it actually is. I argue that the black movement consists of a whole host of overlapping networks of cultural and political practice in which various notions of what it means to be Afro-Brazilian compete, and in so doing I hope to contribute a more nuanced perspective to ongoing discussions of Afro-Brazilian identity politics.

Race and Religion in Brazil

Much of what has been written about Brazilian race relations over the past few decades has focused on establishing that racism and racial discrimination exist in Brazil. It is clear that they do. In some sense, then, this research has helped to debunk the Brazilian "myth of racial democracy," the long-standing fiction that Brazil is a place free of racism. Yet this is a complicated issue: as a Brazilian colleague of mine often says, "The myth is a myth." That is, much of the writing about the ideology of racial democracy has downplayed the extent to which Brazilians are aware of how racism operates in their own country and in their daily lives. Thus, one of the aims of this book is to address the distinctive ways that Brazilians conceive of and struggle against racism and racial discrimination. Often, these ways are not as explicit or as confrontational as those of the American civil rights movement, but that does not mean that Afro-Brazilians are passive dupes of the dominant racial ideologies.

A considerable amount of what has been written about race relations in Brazil takes a comparative perspective, often emphasizing Brazil's parallels and contrasts with the United States. Recent debates about the study of race in Brazil have emphasized the importance not only of examining racism in Brazil, but also looking at what is distinctive about race and race relations there. Some have argued that the very notions of "race" and "race relations" used in many studies are specifically American concepts that obscure the way such things are done in Brazil. (While teaching a course entitled "Race in Brazil," I half-jokingly suggested to the class that we modify the title by adding punctuation: "'Race' in Brazil?"). Brazilians often deny that separate races exist in Brazil—only shades of color. Although I disagree with the contention that the Brazilian black-consciousness movement is a result of U.S. intellectual imperialism (Bourdieu and Wacquant 1999; cf. Hanchard 2003; French 2000), I agree that we need to understand Brazil on its own terms.

Partly because separate racial identities are not generally understood as public and political in Brazil in the same way that they are in the United States, for example, Afro-Brazilians do not tend to link race and politics. Voting patterns do not conform to racial lines as they often do in the United States, and the black-consciousness movement has not gained wide popular appeal in Brazil. As I explore here, Afro-Brazilian identity in Bahia is largely constituted through culture rather than through ancestry or politics, and religion has a particularly important role to play in this respect (cf. Sansone 2003; K. Butler 1998a).

Although I am skeptical about unqualified comparisons between the United States and Brazil, I believe that recognizing what people of African descent in the New World share is crucial. On this issue, anthropologists, especially those who have conducted ethnographic studies in Bahia, have a long history of focusing on African "cultural survivals" in the New World (Herskovits 1941). While such work has been commendable in a number of ways, this book moves sharply away from this approach. I do not discount cultural continuities, yet I stress that they are not simple artifacts passed down from generation to generation (cf. Mintz and Price 1992). That is, I focus on how cultural continuities are constructed in the cultural imaginations of people of African descent rather than on how they are rooted in some primordial cultural substrate. Ultimately, then, my emphasis is more on the common conditions—historical and current—that people of African descent share rather than on any specific cultural content. Although these conditions are often difficult to specify, people of African descent have commonly been affected by and/or involved with processes such as geographical dislocation, sociopolitical marginalization, and, more recently, ethnoracial mobilization.

Bahia, Brazil

My ongoing anthropological fieldwork in Bahia began in the summer of 1998 when I made my first trip to Salvador to study Portuguese. I returned to Bahia to conduct extended fieldwork between 2000 and 2002, and I spent my first eight months living in Cachoeira, a quiet town located in the interior of Bahia. I chose to work in Cachoeira mainly because it is regarded as a center of traditional Afro-Brazilian culture; in addition, it was also a relatively easy and friendly place to live while I improved my Portuguese and got used to living in Brazil.

Eventually I moved to Salvador, Bahia's coastal capital, where I lived for the remainder of my extended fieldwork. If Cachoeira is the home of traditional Afro-Brazilian culture, then Salvador is the center of Afro-Brazilian modernism and social activism. My work in Salvador focused largely on the black-consciousness movement, which, at least in its explicit manifestations, was virtually nonexistent in Cachoeira. A notable exception to this lack of activism in Cachoeira is the festival of the Sisterhood of Our Lady of Good Death (Boa Morte). This yearly celebration draws cultural and political activists from Salvador and beyond and thus forms a "bridge" between rural Cachoeira and urban Salvador. For this reason, the festival of Boa Morte became central to my research, and I returned to Bahia in the summers of 2004 and 2005 to attend the celebration, which I have described in detail elsewhere (Selka 2003). This book, however, focuses primarily on my work in Salvador, and my focus is mainly on religious practitioners involved with the various expressions of the black movement in that city.

During my fieldwork I employed a multi-methodological and multi-sited approach to ethnographic research that involved engaging in participant observation, conducting interviews, and administering questionnaires among the members of different religious communities. My interviews and questionnaires concerned how people perceive racism in Brazilian society and in their own lives, how they relate to anti-racist organizations, and how they interpret different religious discourses about these issues. Most of my research activities took place in churches and temples, in people's homes, and at public religious events and festivals.

Between 2000 and 2002 I taped thirty-one formal interviews and conducted an additional thirty informal interviews in Bahia during my extended fieldwork. These focused on leaders and members of religious organizations, activists, tourism workers (in addition to tourists themselves), as well as Bahians with no particular religious or political involvements. I also administered questionnaires concerning demographic information, past and present patterns of religious practice, different views of Afro-Brazilian ethnic identity, and the ways in which people experience racism. I attempted to divide the questionnaires proportionally among Catholic, Protestant, and African-derived religious organizations. With the help of local assistants I administered fifty-eight in Cachoeira and Salvador. Most of the questionnaire was developed from my preliminary fieldwork, and additional sections were adapted from the Multigroup Ethnic Identity Measure (MEIM) (Phinney 1992) and the Racism and Life Experience Scales (RaLES) (Harrell 1997), which are surveys designed to measure how African Americans perceive their ethnic identities and experience racism.

Religion, Identity, and Politics

This book ultimately concerns the relationship between identity and politics. Provisionally, we might understand identity—or, more precisely, social identity—as the intersection of our personal selves and the social order. Often, we imagine our selves in terms of our desires and dispositions, and we think of the social order in terms of the possible paths we can follow or the roles we can play in life. In this view, our actual identities are formed where these intersect; for example, Afro-Brazilian identity can be understood as the interface of certain kinds of subjectivities with participation in certain kinds of cultural practices.

Yet neither our selves nor the social order are fixed or given. Thus, I contend that we have a hand in defining who we are and that we exercise some agency in shaping our lives. My approach is centered on practice theory, which mediates between two extremes in anthropological studies of identity. At one extreme are studies that focus on individual life histories without situating these narratives within the context of social processes. At the other end are those that center on how the social order is inscribed onto subjectivities while neglecting human agency.

In this book I focus on how processes of identity formation are intertwined with politics. That is, in the process of self-definition and identity construction, agents can work with or against the status quo, and our habits and daily practices tend to reproduce or resist the social order of which we are part. Seen in this way, the construction of identity is at least indirectly political. In fact, identities that may have previously been considered personal are now at the center of politics, as expressed in the dictum "the personal is political." For example, practices or "strategies" such as buying or boycotting certain products, openly affirming one's sexual orientation, or affirming one's ancestry have moved to the center of many social movements. This politics of identity, sometimes labeled by detractors as "political correctness," is an important characteristic of contemporary social movements that I will focus on in the following chapters in my attempt to understand the relationship between religion, Afro-Brazilian identity, and the struggle against racism.

In practice, of course, much of what we do straddles the fence between the reproduction of and resistance to the status quo; any particular action may both resist and reproduce the social order at the same time. A vote for a third-party candidate, for example, is a vote against the current administration, but the act of voting itself endorses the current political system as a whole. Even when social action explicitly aims at overturning the social order, it may ultimately end up reinforcing the status quo. Revolutionary movements in which the vanguard becomes as repressive as the regime it overturns are a good example of this.

The paradoxical interconnection of reproduction and resistance is apparent in the arena of Afro-Brazilian identity politics. In Bahia, debates about the formation of Afro-Brazilian identity tend to center on struggles over classification: for example, mixture versus purity, hybridity versus anti-hybridity, and syncretism versus anti-syncretism. Discourses of mixture, hybridity, and syncretism represent Afro-Brazilian identity as a combination of African and European practices and influences. The strength of this approach is that it denies a categorical difference between blacks and whites; without this difference, many argue, racism has no basis (Sansone 2003).

In fact, the ideology of mestiçagem has long been Brazil's official stance on race relations, and this ideology has worked to buttress the myth of racial democracy. How could racism exist in a place where everywhere—in people's bodies, in the food they eat, in the ways they worship—one sees the melding of the African and the European? As it turns out, however, racism has no trouble existing in places where hybridity is the dominant model for race relations (Hanchard 2003). The trouble is that racism exists in Brazil in spite of the ideology of racial democracy and mixture. In fact, many observers argue that the discourse of hybridity in Brazil obscures and directs attention away from underlying, value-laden oppositions between black and white. In this view, hybrid identities and practices that intend to undermine the basis for racism can end up masking it instead. In Brazil, then, discourses of purity, anti-hybridity, and anti-syncretism transgress the dominant ideology of race relations, while discourses of hybridity may reinforce such ideologies. Thus, many argue that in Brazil, anti-hybridity—a process of separation in which one makes clear what is African and what is not—and Afro-Brazilian ethnic affirmation form the basis of the struggle against racism. Again, things are not so simple: the problem is that the oppositional representations of blackness that emerge are often as essentialist, and perhaps in some ways as constraining, as the racist representations of blacks that they intend to counter.

Here I explore this paradox through an investigation of the intersection of religion, identity, and politics in Bahia. Along the way, I pay close attention to alternative ways of thinking about and constructing black identities in Brazil that are emerging in Afro-Brazilian communities, including those articulated by evangelical Christians. I highlight anti-essentialist approaches to identity and social mobilization that strive to affirm a multiplicity of possible ways of being Afro-Brazilian. I hope that my discussions of these issues will be useful not only to academics and students interested in the politics of identity, but to those involved with movements for social justice as well.

2

Religion and Race in Brazil

For a nation often cited as the most Catholic country in the world, Brazil's religious pluralism is particularly striking. While Catholicism still dominates as the nominal religion of the majority of Brazilians, a significant minority frequent Protestant churches, African-derived religious centers, and even Buddhist temples. This chapter focuses on how people of African descent involved with Catholic, evangelical Christian, and Candomblé organizations have engaged issues of Afro-Brazilian identity and struggled against racism in Brazil. In terms of numbers of members and relevance to the construction of ethnic identity, these are the most important religious groups in Afro-Brazilian communities today.

Brazil has often been referred to as a racial democracy. Proponents of this view have cited as evidence Brazil's lack of de jure segregation, seeming lack of overt racial hostility, and the existence of widespread racial mixture and cultural syncretism in Brazil. Since the 1970s, however, there has been increasing recognition of racial discrimination and major differences between the life chances of whites and nonwhites in Brazil. Especially in Bahia, those involved with the black movement often use religious symbols and practices to affirm a positive Afro-Brazilian ethnicity and to mobilize people against racism. In the chapters that follow I explore some of the complexities and contradictions that arise from the use of ethnic emblems in anti-racist campaigns.

The state of Bahia, where my anthropological fieldwork took place, is located in the northeastern region of Brazil. Bahia is a poor state in the poorest region in the country and is home to the highest proportion of people of African descent in Brazil. Most Afro-Brazilians are concentrated in a coastal area called the Recôncavo, once the home of Brazil's booming sugar plantations and the center of its slave trade. Today this area is an important focal point of racial consciousness in Brazil.

Figure 1. A hilltop view of a typical residential neighborhood in Cachoeira. Across the river is the town of São Felix.

The Recôncavo includes Salvador, the capital of Bahia, known as the Rome of Afro-Brazilian religion, and rural Cachoeira, renowned for its deeply rooted Afro-Brazilian traditions. The rural area of the Recôncavo in which Cachoeira is located, commonly referred to as "the interior," has served as Salvador's agricultural hinterland since the colonial period (Nishida 2003). For centuries, Salvador has represented urban cosmopolitanism in contrast to the rustic provincialism of the interior (Schwartz 1985).

Salvador is the fourth largest city in Brazil, with a population of about 2.6 million people (IBGE 2005). Hailed as the "most African city outside of Africa," Salvador is the cradle of Afro-Brazilian culture and the homeland of Candomblé. In colonial times, Salvador served as Brazil's major slave port, and the surrounding Recôncavo formed the core of the traditional sugar plantation economy. It was here that Afro-Brazilian cuisine and traditional practices such as *capoeira* (an Afro-Brazilian martial art) emerged. Although most major Afro-Brazilian political organizations and movements were founded in Rio de Janeiro and São Paulo, the Afro-Brazilian community in Salvador has done much to define, culturally speaking, what it means to be Afro-Brazilian.

Religion, Race, and Social Mobilization in Brazil

Catholicism has long been an integral part of religious practice in Afro-Brazilian communities. Roman Catholicism was the official religion of Brazil from its initial colonization until the proclamation of the Brazilian republic at the end of the nineteenth century. During most of Bahia's colonial history, Africans and their descendants in Brazil practiced their traditional African religions primarily in the context of the Catholicism of the sugarcane plantation. Thus, it was within the framework of Catholic institutions and practices in a slave-holding society—in other words, in the context of religious and social subordination—that a coherent Afro-Brazilian ethnicity emerged.

Later in the colonial period and during the Brazilian empire, groups of Afro-Brazilians became involved with various forms of resistance that were often based in religion. During the seventeenth and eighteenth centuries, for example, Maroon colonies of escaped slaves (*quilombos*) were common, the largest of which was Palmares, with a population of perhaps twenty thousand (Bastide 1978). The most famous ruler of Palmares was Zumbi, who is still a powerful political and religious icon for many Afro-Brazilians today. African-derived religion and popular Catholicism were central to life in settlements like Palmares. By the nineteenth century, however, armed revolt in the cities became the typical form of African-Brazilian protest, and African-derived religions were catalysts for many revolts during this period (Reis 1993; Bastide 1978).

By the middle of the nineteenth century, a large portion of the Afro-Brazilian population was free and Brazilian born. It is among these Brazilian-born people of African descent who were no longer as bound to the plantations that a new identity began to emerge. This new and truly Afro-Brazilian identity was a fusion of various African cultural and religious elements that were articulated within the framework of Catholicism.

Toward the end of the 1800s, slavery was abolished, and Brazil became a republic in which church and state were formally separated. Thus, the Catholic Church ceased to be an appendage of the government. In this new context, Afro-Brazilian religions began to develop in the cities independently of plantation Catholicism. This contributed greatly to the formation of an Afro-Brazilian identity based in African-derived religious traditions that emerged in the twentieth century.

But African-derived religion was not the only religious influence in Afro-Brazilian communities in turn-of-the-century Brazil. The freedom of religion that came with the proclamation of the Brazilian republic encouraged the growth of Protestantism. In the early 1900s, the Pentecostal movement began to gain many converts among poor Brazilians, the majority of whom were nonwhite.

By the second half of the twentieth century, evangelical Christianity and African-derived religions such as Candomblé became viable competitors with the Catholic Church. Furthermore, for many Afro-Brazilians Candomblé became an emblem of ethnic affirmation in the face of racial discrimination. As I explore in this book, however, the large number of evangelicals of African descent in Brazil today presents a major challenge to images of a unitary Afro-Brazilian ethnoreligious identity.

Race, Racism, and Anti-Racism in Brazil

By the end of the nineteenth century all European and European-derived nations had officially abolished slavery, with Brazil being the last to do so, in 1888. Over the course of the twentieth century, direct colonialism and formal racial domination receded from the world (Bowser 1995). Nevertheless, the results of slavery and colonialism, namely racial inequalities and exploitation, still persist.

Following World War II, anti-racist efforts had two clear targets: segregation in the United States and apartheid in South Africa. The success of these projects could be measured concretely in terms of specific social changes such as the dismantling of formal legal segregation (Guimarães 1995). With regard to Brazil, the postwar focus on formal segregation took attention away from its de facto and "assimilationist racism" (Guimarães 1995, 210) and helped promote the country's image as a racial democracy free from racism.

In the United States and South Africa, de jure and de facto segregation fostered solidarity in black communities and encouraged the creation of alternative institutions parallel to dominant structures. Yet this was not the case in Brazil. Thus, even after activists and researchers began to debunk the myth of racial democracy in Brazil by exposing racial inequalities and discrimination, Afro-Brazilians still lack the "broad-ranging collective identity and a common sociopolitical agenda" (K. Butler 1998a, 59) that are preconditions for a mass movement against racism.

Therefore, in the 1970s, those struggling against racism became centrally concerned with what it means to be Afro-Brazilian not simply as a cultural issue but for the practical purpose of social mobilization. As centers of ethnic affirmation and community solidarity, Candomblé terreiros came to have an important place in the black movement that emerged in Salvador in the 1970s and 1980s. Many activists saw African-derived religion as an important basis for a shared ethnoreligious and sociopolitical identity.

In Catholic communities, such affirmations of Afro-Brazilian culture have been opposed by conservatives and traditionalists but are encouraged by progressive groups such as the Pastoral Afro (African Pastoral). In the view of many evangelical Christian groups, on the other hand—whose members are mostly of African descent in Bahia—Candomblé stands for all that is diabolical in this world. At least for evangelicals, this attitude clearly undermines Candomblé's status as the shared ethnic religion of Afro-Brazilians. This has engendered heated conflicts among evangelical, Catholic, and Candomblé communities and raised questions about the problem of essentialism among scholars and activists.

Some have pointed out, for example, that Brazil's black movement is based more on cultural identity than on a shared ideology (Hanchard 1994). This is especially true in Salvador, where Afro-Brazilian solidarity is largely based on traditional Afro-Brazilian cultural and religious practices. Because Afro-Brazilian culture has been so widely appropriated and commodified in Brazilian society, many believe that it is a shaky foundation on which to build a social movement.

Without some form of collective identity, of course, there can be no mass black movement. In fact, many argue that it is largely because of the widespread appropriation and reification of Afro-Brazilian culture that black communities need to strive to reclaim a positive Afro-Brazilian identity. In this view, cultural strategies for mobilization and consciousness-raising are particularly crucial in Brazil (Crook and Johnson 1999; Santos 1999).

Another obstacle to the black movement is the fact that a large number of people of African decent in Brazil do not identify themselves as black. Many argue that this is because the idea of race does not exist in Brazil, at least in the same sense as in the United States or South Africa. Instead, Brazilians tend to classify themselves into a proliferation of flexible groupings that cluster along the spectrum of color and other phenotypic attributes. Thus, Brazilian classificatory practices are fluid and descriptive, referring to constellations of physical features instead of imposing strict racial categories. Those who hold this view commonly contrast Brazilian classificatory practices to the black/white racial dichotomy that operates in the United States.

Critics of the view that Brazilians simply "describe color," however, assert that people are classified by color only if color has meaning and that the meanings of color are grounded in racial ideologies (Guimarães 1995). In some contexts, for example, the way people are referred to depends on their social as well as physical characteristics, so that, for example, individuals of higher social status are less likely to be referred to as "black" than those of lower status with the same phenotypic attributes. Thus, despite the emphasis on racial mixture in Brazil, it is clear that whiteness is valued over blackness. Racism is a way of naturalizing social hierarchies, and color is the coded name for race in Brazil (Guimarães 1995). Moreover, some observers argue that despite the complex array of color terms used in Brazil, Brazilians readily recognize a basic social distinction between white and nonwhite (Sheriff 2001).

Yet the proliferation of racial categories in everyday discourse, much like the fragmentation of political parties in Brazil, has made consensus difficult among Brazilians of African descent (Reichmann 1999b). Many people of African descent identify themselves not as black but as mulatto, and it is commonly believed that the mulatto is less subject to racism than the black. Yet research has shown that inequalities between mulattoes and whites are nearly identical to those between blacks and whites (Telles 2004; Lovell and Wood 1998; Silva 1985). This evidence supports the view that there is an undeniable dichotomy between white and nonwhite.

Thus, there are multiple and competing discourses about ethnoracial identity in Brazil, some that deny the existence of distinct races based on common ancestry and others that assert a categorical distinction between white and non-white. As I will explore in this book, these competing discourses overlap with one another and are often articulated by the same person in different contexts. That is, recent research has indicated that Brazilians generally recognize a social distinction between white and nonwhite even if they use a wide array of color terms to describe each other in most contexts (Sheriff 2001). Moreover, these representations of racial identity articulate with discourses about the relationship between Candomblé and Christianity in Bahia, including those of syncretism, anti-syncretism, and double belonging.

Religion and Afro-Brazilian Identity

Implicit in my choice to focus on religion in relation to ethnic identity and sociopolitical mobilization is the assumption that religion has a particularly important role to play in the construction of social identities in general and ethnic identities in particular. Since many things can be important in the formation of a group identity, such as shared language, history, and life experiences, what is distinctive about religion?

A traditional starting point for discussions of the relationship between religion and social identity is the work of the classical sociologists. Much of the current thinking about these issues can be traced back to the arguments of Emile Durkheim, Max Weber, and Karl Marx. Simply stated, Durkheim argued that religious practice serves to create social solidarity by fostering feelings of identification with the social group; Weber's approach was more historical and focused on the affinities between specific religious worldviews and the interests of different social groups; and Marx conceived of religion as a force for exploitation through the mystification of the social order.

The ideas of these three classical theorists are echoed in various contemporary theoretical perspectives that I will refer to throughout this book. Durkheim's concern with collective representations and practices, for example, is reflected in Michel Foucault's (1999; Carrette 1999a, 1999b) and Talal Asad's (1993) work on how particular kinds of selves are formed through authoritative discourse and disciplinary practice in religious communities. Weber's (1992, 1968) concern with religion and social differentiation influenced Pierre Bourdieu's (1991) writings on the religious field as an arena of competition over legitimacy. Marx's view of religion as ideology is most fully developed by twentieth-century thinkers of the Frankfurt school and in the writings of Antonio Gramsci. Unlike Marx, however, Gramsci saw religion not as a simple reflection of dominant class interests but as representing ideological conflict and social division in society (Portelli 1974).

As I examine in this book, religion is integral to ethnic identity largely because of the particular ways that religious practice shapes one's self-identity. Religious practices and rituals regularly reemphasize group membership in dramatic ways and help to form distinct kinds of (religious, ethnic) selves. This comes about not simply through the choice to believe in a particular creed, but also through the act of submitting oneself to disciplinary practices through which one comes to embody a particular kind of identity within a structured community of practitioners (cf. Asad 1993).

Furthermore, in pluralistic societies like the United States and Brazil, religious differences can indicate subtle distinctions within similar social groups or asymmetrical relations of power between social strata. In the late modern or postmodern period, as religious pluralism increases, religion is important not only as an expression of explicit beliefs and creeds, but also as part of the politics of identity. Thus, religious identities become a powerful force not only for social differentiation but for social mobilization as well.

Afro-Brazilian Roots: Slavery, Plantation Catholicism, and Confraternities

Judging from the writings of Brazil's most famous twentieth-century anthropologist and historiographer, Gilberto Freyre (1945, 1956, 1959), race relations during Brazil's colonial period were considerably more humane and familial than in comparable slave societies such as the United States. According to Freyre, this was partly due to the frequency and level of acceptance of racial mixture and is evidenced by various forms of cultural syncretism in Brazil. Furthermore, this gentler character of slavery was said to account for the emergence of Brazil's fabled "racial democracy" after the abolition of slavery.

When Brazil's image as a racial democracy began to be exposed as a myth in the second half of the twentieth century, however, scholars also changed their view of the past. More recent studies have argued that the institution of slavery in Brazil was just as cruel, if not more so, than in North America (Conrad 1983; Hasenbalg 1979, 1984, 1986; Degler 1971). Other research has emphasized resistance in the form of slave rebellions (Reis 1993; Schwartz 1991) and runaway slave colonies (Moura 1981, 1986) rather than the humanitarian character of Brazilian slavery.

The social domination of slavery was intertwined with the religious domination of Catholicism in Brazil. Historically, Catholicism has enjoyed a virtually unchallenged hegemony in Brazil's religious arena and has long had a close association with the Brazilian elite. The Catholicism that was carried over from Europe to Brazil, however, was not exactly the same as that of the official Roman Church. At least during most of the colonial period, the religion that was imposed on Africans and Native Americans in Brazil had more in common with the local, medieval Catholicism of European peasants than the orthodox, doctrinal version of the faith originating from Rome.

This emphasis on popular Catholicism arose largely from the Catholic Church's efforts to meet the challenge of Protestantism during the Counter-Reformation, which coincided with the initial period of Brazil's colonization. Missionaries in the New World consciously emphasized the same rites—including certain sacraments, the cult of the saints, and other expressions of popular Catholicism—that the Protestants had suppressed and condemned (Marzal 1993; Bastide 1978). Because Catholicism was imposed rather than developed, church membership came to be "based on social norms rather than personal conviction" (Bruneau 1982, 13–14).

Furthermore, because the pope had turned over much institutional control of the church in Brazil to the king of Portugal under the policy of Patronato Regio (Royal Patronage), the church was not able to develop as an independent institution that could make a deep imprint on Brazilian society (Marzal 1993; Bruneau 1982). As a result, Bruneau explains,

> Church involvement in colonial life . . . was largely at the local level—priests were subservient to the land-owning families in the rural areas and

employees of the irmandades were answerable to the brotherhoods in the cities. The church's control over this weak and essentially rural framework was tenuous and largely unconnected. (1982, 14)

In fact, many of the clergy at the local level promoted this form of Catholicism, since it could prosper without the clerical and institutional support and mediation that the Brazilian church was simply unable to provide (Bruneau 1982).

The Catholic Church has been associated with the elite throughout Brazil's history. During the colonial period, the Brazilian elite filled the ranks of the church. The youngest son of every large family was to become a priest, and daughters who did not marry went to the convent, typically taking with them a couple of slaves as attendants (Bastide 1978). The Jesuits, who formed the most dedicated group among the Brazilian clergy, were the exception to this pattern until they were expelled from Brazil in 1759 (Bruneau 1982; Burns 1980). Not surprisingly, then, the Brazilian peasant viewed the church largely as "an instrument of the upper class, with whom the priest is also identified" (Forman 1975, 220).

Religious Confraternities

During their first three centuries in the New World, the religious life of African slaves in Brazil revolved around this Catholicism of the plantation (Bastide 1978). Slave owners in Brazil were required to do little more by way of religious training than baptize slaves and have them attend Mass. Since the owners showed little interest in keeping up even these simple obligations, the church stepped in and encouraged the slaves to participate in *irmandades* (religious confraternities) devoted to Catholic saints. The local clergy tended to close their eyes to deficiencies in spiritual conformity as long as the slaves participated in the sacraments, and the practice of African religions continued in the context of the confraternities (Bastide 1978; McGregor 1966).

The confraternities typically grouped together slaves of different *nações* (nations, or ethnic groups) corresponding to the slaves' places of origin in Africa (Nishida 2003; K. Butler 1998a; Bastide 1978). The most prominent of these were the Nâgo (Yoruba), Jejê (Ewe), and Angola nações (K. Butler 1998a). Most Africans enslaved in Brazil were originally either Yoruba or Bantu. The Yoruba are part of the Sudanese group that also includes Dahomeans and the Fanti-Ashanti, and the Bantus came either from the Angola-Congo region or Mozambique on the east coast. Islamic Africans, such as the Mandingo and the Hausa, were also brought to Brazil as slaves. Yet it was the Yoruba who had the biggest impact on subsequent African-Brazilian cultural developments, especially in the North and particularly in their contributions to the pantheon of *orixás* or *santos*, the gods of the African-derived religions.[1]

Confraternities were a central means of adaptation for Africans in Brazil. Kim Butler explains,

> They served as cultural orientation centers, support networks, insurance funds, and provided a religious superstructure through which Afro-Brazilians could seek spiritual support from Catholic deities as well as the African deities with which they were syncretized. (1998a, 147)

It was through these organizations that newly arrived Africans and people of African descent were integrated into Brazilian society. Those who were elected to officer positions held much prestige in black communities (Mulvey 1982, 1980).

While confraternities provided a means for integration, they were also vehicles for division and social control. Authorities of the church and state encouraged confraternities based on African ethnic identifications partly to promote interethnic conflicts. This policy was intended to prevent the development of class consciousness (Bastide 1978; McGregor 1966). Ironically, however, the continuation of these practices in this context facilitated the development of African-derived religions that eventually became catalysts for slave protest (Bastide 1978). In tandem with increasing urbanization and the growth of urban slavery during the late colonial period and the empire, however, many African-Brazilians began to transform the religion that was being used to control and integrate them into an instrument of ethnic solidarity and social justice (Bastide 1978).

The Formation of an Afro-Brazilian Identity: Abolition, Nationalism, and Cultural Practice

According to Mieko Nishida (1991), Afro-Brazilian ethnic identity in Salvador passed through four stages before the abolition of slavery at the end of the nineteenth century. In the first stage, during the colonial period, African-born slaves formed the majority of the black population, and the nações provided the most important sources of ethnic identity. After independence, in the second stage (1831–1850), far fewer new Africans were entering Brazil to revitalize the nações. As a result, a new Afro-Brazilian interethnic African identity began to form. In the third stage (1850–1870), this Afro-Brazilian identity solidified after the slave trade ended. In the fourth stage (1871–1888), Brazilian-born mestiços (those of mixed ancestry) finally outnumbered blacks in Salvador (K. Butler 1998a, 53).

Many of these mestiços did not identify with African-derived traditions, and today this lack of identification is a major issue for activists concerned with solidarity among people of African descent in Brazil.

Slavery was completely abolished in Brazil in 1888. A year later the Brazilian republic was formed, and in 1891 the first constitution was promulgated. At the turn of the century, then, Brazil was striving to transform itself from a slave-holding and mostly feudal monarchy into a modern republic. This process necessarily involved a struggle to reformulate the social order after abolition and redefine Brazil's national identity after the advent of the republic. A major issue was the place that nonwhites—blacks and mestiços—would occupy in the new Brazil.

Throughout the twentieth century answers to questions of race in Brazil were often ambiguous and rife with contradictions. In his classic turn-of-the-century Brazilian novel *Os Sertões* (translated as "Rebellion in the Backlands"), Euclides Da Cunha vacillated between praising mestiços as the bedrock of Brazilian society and denigrating them as degenerates (Cleary 1999). Da Cunha was a proponent of positivism, the favored philosophy of the new republican elite. In light of positivism's emphasis on definite stages of societal progress, many saw Africans and their cultural practices as barbaric and antithetical to modernization. Studies of religious syncretism, for example, were used to show that blacks were incapable of being properly acculturated to European Catholicism (e.g., Nina Rodrigues 1935).

This negative view of syncretism was related to the church's desire to distance itself from the popular Catholicism that had thrived on the plantations. Catholicism lost its status as the official religion of Brazil when the constitution of the newly established Brazilian republic declared the separation of church and state in 1891 (Bruneau 1982). Consequently, while the church lost many of the privileges it enjoyed as the official religion of Brazil, it was finally able to establish a direct relationship with Rome unmediated by the Brazilian government.

Now unfettered by the state, the church was actually able to grow and restructure itself. Yet most of the church's new structures and efforts were geared toward the urban middle class, while most of Brazil remained rural. According to Bruneau (1982, 18), the church "remained aloof, or even hostile, to the vast majority of the population and their patterns of popular religiosity." Consequently, a rift occurred between the religion of the church and the religion of the masses—that is, between official, orthodox Catholicism on the one hand and folk or syncretic Catholicism and other popular religious expressions on the other. By the time the Vargas regime established its military dictatorship in

1930, the church had become a powerful potential ally for the government. In fact, it was able to regain some of its former privileges and prestige by pledging support for President Getúlio Vargas' efforts to maintain order and stability under his regime (Bruneau 1982).

The Formative Period for Afro-Brazilian Religions

During this period under Vargas, those involved with African-derived religions continued to be the targets of oppression, persecution, and extortion (Brown 1986). Yet Afro-Brazilian religions eventually came to be protected to some extent by the patronage of those in the middle and upper classes. This patronage emerged from a romantic interest in African and Native American themes and a growing sense of nationalism in which African and Indian culture formed an important part of Brazil's national identity.

While African-derived religions had been developing throughout the periods of the colony and the empire, abolition and the proclamation of the republic ushered in the formative period for the African-derived religions of today. According to Bastide (1978), abolition and urbanization led to increasing social separation of the races that had lived closely together on the plantation. This, together with the Catholic Church's alienation of the lower sectors of society, encouraged African-derived religions to develop in a new social space opening in the cities toward the end of the nineteenth century. The religions that were taking shape during this period, all of which are broadly similar to one another, include Candomblé in Bahia (which I will focus on here), Xango in Recife, as well as Cantimbó, Macumba, and Batuque in other regions.

Candomblé, like other African-derived religions in Brazil, is based on a combination or fusion of similar religions associated with different African ethnic groups, each with its own traditions. The most prominent of these in Bahian Candomblé is the Yoruba nation called Ketu or Nagô, and other important traditions include Angola and Jejê. Candomblé is a complex, hierarchical religion. The participants are predominantly women, ranked by degree of initiation and ceremonial function. Initiation ceremonies in these religions are structured much like traditional African rites of passage (McGregor 1966).

The practice of Candomblé, which is similar to other African-derived religions such as Vodun and Santeria, revolves around the pantheon of orixás (Yoruba gods) and other spirits who possess their devotees in public ceremonies and to whom offerings are made in private rituals. Many terreiros show the marks of Candomblé's long association with plantation Catholicism, which resulted in the popular identification of saints with Candomblé deities, the synchronization of Catholic and Candomblé ritual calendars, and overlapping practices in Afro-Catholic organizations and confraternities. Candomblé and the other African-Brazilian religions are similar to each other in general features, and as a whole they share many characteristics with Vodou and other "Neo-African" religions of the New World, including

> the names and characteristics of African deities, "soul" concepts, ritual objects, drum rhythms, song styles, dance steps, spirit possession, the ritual use of stones, herbs, and water, seclusion and "mourning," animal sacrifices, belief in the immediacy of intervention of supernatural beings in human affairs, utilization of spirits of the dead, and ritual words . . . blended with Christian elements—including the names of Catholic saints, Catholic and Protestant theological concepts, hymns, prayers, Bible verses, the cross and crucifixes, and with spiritualist doctrine—in diverse ways. (Simpson 1978, 61)

Harding writes that the "development of Candomblé as a formalized religion in nineteenth-century Bahia was in many ways correlative to the formation of a nuanced, multi-textured, Afro-Brazilian collectivity in the capital city and in the Recôncavo" (2000, 38). Candomblé in Bahia has passed through four general phases, the first two of which closely paralleled the development of Afro-Brazilian ethnicity. In the first phase, each separate nação (singular of nações) corresponded to its own distinct religious community. The second phase began in the nineteenth century at about the same time that an inter-ethnic Afro-Brazilian identity emerged. During this time Candomblé began to take its modern form as the liturgy consolidated and terreiros multiplied. In the third phase, which began after abolition, the Afro-Brazilian religious community was forced to organize against persecution and assert its religious freedom. Finally, toward the end of the twentieth century, Candomblé became absorbed into Brazil's popular culture (K. Butler 1998a).

In the context of an emerging Afro-Brazilian identity after abolition, Candomblé formed "a vital cross-cutting institution bridging ethnic and color lines and setting the foundation for an integrated Afro-Bahian society" (K. Butler 1998a, 170). In Bahia especially, as in many other parts of the Afro-Atlantic, religion played an important role in the development of new forms of ethnic identity and solidarity that countered dominant definitions of blackness (Harding 2000). Besides ministering to the spiritual needs of the Afro-Brazilian community, leaders of Candomblé terreiros were involved in healing the sick and mediating disputes, among other functions (Harding 2000; K. Butler 1998a). Butler explains,

Long after the abolition of slavery and the disappearance of African-born persons in Bahia's population, candomblés provided the infrastructure for the re-creation of African identity and the foundation of an African-based world that continues to flourish even at the dawn of the twenty-first century. (1998a, 47)

Repression of the newly organizing Afro-Brazilian religions was common in the 1920s and 1930s, as the Catholic Church convinced the government that the practice of these religions was an "offense against public morality" (Brown 1986, 2). In fact, in the discourse of a modernizing Brazilian republic, Candomblé was seen as the "sickness of the nation" (Johnson 2002, 33). Sorcery accusations associated with African-derived religions came to be handled by state-created mechanisms instituted in the Penal Code of the Republic (Maggie 1992). Interestingly, proceedings from these kinds of cases show that the judge's objective was to identify and punish the sorcerer, not stamp out belief in sorcery. Thus, far from undermining the basis for these beliefs, state "regulation" formed the basis of their construction (Maggie 1992; Souza 1986).

The persecution of African-derived religions in Brazil was linked with notions of both religious and racial superiority. As Harding explains,

In the mind of Brazilian elites, blackness and Afro-Brazilian culture represented the antithesis of "civilization" and, especially in the nineteenth century, many of the efforts to destroy Candomblés and other black religio-cultural manifestations were articulated in terms of their supposed nefarious effects on public morale and their inappropriateness for a modernizing society. (2000, xvii)

Especially in Bahia, struggles against racial domination have very often taken the shape of struggles against religious and cultural intolerance. Candomblé has long been denigrated and feared in Brazilian society, and it was not until the 1970s that Candomblé terreiros were legally recognized as legitimate religious centers with the same rights as Christian churches. Since Candomblé was so closely associated with Afro-Brazilian identity, the widespread persecution of African-derived religions during the twentieth century often became a social and political issue.

Racist ideologies influenced the thinking of anthropologists studying religion in Brazil at the turn of the twentieth century. Early discussions of African-derived religious syncretism in Brazil focused on the mixing of African and Catholic "traits," which were eventually further combined with indigenous and spiritist elements (cf. Maggie 1992; Alves Velho 1977). Each of these religious sources was seen as associated with a stage of cultural development, with African religion occupying the lowest stage (since it was associated with the slaves and then with the lower sectors of society, most of whom were and still are African-Brazilians), followed by indigenous religion, Catholicism, and finally spiritism (cf. Birman 1995).

Nina Rodrigues (1935), for example, the pioneer of ethnographic studies of African religion in Brazil, argued that the trance states common in the practice of African religion were a product of the African's weak intellectual development. The works of Arthur Ramos (1942, 1940) and Edison Carneiro (1991) are very similar to that of Nina Rodrigues in their emphasis on syncretism and the survival of African traits, although they are a good deal less racist and more culturally relative. The American contemporary of these writers, Melville Herskovits (1941), introduced the concept of acculturation and a functional perspective to the study of African-derived religions. However, he continued the emphasis on African survivals and the mechanical and unconscious mixing of traits and elements.

Later, Roger Bastide (1958) took a more sociological approach that, in contrast to Herskovits' functionalism, emphasized social conflict. Nevertheless, Bastide continued to focus on African survivals while ignoring the question of whether contemporary practitioners were even aware of their original meaning (Birman 1995). More recent perspectives, such as those espoused by Droogers (2005, 1989) and Stewart and Shaw (1994), pay more attention to the issue of power relations and the role of human agency in analyses of syncretism.[2] As I discuss below, Candomblé practitioners in Bahia have been discussing these issues publicly since the 1980s, when the anti-syncretism movement emerged to challenge the historical relationship between Candomblé and Catholicism and to assert Candomblé's independence as an autonomous religion in its own right.

Early Growth of Protestantism

At the same time that Afro-Brazilian religions were expanding in the cities, the role of the traditional Catholic Church was declining in areas shifting from traditional plantation agriculture to other forms of production and subsistence. Protestant churches began to fill this new niche in the rural areas (Frase 1975). During most of Brazil's history, the Roman Catholic clergy had attempted to keep Protestantism from growing in their domain. Partly because of incursions by Protestant nations into Brazilian territory, Protestants were often viewed as "invading heretics" (Da Silva 1998, 405). Friars during the colony and empire routinely boarded ships to "examine the faith" of incoming immigrants, as evidenced by the newcomer's ability to recite the Hail Mary and the Apostles' Creed and to make the sign of the cross (Freyre 1956).

The constitution of the Brazilian empire promulgated in 1822, however, provided a considerable degree of freedom for Protestantism in Brazil (Farra 1960). Under the reign of the second emperor of Brazil, Pedro II, and to the chagrin of the Catholic Church, missionary activity began to be allowed in the 1850s (Berryman 1995). The earliest denominations in Brazil were the Methodists and the Congregationalists, appearing in 1836 and 1858 respectively (Bastide 1978). Yet the Protestant groups that became most significant numerically were the Presbyterians, the Baptists, and the Pentecostals, the first churches of which were established in 1863, 1882, and 1910 (Costa 1979).

The founding of these first churches coincided with a push for economic modernization, the abolition of slavery, and the establishment of a Brazilian republic (Costa 1979). An important factor in the success of Protestantism at the end of the nineteenth century was the liberal ideals popular among the Brazilian bourgeoisie. Positivism, with its emphasis on progress, modernization, rationalism, and the liberalization of society and the state following the model of the United States, was particularly influential around the time of abolition and the proclamation of the Brazilian republic at the end of the nineteenth century. Protestantism was seen as embodying these ideals. Furthermore, Protestantism was opposed to the conservative worldview of Catholicism and to the mysticism of Afro-Brazilian religion, which many immigrants and members of the Brazilian middle class viewed as culturally inferior (Da Silva 1998).

While certain strands of mainline Protestantism had an affinity with the ideology of the liberal elite, other more grassroots churches, especially Pentecostal ones, appealed to the poor who were marginalized in the process of Brazil's modernization. Broadly speaking, Pentecostal churches differ from historical or mainline Protestant denominations in their emphasis on the manifestation of certain "gifts of the Holy Spirit" such as speaking in tongues and faith healing by the laying on of hands. Pentecostal discourse emphasizes the literal interpretation of the scriptures, the imminent second coming of Christ, and the separation of the faithful from the ways of this world (Freston 1994; Novaes and Floriano 1985; Costa 1979).

Pentecostal churches in particular ostensibly provided a kind of haven during the transitions and crises associated with economic modernization, and early missionary efforts appear to have focused mainly on those displaced and disoriented in the wake of change and adversity that modernization brought to Brazil (Costa 1979). According to Ronald Frase, the development of Protestantism in Brazil has always been connected with "marginal groups created by structural changes occurring within that society" (1975, 17). Many Protestant churches explicitly targeted those affected by the social changes brought about by major social and economic shifts. A disproportionate number of the people affected by these shifts were of African descent, and in the twentieth century the remarkable Pentecostal growth would depend heavily on such communities. Thus, Pentecostalism (and evangelical Christianity in general), along with African-derived religion and Catholicism, became an important part of the religious context in which Afro-Brazilian identities were formed.

Indeed, at the same time that an interethnic Afro-Brazilian identity was forming, Protestantism and Pentecostalism were beginning to gain adherents in the same black communities where Candomblé was expanding. At first such gains were modest. At the turn of the century, there were fewer than one hundred thousand Protestants in all of Latin America, most of whom were European immigrants (Clawson 1984). According to Frase (1975), those Brazilians who converted to Protestantism in the nineteenth century were mainly a small number of disaffected members of the middle class. Many of these converts embraced Protestantism because it sanctioned the values of small, independent landowners and the urban industrial middle class.

After the proclamation of the republic and the separation of church and state, however, Protestantism began to gain ground rather quickly considering Brazil's strong Catholic traditions (Bastide 1978). According to Robert Farra (1960), the new political and religious freedoms that came with the republic fostered a strong national spirit among Brazilian Protestants as well as the drive to develop their own churches independent of foreign missionary organizations.

Two decades after the proclamation of the republic, Brazil's first Pentecostal church was founded in São Paulo by Louis Francison, an Italian American immigrant from Chicago. As a Presbyterian minister, Francison was originally inspired to move to Argentina to spread the word of the works of the Holy Spirit to Italian immigrants. He moved to São Paulo in 1910, where his ministry split from the Presbyterian Church to form the Congregacão Cristo no Brasil (Read 1965). Yet the growth of Pentecostalism during the first republic was comparatively modest. Missionary activity until the 1930s came mostly from the mainline churches of the Presbyterians, Lutherans, Baptists, Episcopalians, and Methodists.

By the 1930s, however, the major boom-and-bust economic cycles that had been associated with the initial development of Protestantism in Brazil came to an end. From 1930 on, Brazil's attention turned to industrialization and diversification of the economy—which meant increasing urbanization and more internal migration than ever before (Costa 1979). It is in this context that Protestantism, and Pentecostalism in particular, began to grow at an increasing rate.

It is estimated that by 1930 the Presbyterians had established 354 churches; the Baptists, 494; and the Pentecostals, 223. By 1963, the Presbyterians had 1,080 churches; the Baptists, 1,654; and the Pentecostals, 2,134 (Costa 1979). During Vargas' regime, growth was particularly marked in rural areas shifting to modern commercial agriculture and in the major metropolitan centers of Brazil. The majority of those living in these areas and those most profoundly affected by the changes occurring in Brazil were people of African descent.

After 1930, Pentecostalism began to outgrow the mainline Protestant denominations. While the Presbyterians and Baptists were busy attempting to consolidate their local churches and bring together their denominational structures, the Pentecostals were tapping into currents of "religious discontents and religious hopes" in places like the economically depressed and politically marginalized northeast (Costa 1979). Here the Pentecostals developed a Protestant version of popular folk Catholicism that would appeal to the increasingly dislocated masses. Pentecostal churches such as the Assembly of God, however, also expanded in the urban centers of the southern states, where Pentecostalism appealed to socially and spatially displaced members of the new industrial working class.

As for the rural regions of Brazil, the role of the traditional Catholic Church in these areas began to diminish in the context of rapid modernization associated with the shift from small-scale, traditional plantations to large-scale, modern commercial agriculture. According to Curry (1969), Pentecostal churches came into these rural communities during the 1930s and 1940s and created labor networks that were linked to the new economic elites and political bosses of the modernizing Brazilian state through the personal connections of their pastors. In both rural and urban areas, membership in the Pentecostal church provided job opportunities for its members in the context of rapidly changing economic and social conditions, while at the same time replicating the traditional patron-client relations that have long characterized Brazil's political economy.

Early Afro-Brazilian Political Involvement

Any Afro-Brazilian social or political movement in early twentieth-century Brazil confronted two powerful discourses about race relations. The first authoritatively asserted the inferiority of blacks, and the second claimed to value the black contribution to Brazilianness but denied that racism existed in Brazil.

Both the discourses of whitening and of racial democracy seemed to negate the claims of Afro-Brazilians who demanded equality, since according to these dominant ideologies racial inequalities were either viewed as natural or seen as really related to class rather than race.

Furthermore, Brazil's deep-seated political culture of patronage has always made group activism rare, since Afro-Brazilian initiatives are often co-opted by elites (K. Butler 1998a). This is especially true in Salvador, where there was no wave of industrial modernization to correspond with that in São Paulo in the early twentieth century. In addition, in Salvador the most important organizations in the Afro-Brazilian community are little concerned with political power. Early Afro-Brazilian activism after abolition in Salvador was primarily concerned with the protection of the cultural freedoms of Afro-Brazilian organizations such as Candomblé terreiros.

Nevertheless, Afro-Brazilian groups did emerge against the grain of dominant ideologies and political obstacles. The Frente Negra Brasileira (FNB) was the first explicitly political Afro-Brazilian organization. It was founded in São Paulo in 1931 and later spread to other states in the country, including Bahia (Reichmann 1999b). The FNB "sponsored literacy and vocational courses, health clinics, legal aid, and credit unions for its members, and lobbied to promote Afro-Brazilian rights" (1999b, 14).

The FNB did not last long in the political climate of Bahia. Soon the populist politician Juracy Magalhães absorbed the organization into the government's Ação Social Proletária (Proletarian Social Action) program, which was much more focused on labor than racial issues (K. Butler 1998a). A major problem for the FNB was the fact that Salvador, in contrast to São Paulo, had a large black middle class that was unsupportive because its members preferred assimilation and social ascent by conventional means.

In any case, Vargas banned political parties in 1937, and the FNB was disbanded (Reichmann 1999b; Hanchard 1994). For several decades after, there were no Afro-Brazilian political parties. In the 1940s and 1950s blacks took part in union and populist and leftist party politics, but race generally was not raised as a separate issue (Reichmann 1999b). During this period Afro-Brazilian initiatives like the Teatro Experimental do Negro (TEN) emerged in São Paulo and Rio as a counterpart to the Négritude Mouvement in Francophone Africa.

The TEN was based mainly on cultural expression, and its politics were widely divergent. Many criticized the TEN as being elitist and too driven by intellectuals (Barcelos 1999). Academics such as the anthropologist Gilberto Freyre were involved in the movement, one of the aims of which was to mediate artistic and intellectual abstraction with black sensuality and passion (Hanchard

1994). Some complained that this essentialist view reinforced the notion of the primitive black.

There has long been an association between culture and activism in black communities, which has often given rise to debates about cultural essentialism. Some contend that although discourses about negritude aim to reverse negative stereotypes, they frequently replace them with positive ones that are equally essentialist. Moreover, as I discuss below, the tendency to naturalize the connection between race and cultural practice has complicated racial mobilization in Brazil.

Contemporary Brazil: Religious Diversity, Afro-Brazilian Identity, and Black Consciousness

It was not until the second half of the twentieth century that researchers began to acknowledge the existence of systematic racial discrimination in Brazil. Ironically, many of the initial studies that challenged the myth of racial democracy, which were commissioned by the United Nations Educational, Scientific and Cultural Organization (UNESCO) in the 1950s, were originally meant to highlight Brazil's harmonious race relations (Hanchard 1994; Skidmore 1992, 1993). At first, most commentators interpreted racial inequalities in terms of class differences and not as indicating racism per se. In fact, in the 1960s, 1970s, and 1980s, many followed the Marxist-derived assumption that race is epiphenomenal and assumed that class shapes social relations more than skin color.

The work of Florestan Fernandes (1969) was considered especially groundbreaking for its acknowledgment of racial inequalities. He and other researchers from what came to be known as the São Paulo school of sociology completely devastated Freyre's arguments about racial democracy (Cleary 1999). Nevertheless, Fernandes maintained that racial inequalities in Brazil were due not so much to racial discrimination as to the fact that freed slaves were unprepared for the kind of discipline needed for wage labor in a modern capitalist society. This left Afro-Brazilians at a distinct disadvantage in the competitive labor market, thereby relegating them to the underclass (Fernandes 1969).

Later researchers, however, refuted this "dysfunctional negro" explanation that Fernandes advanced for the marginalization of Afro-Brazilians after abolition (Hanchard 1994, 33). Hasenbalg's work examined the societal mechanisms that reproduce racial inequalities, focusing on racism and discrimination for his explanations rather than the "legacy of slavery" (1979, 21). Later, Andrews (1991) showed how the state and landowning elite conspired to skew the labor market against blacks through immigration policies and discriminatory practices on the job.

In the 1980s, Hasenbalg and Silva's (1988) work showed definitively that explanations based on class and the labor market were not sufficient to explain racial inequalities in Brazil. They provided conclusive evidence of systematic racial discrimination by documenting "inequalities in social mobility, employment, wages, and showed that blacks achieved lower financial returns than whites on their investments in education, particularly at higher education levels" (Reichmann 1999b, 26).

In addition, Silva's (1985) landmark work refuted the influential theory of the "mulatto escape hatch" that had been championed by Carl Degler (1971), who argued that the key to differences in race relations between the U.S. and Brazil is the existence in Brazil of a middle group between black and white (hence the "mulatto escape hatch") that makes segregation impossible. Although he did not accept the myth of racial democracy, Degler claimed that the lack of a clear caste-like boundary between blacks and whites and the acceptance of racial mixture made Brazil exceptional. Nevertheless, Silva (1985) showed that levels of inequality between blacks and mulattoes are much less significant than between whites and nonwhites taken as a whole, supporting the view that there is actually a clear division between whites and nonwhites in Brazil.

Even considering these groundbreaking studies in the 1980s, until the late 1990s most Brazilian scholarship steered clear of addressing contemporary racism and racial inequalities (Reichmann 1999a). Instead, scholars typically focused on cultural, religious, and linguistic syncretism; slavery and forms of slave resistance; and race relations during the transition to free labor in the immediate post-abolition period. At worst this work has reduced a vibrant and dynamic culture to a static specimen of idealized folklore, and at best it has documented the resilience of African culture by detailing African survivals while attesting to "the enormous impact of black experience on Brazilian culture and identity" (Reichmann 1999b, 24).

More recent work, however, has directly addressed racism in Brazil.[3] From the 1960s to the 1980s, researchers compiled abundant statistical data showing that inequalities based on racial discrimination exist in Brazil. In the 1990s, anthropologists and others fleshed out these numbers with ethnographic studies of racism and anti-racism in Brazilian communities. Many of these studies sought to debunk the "myth of racial democracy" and drew parallels between race relations in Brazil and the United States. Research in recent years, however—including mine—has sought to understand what is distinctive about how race and racism work in Brazil while emphasizing the transnational processes that influence local discourses about race.

Afro-Brazilian Mobilization

Despite growing recognition of sharp discrepancies in resources and life chances between whites and nonwhites, Brazil's image as a racial democracy still lingers. As Michael Hanchard asks, how could Afro-Brazilians "struggle against an ideology that claims there is no need for such strivings in the first place?" (1994, 21). Clearly the hegemony of discourses about Brazil as a racial paradise has been a major obstacle to Afro-Brazilian mobilization.

Nevertheless, movements that resist dominant racial ideologies have emerged in Brazil. In the 1960s, for example, the Black Soul movement appeared. Heavily influenced by developments in the United States, Black Soul focused on African-style clothing and hairstyles, the adoption of African names, and the teaching of African and Afro-Brazilian histories in schools (Hanchard 1994). The movement was criticized, however, on the basis that the celebration of culture should be a means of raising consciousness and not an end in itself. Although Black Soul was a form of resistance, it was also appropriated as a form of popular culture or entertainment that could be consumed as a commodity.

In the late 1970s, when Brazil slowly began to move toward democracy and civilian rule, a revitalized black movement emerged. It began as a collection of relatively low-profile study groups and cultural organizations but eventually included "a heterogeneous mix of explicitly political organizations" (Reichmann 1999b, 15). The Movimento Negro Unificado (MNU), for example, was founded in 1978 and became the first national Afro-Brazilian organization since the Frente Negra Brasileira disbanded in 1937. Like other similar movements, it emphasized two traits shared by blacks everywhere: a common oppressor over the last three hundred years in Africa and the Americas, and Africa as a place of common origin (Hanchard 1994).

The MNU began in São Paulo, then spread to Rio, and soon "struggle centers" were established in locations including samba schools and Candomblé terreiros in major cities such as Salvador, Porto Alegre, and Espirito Santo (Hanchard 1994; Jones 1995). The MNU's first national congress was held in 1979 in Rio, during which regulations about organization and structure were enacted (Hanchard 1994). The MNU became a national organization that through publications, demonstrations, academic debates, cultural events, and, to a lesser extent, mainstream politics "stressed black consciousness and an adversarial stance vis-à-vis the dominant political, social, and cultural institutions and values in Brazil" (Covin 1996, 43).

While MNU had begun as an umbrella organization, by the late 1980s it became just one among many because of the proliferation of Afro-Brazilian groups (Hanchard 1994). Black organizations continued to flourish in the 1990s, and most of these groups focused on the celebration of Afro-Brazilian culture. Only a small number of organizations, most of them in São Paulo, remained explicitly political. Unfortunately, no national organization has emerged whose explicit purpose is to lobby for racial issues (Hanchard 1994).

Those who initiated the black movement in Brazil in the 1970s were painfully aware of the irony that the country with the largest black population in the New World was also the one with the lowest levels of racial consciousness (Hanchard 1994). Not only were both white and nonwhite Brazilians likely to deny the existence of racism, but many Brazilians of African descent did not identify themselves as black. For activists, this lack of recognition of and resistance to the discourse of anti-racism continues to be an obstacle to mass participation in the black movement.

Furthermore, the preemptive efforts of the Brazilian elites have helped to keep mass mobilization at bay. In the face of glaring racial inequalities, Guimarães explains,

> Brazilian elites turn to denial and disguise, appropriating Afro-Brazilian experience (i.e., "culture") as their own. This device, designed to avoid social polarization, requires whites to engage in ritualized roles that gush with Brazil's traditional cordiality and emphasize a mediating common ground—a role filled nicely by the pervasive color term, moreno [brown]. Roberto Da Matta has described this phenomenon as an encompassing approach to conflict, intrinsic to the national character. (1999, 5)

The appropriation of Afro-Brazilian culture is linked with the appropriation of ancestry, as expressed in the common saying that racism cannot possibly exist in Brazil because all Brazilians are of mixed blood. Despite such obstacles and resistance, however, Edward Telles argues that by the end of the 1990s the black movement had succeeded in accomplishing three important things in Brazil: 1) discrediting the myth of racial democracy in the general population; 2) changing the thinking of elites about who is black and who is white; and 3) engaging the government in discussion of public policy dealing with racism (2004, 322).

Race in the Contemporary Religious Arena

Closely related to the ideals of racial democracy and racial mixture in Brazil are those of religious pluralism and syncretism. The coexistence and frequent hybridization of European and African religions is often referred to as a metaphor for the cordial and conciliatory relations between races in Brazil. Yet in Brazil's contemporary religious arena, Catholicism, Protestantism, and African-derived religions are by no means equal competitors with one another.

According to David Hess (1985, 180–81), the contemporary religious arena in Brazil has two poles. The Catholic Church is located at one end and the African-derived religions of Brazil are at the other, while Pentecostalism occupies a position in between. The historical hegemony of white male elites and the colonial legacy of racism and slavery are reflected today in the dominance of Catholicism and the relatively marginal status of Candomblé. Although Hess' characterization is accurate in a general way, the religious arena in Bahia today is very complex. In the second half of the twentieth century, for example, the Catholic Church in Brazil became more concerned with social issues, and, more recently, with specifically racial problems.

The initial impetus for the church's turn toward these issues came at the end of its alliance with the Vargas regime. After democratic rule was reinstated in 1945, the church was forced to rely on grassroots efforts to maintain its influence. In 1952, Bishop Hélder Câmara formed the National Council of Brazilian Bishops (CNBB), an organization committed to coordinating pastoral action in Brazil (Adriance 1986). Under the guidance of the CNBB, the Catholic Action movement, which had been organizationally fragmented in the 1940s and 1950s, finally came together by the 1960s (Azevedo 1987).

In contrast to earlier versions of Catholic Action in Brazil, this new movement divided laypeople into different groups that focused on evangelization within a certain social milieu. From the point of view of the conservative bishops within the church, the movement was a response to the spread of socialism among factory workers. But for others, the movement represented a vehicle for social reform, and eventually the CNBB allowed the progressive bishops to come together, break the church's alliance with the upper classes, and turn its attention to the poor (Adriance 1986).

In 1964 the military once again took control of the government. Although the upper levels of the Brazilian Catholic hierarchy were filled with traditionalists after the coup, the church's old alliances with the economic and military elites, such as it enjoyed under Vargas, would not return. In the early years of the new regime, the conservative bishops supported a military government they saw as ending the "communist threat" (Adriance 1986). Eventually, however, the military began to violently repress the social activism of the church's progressive wing. Between 1968 and 1973 there were 395 arrests and 34 documented cases of torture of the clergy, and 7 priests as well as 200 laypeople were killed. Consequently, the church as a whole began to reconsider its support.

While the church's concern with the lower classes in the late 1950s and early 1960s may have represented a conservative response to socialism and evangelical Protestantism, its "option for the poor" in the context of authoritarian regimes turned out to be a vehicle for land struggles, organized labor, and other progressive movements (Adriance 1986). This progressive current gained momentum during the Second Vatican Council (1962–1965), which was a turning point in the relationship of the Catholic Church as a whole to the modern world and had a profound impact on the Brazilian church.

Following Vatican II, at the Episcopal Conferences at Medellin (1968) and Puebla (1979), those in the Brazilian church became painfully aware of the extent to which the church itself supported an unjust social order that generated poverty and oppression (Azevedo 1987). Thus, the church made a "preferential option for the poor," embracing the project of liberation and the struggle for freedom from oppressive sociopolitical structures (Burdick 1993).

The church soon realized that its lay groups were no longer viable or effective for implementing the new projects of the more progressive church. Catholic brotherhoods, devotional associations, and movements, including Catholic Action and more recent movements such as Charismatic Catholicism, had succeeded in reaching the poor but had stayed clear of controversial social issues (Azevedo 1987). In response to this, base ecclesial communities (CEBs) emerged, based on the church's more progressive discourse, liberation theology, and its preferential option for the poor.

By the early 1980s, CEBs had reached their height in Brazil and were stronger there than in any other nation in Latin America at the time (Clawson 1984). Yet by the middle of that decade, when Brazil returned to civilian rule and democracy, CEB growth slowed significantly while Pentecostalism continued to expand rapidly (Vasquez 1997). According to Vasquez (1997), during this period the material conditions of the lives of most Brazilians, especially the poor, severely deteriorated as a result of Brazil's financial crisis and restructuring. In this context, the abstract theologies and social teachings of the progressive church lost meaning and were of little use to many poor and uneducated Brazilians (Burdick 1993; Azevedo 1987).

According to John Burdick (1993), a number of factors seem to have contributed to the appeal of Pentecostalism over the CEBs. First of all, Pentecostal discourse shifts responsibility for suffering and misfortune, as well as for its alleviation, from the individual to another agent, supernatural or otherwise, thereby offering a level of comfort in the face of suffering not provided by Catholicism. In addition, Pentecostalism appeals to those who are alienated by the heavy emphasis on literacy in the CEBs.

For young people, Pentecostalism provides a distinct break from a competitive and consumerist youth culture that many find undesirable, whereas the social circles of the CEBs tend to overlap with these domains of mainstream culture. In terms of race relations, the Catholic Church's attempt to erode racism has been met by resistance from blacks who point out that the leadership of the church continues to be dominated by those with lighter skin; alternatively, some see in Pentecostalism the potential for a more powerful counterdiscourse to racism (Burdick 1993; cf. Chesnut 1997).

Regarding gender, Burdick (1993) observed during his fieldwork that although participants in CEBs are predominately female, women were much more likely to belong to Pentecostal churches than to be active in CEBs. To account for the apparently greater appeal of Pentecostalism, Burdick suggests that Pentecostal churches provide opportunities for women's participation not available in the Catholic Church and give women an ideological or moral basis on which to increase their spiritual authority in the household.

In summary, then, the decline of the CEBs was partly related to the failure of "progressive" Catholic discourses and practices to resonate with a significant number of Brazilians, including many young people, blacks, and women. In addition, at the institutional level, the drop-off of dynamism in CEBs in the mid-1980s was also a result of conservative pressure from the Vatican and the highest positions in the Brazilian church. By the late 1980s, the Brazilian church turned its attention away from CEBs and sociopolitics and toward revitalizing the popular religiosity of the masses (Burdick 1993). To some extent, the reform function of the CEBs seems to have passed to secular groups and political parties.

On the local level, many Catholics, old and young alike, have always been wary of the post–Vatican II progressive discourse. Many objected to the "mixing" of spiritual and worldly (political and social) matters, this being perceived as a departure from scripture (Burdick 1993). In addition, those involved with the CEBs are not permitted to be involved with Pentecostal prayer healers or Candomblé terreiros, otherwise they suffer gossip and lower standing in the church—whereas formerly Catholics could participate in other religions without drawing much attention.

Like the CEBs, many of the Catholic groups that emerged in the early 1980s to address racial issues eventually dissolved largely because of their ideological emphasis (Burdick 1998a). By the late 1980s, the emphasis of the Catholic antiracism movement had shifted from grand ideological projects and grassroots organizing outside of the church to establishing a black pastoral as an institution within the structures of the church. Partly because of church politics, such an internal pastoral organization did not appear in Bahia until the late 1990s.

In 1999 the Centro Arquidiocesano de Articulação da Pastoral Afro (the Archdiocesan Coordinating Center for the African Pastoral), or CAAPA, was founded in Salvador. Its stated purpose is to address racism and the under-representation of blacks within the church, to assist the black community through educational programs, and to affirm a black identity based in the Afro-Brazilian heritage—including through dialogue with Candomblé practitioners. These objectives have been complicated by the fact that many are suspicious of representatives of the white-dominated church. Nevertheless, many embrace CAAPA as the end of the Catholic Church's history of racial discrimination and religious persecution.

Although racism was named an official concern of the Brazilian Council of Bishops in the 1970s, it was decades before an official anti-racist organization appeared in the church in Bahia. Concern with racism gained public legitimacy when the Brazilian government hosted an international conference on diversity, multiculturalism, and affirmative action in 1996. At this conference President Cardoso, a sociologist who had studied Brazilian race relations, was the first to officially recognize these concepts and the problem of racial inequality in Brazil (Reichmann 1999b). It appears that the church began to focus on racism in Bahia just when the political climate was right.

One of CAAPA's main objectives is to create a dialogue with the Candomblé community. While Afro-Brazilian religion is still denigrated in Brazilian society, it has gained legal and cultural recognition in the past several decades. Beginning with the return to democracy in the 1940s, overt religious persecution by the state eased, and African-derived religions were practiced more or less openly. During the 1950s, however, the Catholic Church took a strong stance against these religions, associating them with superstition, heresy, and communism (Brown 1986). After the Second Vatican Council first met in 1962, the church backed off and began to adopt a stance of "liturgical pluralism" (Brown 1986, 162). It made attempts to appease rather than alienate practitioners of African-derived religions and often attempted to capitalize on forms of syncretism it formerly denounced in order to extend its influence to the lower sectors.

Contemporary Developments in the Candomblé Community

By the 1970s Candomblé terreiros in Bahia were freed from the requirement to register with the local police before their ceremonies. Subsequently, ceremonial performances were transformed into tourist attractions at the same time that many of these religions were associating themselves with movements for racial equality. Like Pentecostalism and evangelical Christianity in general, African-derived religions continued to grow at a fast pace in the 1990s. Burdick (1993) sees the popularity of Afro-Brazilian religions vis-à-vis Catholicism as partly due to their promise, like Pentecostalism, to provide prompt relief from suffering without stigmatizing the sufferer. Furthermore, such religions provide African-Brazilians with a powerful counterdiscourse to racism, as Candomblé terreiros are places in the Afro-Brazilian community where people proudly celebrate their African-derived cultural and religious heritage.

According to research on the nationwide census that Prandi (1995) conducted in the 1990s, about 1.3 percent of the Brazilian population reports being involved with Candomblé. This modest statistic, however, probably reflects only those who are formally initiated. Initiation is a lengthy and expensive process, and thus few participate in the daily activities of the terreiro, most of which are not open to the public. A significantly larger number of people attend or have attended public Candomblé ceremonies or have consulted with a Candomblé practitioner for a number of possible reasons, including problems with heath, money, or relationships. Judging from questionnaires I distributed (Selka 2003) and conversations with people in the field, I would estimate that somewhere between one-third to one-half of Bahians living in Cachoeira and Salvador had visited a terreiro at some point in their lives.

The path to full participation in Candomblé is initiation. Initiation ceremonies in Candomblé and similar religions are structured much like traditional African rites of passage (McGregor 1966; Bastide 1958). Often, candidates are initiated together as a group. Traditionally, each candidate enters into seclusion in his or her own sanctuary—usually a room in a hut or other building—for between three to twelve months (although this period is often much shorter today). During this time, the *mãe* or *pai de santo* (leaders of the terreiro) conducts ceremonies (e.g., animal sacrifices, food offerings, sacred baths, and shaving, cutting, and decorating the head—the "seat" of the spirits who "ride" their devotees) that bind the initiate to his or her orixá. Everyone, initiated or not, "belongs" to a particular orixá or set of orixás, but some people formalize and deepen this relationship through initiation. Many candomblecistas undergo initiation in response to an illness that is interpreted as a sign or beckoning from one's orixá. At the end of the initiation period, the new initiates (*filhos de santo*) emerge from seclusion in a spectacular ceremony often referred to as a kind of rebirth.

Day-to-day life at terreiros revolves around private and public activities, rituals, and ceremonies. Private activities consist mainly of fulfilling *obrigações* (ritual obligations), including animal sacrifices, food offerings, and other such rituals, to the orixás and other entities (Carneiro 1991; Bastide 1958). These obligations are due on days that are dedicated to particular entities, before public celebrations, as part of the requirements of initiation, for healing, or other special purposes—usually to do some kind of "work" on behalf of a client. Such work ranges from love spells to magic that aims to harm someone.

By far the most prominent of public Candomblé ceremonies is the public *festa* (feast or festival), also called a *toque*. Festas are dedicated to particular deities, and their timing is determined by the yearly ritual calendar that sets out the special days for each santo (a generic term for Candomblé god or spirit, including African orixás and indigenous Brazilian *caboclos*). These are elaborate events that people attend for a variety of reasons. Some come out of religious devotion, others to "see the beauty of the festival," and others to socialize. For the members of the terreiro, Candomblé festas require much planning and preparation. Food, decorations, clothing, and ritual items must be properly arranged. All of the available members of the house, and often friends and patrons as well, come together to help.

During festas, most, but not all, of the initiates present will "dance"—that is, participate fully in the celebration and become possessed by their deity. In addition to the filhos de santo and the mãe and pai de santo, others who have important duties include the *ogã* and *ekédis*, male and female helpers with special functions to fulfill in the terreiro, such as preparing offerings, playing *atabaques* (Afro-Brazilian hand drums), and helping the filhos de santo prepare for the festa, but who do not themselves become possessed during the celebration.

On the night of a typical festa in a Nagô terreiro, for example, guests begin arriving an hour or two before the ceremony begins. The terreiro is often decorated with streamers or palm fronds hanging from the rafters of the ceiling and sacred leaves placed on the floor; in addition, pictures of Catholic saints often hang on the walls. Before the ceremony begins the guests socialize, gossip, and compliment the terreiro leaders on the decorations. As the time to begin approaches (usually between 9:00 p.m. and midnight) the guests take their seats on benches around the *barracão*, or the large room in which the terreiro's public ceremonies take place. Traditionally, men sit on one side and the women on the other. On one side of the room large chairs are arranged for the leader and dignitaries of the terreiro, usually in front of the space set aside for the three drums that play during the festa. Veiled doorways lead to the back rooms where the initiates prepare for the ceremony.

Outside, the loud report of fireworks signals that the ceremony is about to start. The festa begins with the *padê*, or an offering made to the messenger orixá Exu, to establish a connection between the world of humans and the realm of the gods (as well as to prevent Exu from disrupting the ceremony). After the padê the filhos de santo file out of the back room and dance in a circle around the

Figure 2. These Cachoeiran women are participating in a *toque*, a public Candomblé ceremony. These particular Candomblé adepts are dancing for Oxum, the orixá associated with rivers and other bodies of fresh water.

center of the terreiro. The first half of the festa consists of the filhos performing the dances of each of the different santos (most commonly orixás or caboclos).

Each dance incorporates distinctive body and hand movements, drumbeats, and call and response songs, most of which are sung in Yoruba. Usually the mãe or pai de santo calls out the songs, and the filhos—along with many of the guests—respond. One after another, the filhos engage in ritual prostrations and salutations in front of the mãe or pai de santo. Toward the end of this first half of the ceremony, which can last several hours, the drumbeat quickens and the filhos who are not already possessed are "mounted" by their santo. This can be quite dramatic, especially after hours of repetitive dancing; the possessed often shake, swoon, and shout in ways that leave no doubt that their santo has arrived. Ogãs and ekédis help restrain those who are becoming possessed and secure a special cloth around the filhos' torsos. The filhos are then led to the back rooms of the terreiro, after which there is an intermission during which traditional Bahian foods are served.

After the break, each filho exits the back room dressed in the paraphernalia of his or her santo. These accouterments usually include vests or dresses of distinctive colors and styles, headdresses, and hand-held items that represent objects associated with the spirit, such as mirrors, swords, or bows and arrows.

Figure 3. This new Candomblé initiate is emerging from seclusion to make a public debut during a toque. Having one's head shaved is a central part of the process of initiation. (Photo by Chris Dunn)

One by one, each of the filhos comes to the center of the barracão and performs the dance of his or her santo. Sometimes onlookers become possessed and are taken to the back until the possession passes or to be fitted with the appropriate paraphernalia for dancing. When the last dance is finished, which is often in the early morning, the ceremony ends and people walk or ride home together discussing the night's events.

In addition to festas, consultations are another important activity that Candomblé terreiros provide for the public. Consultations typically center on a personal problem, such as physical or emotional illness, financial troubles, and romantic difficulties. Some terreiros hold regular hours for visitors seeking to have services performed, while others work only by appointment. Often these spiritual services account for a large portion of the terreiro's income. Consultations usually begin with the *jogo de búzios*, a divinatory technique used to discover spiritual imbalances as well as what weapons are being used against the person by his or her enemies. The jogo reveals who one's spiritual protectors and enemies are and what needs to be done to restore one's spiritual balance. People who come with specific complaints about their health are often prescribed ritual baths for purposes of purification. Some clients with grave problems are told that they must become initiated into Candomblé in order to end their suffering. Other kinds of services include defense against harmful spells, which many people claim can kill. Most practitioners will not openly admit that they practice harmful magic and insist that they "faz por bem" (practice for good) rather than "faz por mal" (practice for evil).

Candomblé is often described as a syncretic religion, and thus many people who witness a Candomblé festa for the first time are often surprised at how peripheral Catholic symbols and practices are in most terreiros. Although many terreiros have small Catholic shrines on their grounds and saints' images on the walls of the barracão, the influence of Catholicism may not at all be visible in ritual practice, most of which is African-derived. At least in the practice of Bahian Candomblé, the mixing or blending of religious elements is peripheral; in fact, the term that best describes Candomblé practice in Bahia is "syncretism in mosaic" (Bastide 1978). In other words, Candomblé ceremonies are seen as something separate from Catholicism even though Catholic Mass may be an integral part of a candomblecista's weekly religious practice, for example.

In fact, syncretism is most publicly visible during popular Catholic festivals in Bahia (including the Lavagem do Bonfim, the Festa da Nossa Senhora da Boa Morte, the Festa de Santa Barbara, and especially Carnaval), in which the participation of the Candomblé community is central. These festivals, which celebrate Catholic feast days and other holidays, typically involve large street processions or parades, along with plenty of "worldly" celebration (eating, drinking, and dancing) to accompany the religious festivities. Such celebrations are focal points of the Bahian calendar and in many ways appear as microcosms of Bahian society, often featuring both white elites (usually politicians and priests) and poor Candomblé practitioners marching side by side. Elements of Candomblé (symbols, certain kinds of clothing, drum rhythms, etc.) are often integrated into the festivities, and thus the celebrations often take on multiple meanings, some derived from Catholicism and others from Candomblé. The different meanings attributed to these festivals are often bridged through the identification of particular Candomblé santos with certain Catholic saints. This kind of identification, however, which is often cited as the epitome of syncretism, is a controversial issue for many candomblecistas. Some prominent practitioners have insisted, in order to emphasize that Candomblé is a legitimate religion in its own right, that candomblecistas abandon the tradition of celebrating Catholic festivals.

In fact, syncretism and the questions of cultural appropriation it raises have become heated political issues for many practitioners of African-derived religions. Some argue that the identification of African orixás with Catholic saints in Candomblé terreiros and the patronage of African slave-spirits by white Umbanda practitioners obscures unequal power relationships and in fact reinforces a social order based on hierarchy and inequality (Birman 1995; Brown 1986). Like the appropriation of Native American spirituality by whites in the United States, such practices often trivialize the cultures of dominated peoples and marginalize their efforts to represent their own cultural heritages (Churchill 1996).

In response, many African-Brazilians have been attempting to "Africanize" Umbanda (while at the same time many white middle-class *umbandistas* have been trying to deemphasize Umbanda's African origins) and to "re-Africanize" religions such as Candomblé (Brown 1999, 1986). In the last few decades, this cultural appropriation and reappropriation has become an important racial, religious, and political issue. As I discuss in the following chapters, practitioners of African-derived religions have strongly objected to inappropriate and unauthorized uses of ritual performances and esoteric knowledge, which, again, is also a major concern among Native Americans in the United States (Nason 1997).

An important milestone in the re-Africanization or "anti-syncretism" movement occurred in the early 1980s, when a group composed of prominent leaders in the Candomblé community in Bahia asserted Candomblé's independence from the Catholic Church. In a conference and a subsequent newspaper article, the leaders declared that Candomblé "is a religion and not a syncretic sect" and denounced syncretism as an artifact from the time of slavery (Ilé Axé Opô Afonjá 2002, translation mine). Many Candomblé practitioners subsequently removed Catholic paraphernalia from their ritual spaces, stopped attending Mass, and no longer participated in popular Afro-Catholic festivals.

The anti-syncretism movement aimed not only to establish Candomblé as an independent religion in its own right, but also to protest the rampant commodification of Afro-Brazilian religion and culture by the tourist industry in Bahia. Because it affirms a sacred cultural tradition separate from the white elite, the anti-syncretism movement has an affinity with the outlook of some Afro-Brazilian political groups. In fact, many activists involved with political groups such as the MNU are involved in the Candomblé community. While those involved with the black movement emphasize that there is no formal link between any particular religion and the movement, Candomblé is often closely associated with anti-racist initiatives.

Contemporary Evangelicals

The connection between Candomblé, Afro-Brazilian identity, and anti-racist struggle is complicated by the striking growth of Pentecostal Christianity in Brazil. An estimated 15 percent of Brazil's population is Protestant, about two-thirds of whom are Pentecostals and make up the fastest-growing religious group in Brazil today (Freston 1994). Pentecostals avoid African-derived religious practices and therefore generally keep their distance from the mainstream black movement. Because the majority of Brazilian Pentecostals are of African descent (Prandi 1995), this presents a challenge to racial solidarity and mobilization, at least on the basis of religion.

The striking rates of growth of Protestantism in Brazil today began in the 1950s and 1960s. Protestant growth during this period was primarily an urban phenomenon (Costa 1979). The democratic government's projects of modernization, development, and building a strong, unified nation became increasingly relevant to the lives of members of the rapidly growing lower and middle classes in the cities. Protestantism, particularly Pentecostalism, was growing at its fastest rate among these same social groups during this time.

During the 1950s and 1960s, when the patron-client networks of the Brazilian political economy were breaking down in many places, a schism within the Assembly of God led to the formation of the Brasil Para Cristo movement. This movement was an early expression of what has been called "theology of prosperity" in a perverse reference to the theology of liberation in the Catholic Church. By emphasizing upward mobility and material success as a reward from God for good conduct, this movement targeted those among the urban proletariat who sought to distance themselves from patron-client relationships and traditional values (Costa 1979). Even within the Assembly, the increasing number of members from the middle and professional classes contributed to a more "modern" perspective and organization that articulated with the changes occurring in Brazilian society.

Pentecostal discourse in general during the 1950s and 1960s was anti-Catholic, as evangelical Christians increasingly came to see Catholicism as undermining the foundations of true democracy (Costa 1979). Some Protestant churches began to develop their own community improvement programs, like those of the Catholics, including social services for the needy. These groups, however, advocated "ordered social development," and in contrast to the developments within the Catholic Church during the 1960s, radical social politics were excluded from Protestant discourse (Costa 1979, 413–14).

The succession of military governments in the 1960s and 1970s brought both political stability and continued economic development, if only for the ultimate benefit of the elite (James and Minkel 1986). During this period, the growth of Protestantism was staggering. From 1960 to 1970, the Protestant population grew by 77 percent and from 1970 to 1980 by 155 percent (Stoll 1990). Pentecostals account for most of this increase, and some have attempted to explain this growth by arguing that the supposedly individualistic, liberal ethos of Pentecostalism, in contrast to the more traditional worldview of Catholicism, articulated well with the increasing modernization resulting from capitalist development (see Martin 1991; Manning 1980).

On the other hand, Margolies (1980) and Hoffnagel (1980) point out that in the context of the rural to urban migration associated with increasing economic growth due to industrialization, Pentecostal organizations replaced disrupted extended family ties with an ethic of reciprocity and mutual aid. From this perspective, Pentecostalism replicates rather than contradicts the principles of traditional community life. More recent studies (Stewart-Gambino and Wilson 1997; Berryman 1995; Campos Machado 1996; Freston 1994; Burdick 1993; Garrard-Burnett and Stoll 1993; Novaes and Floriano 1985; and Rolim 1985) approach Pentecostalism as a more dynamic phenomenon and emphasize the variations between and within Pentecostal churches. These authors focus on the variety of factors that lead people in particular times and places to become involved with Pentecostalism.

Generally, during the military regime evangelical Christians appear to have kept a low political profile or embraced the status quo, unlike their progressive Catholic neighbors. Many Pentecostal pastors during this period were entangled in the elite and involved in conservative political parties. Local church members, however, often passively accepted their pastor's mediation for them in political affairs (Ireland 1991). Thus, public Pentecostal politics under the military regime ranged from conservatism to apathy, leaving little room for progressive initiatives.

It is important to remember, however, that during this period leftists, reformists, and others who challenged the government were considered radical and subject to prison or exile. As Stewart-Gambino and Wilson (1997; cf. Berryman 1995) point out, because Pentecostals were regarded as a marginal religious group, avoiding open conflict with the government made some sense. Yet they note that, more recently, some Pentecostal groups have backed reformist candidates in Brazil and elsewhere in Latin America.

By the 1990s, the future of Brazilian religion clearly appeared to belong to Pentecostalism rather than the CEBs (Berryman 1995). In greater Rio de Janeiro, five new Protestant churches were established each week between 1990 and 1992, 90 percent of which were Pentecostal; yet during this time, only one new Catholic parish appeared (Berryman 1995; cf. Freston 1994). Furthermore, Pentecostalism has become truly "nativized"—according to Paul Freston (1994), thirty-seven out of fifty-two major Pentecostal denominations originated in Brazil, and no foreign denomination has succeeded in building a significant presence in Brazil in the last forty years. By 1994 it is estimated that 15 percent of Brazil's population was Protestant, 60 percent to two-thirds of whom were Pentecostal.

In the 1990s Pentecostals broke into the political arena after decades of being characterized either as diehard reactionaries or as politically apathetic. Evangelical congressional representatives have come to make up "one of the most important blocs in the Brazilian Congress" (Freston 1994, 10). Furthermore, their recent political activities have forever dispelled the stereotype of Pentecostals as uniformly conservative, since Pentecostals have become involved with questioning the status quo and protesting social inequities (Rolim 1985).

The recent emergence of progressive evangelical politics raises the question of whether this is a new phenomenon or whether leftists in the past were simply keeping a low profile under the threat of persecution. Surely some evangelicals have always held progressive views, yet the increased diversity and public expression of political ideas in evangelical communities today is unprecedented. This political "opening" has paralleled the expansion of democracy and the gradual maturation of civil society in Brazil since the 1980s. As I discuss in chapter 5, it appears that the growth of progressive evangelical politics is more a result of the influence of political changes in Brazilian society—including the proliferation of leftist parties, social movements, and nongovernmental organizations (NGOs)—than of the release of a repressed leftist tendency within Pentecostalism itself.

Whether conservative or progressive, most Pentecostals share similar socioeconomic characteristics. Recent demographic studies of Pentecostalism show that while it has grown among the middle and upper sectors, most Pentecostals are still from the lower classes (Chesnut 1997; Freston 1994; Novaes and Floriano 1985). Compared to their non-Pentecostal counterparts, Pentecostals are disproportionately represented in service-sector jobs (Chesnut 1997). But as Novaes and Floriano (1985) emphasize, the repercussions of Pentecostal doctrine vary in different areas of social life and according to the interests of different social groups, making it difficult to claim that involvement with Pentecostalism affects subjectivities in some uniform way or that there is a singular Pentecostal worldview.

On the whole, it is apparent that evangelical Christianity has "arrived" in all areas of Brazilian life, as it has become highly visible on television, in the realm of sports, in the business world of the executive, and in politics (Freston 1994). Moreover, within the past several decades a new "third wave" of Pentecostalism has been surging in Brazil. The first wave was associated with the first Pentecostal churches founded in Brazil at the beginning of the twentieth century and the second with Pentecostal movements that began to emerge from mainline Christian denominations around the 1950s (Campos 1996).

The third wave began in the 1970s and can be seen as an extension of the theology of prosperity. Third-wave churches like the Igreja Universal Reina de Deus (Universal Church of the Kingdom of God; IURD) represent a sort of postmodern adaptation to the sensibilities of a society of consumption and to the demands of a competitive religious marketplace (Freston 1994). The IURD uses an "entrepreneurial" approach to church growth and is quite effective at using the mass media for the purposes of evangelization (Campos 1996). In fact, as of 1997, the IURD owned forty-seven television and twenty-six radio stations throughout Brazil.

Some commentators argue that IURD is a prime example of truly Brazilian Protestantism (Da Silva 1997). Da Silva argues that the IURD is very well attuned to elements of the Afro-Catholic "minimal religiosity" in Brazil (1997, 11). Services often incorporate mystical materials such as blessed water (made holy by the prayers of the congregation, not by the pastor), anointed oil, and salt that can be used to expel demons. On Fridays, which are days of reverence in Afro-Brazilian religion, all IURD churches host exorcism services in which people possessed by demons (orixás) are "liberated." The IURD's enterprising approach that incorporates elements and themes from Brazilian popular religion has made it one of the country's largest and fastest-growing churches.

Nevertheless, the IURD is virulently hostile to certain fundamental expressions of Brazilian culture. Although it incorporates elements from the Afro-Catholic religious universe, the IURD reviles Candomblé as the religion of the devil. Furthermore, in 1995 an IURD pastor kicked an image of Nossa Senhora da Aparecida—the patron saint of Brazil—on national television. The iconoclastic pastor defiantly declared that the image was nothing but a powerless piece of plaster. This caused a tremendous uproar, and eventually the founder of the IURD publicly apologized for the excess of the young pastor (Da Silva 1997).

As scholars and activists have argued, the growing popularity of Pentecostal-ism is, or should be, of major concern to activists in the black movement (cf. Burdick 1999, 1998a, 1998b; Myatt 1995). With respect to mobilization, Pentecostals are often perceived as politically apathetic, despite ample evidence to the contrary (Cleary and Stewart-Gambino 1997; Freston 1994). Nevertheless, Pentecostals are underrepresented in major black-consciousness groups. Part of the reason for this is that Pentecostals generally shun the cultural (capoeira, samba) and religious (Candomblé) components of Afro-Brazilian identity that are often at the center of the black movement.

As Burdick points out, the antagonism between the black movement and Protestant Christianity stems from four main sources. First, many activists "reject Christianity in general because of its historical links to slavery" (1998a, 119). Second, Protestantism is widely regarded as a religion of ethnic assimilation into white culture. Third, Pentecostal Protestantism's emphasis on both individualism and universalism is often seen as opposed to ethnic and other group identities. Finally, as I mentioned above, Pentecostalism is particularly hostile to traditional Afro-Brazilian culture.

Because of this hostility, some openly accuse Pentecostals of racism. As Burdick notes and as I discuss in later chapters, in recent years Candomblé terreiros have increasingly been the target of evangelical verbal and even physical attacks. Many black activists equate such intolerant and hateful attitudes toward African-derived religions with racism. In a document Burdick cites, for example, the Movement for African Religious Freedom and Citizenship condemns these assaults on Afro-Brazilian religions by "nazi-pentecostal churches" (1998a, 119).

Academic studies have tended to reinforce the black movement's negative assessments of evangelical Christianity. Pierre Verger, a famous ethnographer and photographer of Afro-Bahian culture, wrote that "adhesion to the religious values of the Protestants" leads to "alienation from African values" (1992, 19; translation mine). Likewise, Roger Bastide (1978) has contended that Protestantism assimilated blacks to white culture. Novaes and Floriano (1985) cited numerous black Protestant informants who claim that skin color is unimportant in their churches and who maintain that by drawing a distinction between blacks and whites, the black movement causes racism rather than ameliorates it. Similarly, Contins (1992) contends that black identity is simply not an issue for Pentecostals.

Yet Burdick argues that given the rapid growth of evangelical Christianity among people of African descent, it is worthwhile to examine if the portrayal of

Pentecostalism "as irredeemably corrosive of black identity and political struggle is accurate or exhaustive" (1998a, 121). He suggests that although evangelical Christianity is generally hostile to racial identities, it might foster other forms of anti-racism through its discourse of human equality (1999, 1998a, 1998b). Many black Pentecostals tell of overcoming shame about their physical appearance, for example. As Chesnut points out, Pentecostal belief "may not cure the scourge of racism, but it provides a space and community where African Brazilians are immune from its most malignant forms" (1997, 124).

Furthermore, initiatives such as the Movimento Evangélico Progressista (Progressive Evangelical Movement; MEP) provide possible points of articulation between evangelical Christianity and the black movement. The members of MEP in Bahia, many of whom are affiliated with the leftist Workers Party, are concerned with issues of social and economic justice. As evangelicals, they question the natural connection between being black and involvement with Candomblé. Like other Christians, the members of MEP attempt to live their lives according to the Bible. Yet they interpret the scriptures from a clearly progressive perspective.

As I discuss in more depth below, members of MEP emphasize the historical connections between Protestantism and political democratization and often cite the involvement of Protestant groups with progressive social causes such as abolition, feminism, and the civil rights movement. American civil rights leaders such as Martin Luther King, Jr., provide the paradigm for struggle against racism. In this way, progressive evangelicals such as the members of MEP attempt to construct a politically engaged identity that is based on the common experiences—but not a shared traditional religion—of blacks throughout the diaspora. As I have already indicated and as we will see in the following pages, this approach goes against the grain of popular understandings about the connections among religion, Afro-Brazilian identity, and anti-racist politics in Bahia—particularly those that focus on Candomblé terrerios as privileged sites of Afro-Brazilian identity construction and resistance to racism.

3

Catholicism and Afro-Brazilian Identity

Founded in 1549, Salvador da Bahia was Brazil's first major port and the capital of colonial Brazil for almost two hundred years. The surrounding region became one of the most productive areas in Brazil by the end of the sixteenth century. During the early colonial period, the port of Salvador bustled with activity—namely the exportation of sugar and the importation of slaves. From the seventeenth to the early eighteenth centuries, the northeastern sugar plantation area, with Salvador as its center, was the most important economically, socially, and politically in Brazil (Tavares 2001; Skidmore 1999; Burns 1980; Wagley 1963; Hutchinson 1952).

While the importance of Salvador and the Recôncavo eventually declined as the center of economic and political power moved to the south of Brazil in the 1700s, to a significant extent the core economic, political, and social structures of the plantation economy have persisted until today. Although Bahia has undergone significant industrialization in recent decades and commercial agriculture has had a major impact on farming practices, the agricultural sector is still an important source of jobs in the northeast.

As in the past, Bahia today continues to be dominated by patron-client politics and certain prominent families. Recent high-profile scandals seem to indicate, however, that there is less tolerance for corruption than before. In addition, although many of the elite who live in Salvador still own their *fazendas* (plantations) in the interior, which they visit on the weekends, the members of the middle and upper middle classes in the city are more likely to be employees of modern corporations than owners of agricultural land. Thus, economic practices and social relations are changing under the rubric of modernization, albeit in characteristically Bahian ways.[1]

Salvador, the capital of Bahia and the fourth largest city in Brazil, is a complex urban landscape with about 2.6 million inhabitants (IBGE 2005). The downtown section of the city is divided into the upper and lower cities—separated by a precipitous cliff—which were connected by elevator in the 1870s. The lower part of Salvador serves mainly as the business and financial district while the upper city is the governmental, ecclesiastical, and tourist center. Pelourinho, the recently restored historical district in the upper city, is a popular tourist destination that has been deemed part of "the heritage of humanity" by the U.N. in recognition of its sixteenth-century colonial architecture. Until the 1980s, however, Pelourinho was a lower-class residential district where many Afro-Brazilians lived.

Today, besides being a tourist attraction, Pelourinho remains a center of social life for many Afro-Brazilians who live in the surrounding bairros (neighborhoods), such as Liberdade, where the headquarters of such prominent Afro-Bahian institutions as Ilê Aiyê and the MNU are located. Residential segregation is perhaps not as clear in Salvador as in some North American cities, but in general the further one goes into the periphery of the city, the higher the proportion of Afro-Brazilians in the population. On the other end of the racial and socioeconomic spectrum, the lighter-skinned members of the middle class usually live in the swank bairros along the city's extensive coast.

The importance of religion is clearly visible in Salvador. A popular but exaggerated local saying is that there are 365 Catholic churches in the city, one for each day of the year. Some of the older churches are decorated in an elaborate baroque or rococo style that reflects the opulence of the times in which they were built. Today, Catholic street festivals are a major form of religious celebration in the Bahian capital. The Lavagem do Bonfim, for example, draws crowds of tens of thousands who march through the main streets of the city each year to make a pilgrimage to the church of Salvador's divine patron, Senhor do Bonfim.

The number of Catholic churches and chapels in the city is surely rivaled by the abundance of evangelical churches. While most of the latter are simple and humble in comparison with the elaborate styles of many Catholic buildings, the size of the Universal Church of the Kingdom of God's "Cathedral of Faith" rivals that of any Catholic structure in Salvador. Moreover, the Cathedral of Faith is located off of a major highway next to the city's interstate bus terminal and across the street from the largest and busiest mall in town. Thus, evangelicals are becoming more visible, and in recent years evangelicals have even celebrated an alternative Carnaval in the streets of Salvador.

Salvador, however, is perhaps best known as the Rome of Afro-Brazilian religion. During the colonial period Salvador and the surrounding Recôncavo made up the cradle of Candomblé, and today many of the oldest and most famous of Brazil's Candomblé terreiros are located in and around the city. Because of Salvador's large population of African descent and its strong Afro-Brazilian cultural traditions, it is also a center of racial consciousness in Brazil.

Salvador and São Paulo were perhaps the two most important centers of Afro-Brazilian consciousness and activism in the twentieth century (K. Butler 1998a). Yet the two cities are different in this regard, as São Paulo has been a center for political activism, whereas Salvador is known as the African capital of Brazil. Moreover, black communities in both cities differ in how they construct Afro-Brazilian identity, as Kim Butler explains.

> In response to different historical trajectories and modalities of ethnic exclusion, the African-descended population in São Paulo developed an identity based on racial differences, whereas that of Salvador was predicated on cultural differences. The strategic use of identity in each community, however, was remarkably similar. In each case, Afro-Brazilians appropriated the identity of exclusion, a tool of oppression, and used it as a strategy of empowerment. (1998a, 218)

Today Salvador is an important center of Afro-Brazilian cultural awareness and, perhaps to a lesser extent, political activism.

In this and the following chapters I explore how ethnic consciousness is constructed and how anti-racist activism is enacted in the context of different religious, cultural, and political groups in Salvador. Rather than assuming that black identity is something unitary and uncontested, I focus on different discourses about Afro-Brazilian identity among various Catholic, Candomblé, and evangelical Christian groups. Again, debates about Afro-Brazilian identity are often based in struggles over classification. In the religious arena, such struggles concern how African-derived religion is categorized and characterized, its relationship to Christianity, and, ultimately, its role in the construction of Afro-Brazilian identity and the battle against racism. Furthermore, outside the religious arena proper, in the context of Afro-Brazilian cultural affirmations and political activism, many with whom I spoke see these issues as centrally relevant to the black movement.

Catholicism and Afro-Brazilian Identity

Although I spoke with a wide range of Catholics while I was in Salvador, I worked most closely with members of the Irmandade da Nossa Senhora do Rosário dos Pretos do Pelourinho (Confraternity of Our Lady of the Rosary of the Blacks of Pelourinho) and the Centro Arquidiocesano de Articulação da Pastoral Afro (Archdiocesan Coordinating Center for the African Pastoral; CAAPA). The Irmandade do Rosário is a lay organization that is several centuries old; the Pastoral Afro, which consists of Afro-Brazilian clergy, was founded in 1999. Although these groups have very different histories, they are both centrally concerned with Afro-Brazilian identity and the struggle against racism. Furthermore, as Afro-Brazilian organizations within the church, these groups are closely associated and often coordinate their practices.

Irmandade da Nossa Senhora do Rosário dos Pretos do Pelourinho

The Irmandade do Rosário was established in Salvador in the late seventeenth century. Nossa Senhora do Rosário was an important figure for Brazilian slaves, many of whom believed that she relieved the suffering inflicted by their white masters. In the sixteenth century, the first slave confraternity in Brazil was dedicated to her, and since then Nossa Senhora do Rosário has been the most popular patron of black confraternities in Brazil (Kiddy 2005, 1998; Mulvey 1980, 1982).

The members of the Rosário confraternity in Bahia began the construction of the church of Nossa Senhora do Rosário in Pelourinho in 1703. The church was built by slaves—who were not allowed inside the churches of the white elites—as a place of their own where they could worship freely. The building is said to have taken almost one hundred years to complete, as construction could be done only on Sundays, on holy days, and at night after the slaves had finished their daily work (Mulvey 1980, 268).

Largely built in the rococo style, today the church of Nossa Senhora do Rosário is one of Pelourinho's most impressive landmarks. On the walls inside the church, murals composed of blue and white tiles imported from Portugal depict the Virgin Mary holding the rosary as she appears to her devotees. Although the people portrayed on these tiles are invariably white, above the tile murals are paintings of the stations of the cross in which Christ and the other figures are depicted as black. Also along the walls of the nave are statues of various black saints, including St. Benedict the Moor. To the left of the altar stands a statue of Nossa Senhora da Aparecida, the patron of Brazil, who is black as well.

Outside in the courtyard in back of the church is a shrine to Anastácia, who is a central figure in Brazilian popular Catholicism. Anastácia, who ostensibly lived as a slave in colonial Brazil, was a dark-skinned young woman who was considered especially beautiful because of her mysteriously blue eyes. There are many versions of her story, but in all of them she was repeatedly and brutally raped throughout her short life. Eventually she was martyred after being placed

Figure 4. The church of Our Lady of the Rosary of the Blacks in the Pelourinho neighborhood of Salvador. The church was built by slaves in the eighteenth century to provide a place of worship for blacks.

in a mask and iron collar for some transgression, perhaps denying her affections to her overseer or tasting the sugar that she was forced to harvest. While the stories of her life and death speak of the horrors of slavery, Anastácia is always portrayed as stoic and docile despite the intensity of her sufferings. Today, many Brazilians consider Anastácia to be a saint. Some activists, however, see devotion to Anastácia as working at cross-purposes with the aims of the black movement because of what is characterized as her passivity in the face of white domination (Burdick 1998a).

In the backyard of Nossa Senhora do Rosário many devotees have placed their votive candles in a metal contraption near the shrine; yet candles, vases, and small statues of Cosme and Damião (the twin saints Cosme and Damian) are strewn around the area and along the wall in front of Anastácia's image. As is common in popular Catholicism in Brazil and Latin America, the relationship between Anastácia and her devotees is one of reciprocity. Many come to her

Figure 5. A shrine devoted to Escrava Anastácia at the church of Our Lady of the Rosary of the Blacks. Anastácia is an important patron saint in popular Catholicism in Brazil, especially among Afro-Brazilians.

seeking patience and peace of mind in the face of suffering, while others leave candles and other items at the shrine hoping for miracles.

Devotion to black saints like Anastácia and Benedito sets the Rosário church apart from most other churches in Salvador, as does the incorporation of "African" elements into the celebration of Mass. On one of my first visits to the church, I met a local tour guide who explained that the church was originally built for Candomblé purposes. He was adamant, however, that although most people who belong to the irmandade are involved with Candomblé, today there is no such mixing of Catholicism and African-derived religion in the church. When I asked him about "inculturated" Masses, he said that Mass at Nossa Senhora do Rosário is just like anywhere else. "At some celebrations they play *samba de roda*, but that's the only big difference," he insisted. Although it is true that Candomblé rituals probably do not take place in the Rosário church today, the tour guide was downplaying the extent to which Mass has been "Africanized."

Inculturated Mass at the Rosário Church

Every Tuesday evening, the Rosário church celebrates inculturated Masses that incorporate African musical instruments and song. Broadly speaking, inculturation refers to "the process of incorporating cultural elements from the traditions of the cultures of the people making up the Church community in a particular context into the ceremonies and celebrations of the Church" (Myatt 1995, 199). Starting in the late 1970s, at about the time that the MNU emerged in Brazil, progressive priests began integrating Afro-Brazilian cultural elements into the Catholic liturgy. Nevertheless, the inculturation movement did not become popular in the mainstream church until the late 1980s, when Rome was increasingly confronting the difficulties of maintaining its influence in a world where most Catholics were non-European (Burdick 2003).

In fact, the Pastoral Afro, ostensibly the official organization within the church involved with inculturation, did not appear in Salvador until 1999. Yet it is important to note that while inculturation as an official Catholic discourse is a relatively recent development, as early as the 1700s the Rosário confraternity in Bahia was integrating African songs and dances with Catholic feast days (Mulvey 1982, 46–47).

Tuesday evening inculturated Masses at the Rosário church are celebrated in honor of Santa Bárbara, who is often associated or identified with the orixá Iansã (whose day of honor in Candomblé is Tuesday). The president of the Rosário confraternity explained to me that Santa Bárbara was the patron of a nearby market that closed many years ago. The merchants and vendors of that market used to have Masses said for their patron at the Rosário church, and when the market closed, the images of Santa Bárbara were moved to the church and are now displayed in the halls.

What is perhaps most distinctive about the inculturated Masses at the Rosário church is the style of the music that accompanies the hymns. During the Mass for Santa Bárbara/Iansã, a group of singers and musicians assembles to the left of the altar. The group includes worshipers playing tambourines, rattles, and a number of other percussion instruments like those played in Candomblé terreiros. The rhythm of the music is often recognizably Afro-Brazilian and similar to that which one hears played in Candomblé toques. Moreover, the singers frequently employ a call and response style that is common in African-derived vocal performances. In effect, the energy of the Mass is ebullient and joyous in contrast to the traditionally stern and solemn liturgy of traditional Masses.

During the Mass, a procession of women carrying bread in straw baskets dances up the aisle in a way very similar to what one would see in a Candomblé terreiro. Although the tone of the Mass is decidedly Afro-Brazilian, many of the hymns are reminiscent of evangelical songs and are accompanied by hand and body movements as in evangelical churches. As opposed to Masses in other churches in Pelourinho, practically everyone who attends would be considered black from the North American point of view. With respect to skin color, I would estimate that half or more of the parishioners who attend inculturated Masses at the Rosário church would be called *preto* (black), while the others, who were lighter-skinned, would most likely be referred to as *moreno* (brown).

Festival of Santa Bárbara

In addition to weekly Masses, many people from the Afro-Brazilian community—including large numbers of Candomblé adepts—gather around the Rosário church for yearly festivals in honor of various saints. Not surprisingly, one of the yearly festivals celebrated at the Rosário church is that of Santa Bárbara. In December 2001, I attended the festival along with huge crowds of people dressed in red (Iansã's color) and packed into the winding cobblestone streets of Pelourinho. Locals set up their *barracas* (stalls or stands) along the Largo of Pelourinho, the wide street in front of the church, where they would sell necklaces, red roses, and T-shirts bearing images of Santa Bárbara. Many of the vendors were women dressed in the traditional Bahian white lace dress with red accessories in honor of Iansã.

The festival of Santa Bárbara is one of the most popular syncretic festivals in Bahia. As a local newspaper reported, "in communion, Catholics and Candomblé adepts sung with one voice and showed that faith in the entity—Santa Bárbara or Iansã—is independent of religion" (*A Tarde*, December 5, 2001; translation mine). The festival that I attended in 2001 began with music, as is common in popular celebrations in Bahia, and the musicians launched the festivities with a samba beat played on drums and cowbells.

Dom Geraldo, the bishop of Salvador, presided over the celebration. Before Mass he spoke over a loudspeaker about the connection between Santa Bárbara and the Afro-Brazilian community. Dom Geraldo announced that people often ask him about the importance of Santa Bárbara. He said that he explains to them that she was a martyr who endured much suffering like so many people of African descent in Bahia. Africans were taken from their land, enslaved, separated from their families and culture, impoverished and discriminated against. Thus, Dom Geraldo suggested that people of African descent, perhaps more than others, could identify with the incomprehensible suffering of Santa Bárbara.

By the time Dom Geraldo finished speaking, the church had filled to capacity. More than a thousand people were congregated outside, and I was one of the many not able to work my way inside the building on this occasion. As the Mass began, fireworks exploded, and around the corner a drum troupe of young boys played songs reminiscent of the music of the popular Afro-Brazilian group Olodum. During Mass those of us outside in front of the church socialized, bargained with the vendors, and enjoyed the vibrant atmosphere of the festival.

After Mass ended, a procession left the church carrying a parade of small statues of saints set on beds of plants and flowers. As the procession came out of the church and wended its way up the Largo do Pelourinho, a man sang out each of the saint's names over a loudspeaker: Santo Antonio, Cosme and Damião, São Lazaro, and so on. At the end came the little statue of Santa Bárbara, perhaps ten inches tall, atop a bed of plants and red roses. The announcer sang "Viva Santa Bárbara!" as people cheered and threw rice in the air. The procession went up the hill that leads from the Rosário church to the Praça da Sé (the main square in Pelourinho), which was filled with still more people who came out for the festival.

In addition to the integration of Afro-Brazilian symbols and practices into the liturgy, Afro-Brazilian themes were often featured prominently in the priest's homily during Masses I attended at the Rosário church. As I mentioned above, Dom Geraldo argued that there is a close connection between the suffering of Santa Bárbara and that of the Afro-Brazilian communities. On a different occasion, another presiding priest compared the history of the Irmandade do Rosário to a story of a black slave who overcame racism in the church. Most strikingly, the priest argued that if God is present in nature and everything else, why not say that He also is present in the force of the orixás?

The Irmandade do Rosário

Alberico, the head of the Irmandade da Nossa Senhora do Rosário dos Pretos do Pelourinho, is a large, stout man, perhaps a little under six feet tall. Despite his position of authority in the irmandade, he is rather soft-spoken. Sometimes his words are hard to make out—he mumbles a bit—but he is articulate and knowledgeable about the Irmandade do Rosário. From what he told me, it seems that he spends most of his time at the church and that his life revolves around the irmandade.

In my interviews with him about Catholicism and the Afro-Brazilian community, Alberico maintained that the Catholic Church has recently made progress in its position toward people of African descent. Inculturated Masses, which he describes here, are a major sign of this progress.

> In the inculturated Masses we just change the rhythm of the songs, we add the musical sounds of black culture, and also, generally, we have a lot of applause, clapping, and dancing.

But support for inculturation is not unanimous in the church.

> We have had many problems with groups that are not open [to incultura-tion], there are also some intolerant priests. But in general there has been progress: at least two times a week we have inculturated Masses.

Although some criticize inculturation as a way to bring Candomblé into the church, Alberico says there is no mixture with Candomblé.

> The Irmandade in itself has no connection with Candomblé. . . . Now, the members of the Irmandade, I would say that 95 percent of them have a double religious belonging: to Catholicism and to the religion of the orixás that is called Candomblé.

Yet this double belonging is something distinct from syncretism, which, as I examine throughout this chapter and as Alberico points out here, is often looked upon disparagingly.

> You have seen that, at least here in Bahia, it [syncretism] has a pejorative connotation . . . [yet] even the Catholic religion is syncretic because it uses many Greco-Roman things. But here in Bahia people started a move-ment in the 1980s to end syncretism because, in reality it was a necessary

evil in the past. Today it is no longer, it is no longer necessary. . . . There is double belonging, there is ecumenism, but as for syncretism—nothing absorbed anything from anyone.

The Irmandade do Rosário shares this emphasis on the discourse of double belonging with the Pastoral Afro, just as both organizations stress their involvement with raising black consciousness. Alberico maintains, for example, that the Irmandade takes part in the wider struggle against racism by providing an affirmative space for Afro-Brazilians.

We fight against racism by raising the self-esteem of blacks. Because blacks come and get married here because they find it more accessible, they get baptized here, have their funerals here, have festivities here, and all the festivals that we have here bring people together with the priest. So, they [blacks] feel their self-esteem go up!

While the Irmandade do Rosário is centrally concerned with black self-esteem, Alberico denied any connections to formal political groups like the MNU.

I don't have [this connection with the MNU] and neither does the brotherhood. . . . There are no members of the brotherhood who are from the MNU. I was one of the founders of the MNU! But, when the MNU became, and I don't know if it still is, sectarian . . . it started to become very closed and had ideas that were a little crazy, fighting against racial discrimination and continuing to discriminate behind this, at that time I left! But . . . I am friends with everyone, from the past and from the present. All of the blocos afros are part of the black movement. Look, I think that the Rosário church is part of the black movement, not with that label, but it is!

Thus, Alberico identifies the Irmandade with the black movement in general but not with its political wing, as represented by the MNU. He laments that many people see the black movement only as a political phenomenon.

Generally, people say: "Ah, but the black movement is only run by the MNU and it is political. . . ." This is misguided thinking because I have yet to see [any results]. All they do is argue about politics and education, but they don't educate, and this is no good! . . . The MNU should create a school to train professors or have a group of students, but they don't do that. They just keep arguing, hurting themselves, complaining without doing anything to change the picture.

By contrast, the Irmandade's emphasis is on religion and culture, and Alberico clearly prefers this to MNU politics.

> Here in the church we work with black politics, we work with the spiritual side, with music and even with art. Because people also have a way of dressing, because blacks come here for a celebration and to do things: African dance, African clothes, that whole business, African elements. . . . For me it is much better to be here . . . it is much better than just arguing and arguing.

As I examine in more depth in my discussion of the Pastoral Afro later in this chapter, the discourse of inculturation that underlies Alberico's comments is particularly interesting because it works to pull religion and culture apart. That is, inculturation entails the abstraction of elements of the African way of being from Candomblé and their integration into a Catholic context. Moreover, in order for this to work, one has to affirm that despite Catholicism's European (Roman) origins, one can be Catholic in an African way. Thus, we can see at least three parallel oppositions at work: between white and black, Europe and Africa, and Catholicism and Candomblé.

With respect to double religious belonging, my conversations with Alberico and others piqued my curiosity (not only as an anthropologist but as a person who has a double religious belonging myself) about the different meanings or purposes that multiple religions might have in people's lives. When I asked Alberico about this he responded by proclaiming, as Brazilians often do, that "Deus é um só" (there is only one God). In the context of popular Catholicism and Candomblé, this phrase is often invoked to argue that all religions worship the same God and therefore they are equal. (By contrast, in the context of Pentecostalism it is more typically deployed to make the argument that there is only one proper God, that of the Bible.)

Thus, Alberico argues that Catholicism and Candomblé are equally valid and contends that double belonging is a cultural issue (as opposed to a theological one, for example). He explains that Afro-Brazilians see their heritage as grounded in both Candomblé and Catholicism, but in different ways. Candomblé is derived from the religion of the African ancestors, while to a large extent Catholicism has formed the public framework of Afro-Brazilian religiosity since the sixteenth century. Alberico claims that Candomblé is generally seen, in contrast to Catholicism, as an ecologically oriented religion—it deals with the forces of nature, incorporates extensive knowledge of plants, involves animal sacrifices, and centers on ideas of balance and reciprocity. In addition, he argues that for people of African descent, Candomblé forms a true brotherhood—as opposed to the Catholic Church, which is a brotherhood only for the priests.

Other members of the Irmandade do Rosário expressed similar views. One older brother who is a member of a prominent terreiro in Salvador contended that Catholic and Candomblé priests do essentially the same thing (they perform the same function of mediating between the faithful and the divine), and the Pastoral Afro is striving for recognition of this fact in the church. By contrast, he said, evangelical Christians do not see themselves as equals with candomblecistas. Thus, he argues that evangelicals of African descent do not properly recognize their roots in African religion, as do many Catholics.

Pastoral Afro

In the 1960s the Catholic Church made a "preferential option for the poor." By the end of the decade, the progressive wing of the church in Brazil had opposed itself to the repressive military regime that had taken power in 1964. Yet it was not until the late 1970s, at a National Brazilian Bishops' Conference, that racial issues became an official concern of the church in Brazil (Burdick 1998a). Moreover, not until the early 1980s did the first Catholic anti-racist group emerge, the Grupo de União e Consciencia Negra (Black Unity and Consciousness Group) or GRUCON. Because of widespread suspicion of the church's motives for getting involved with the black movement, GRUCON was formed with the objective of creating projects outside of the church. Some clergy, however, sought to create an internal black pastoral group (Burdick 1998a). To this end, a group of priests concerned with anti-racism formed the Agentes de Pastoral Negros (APNs) at a meeting in São Paulo in 1983. Over the course of the 1980s, GRUCON faded into the background because of arguments among Catholics involved with the black movement about how closely to work with the Catholic hierarchy. By the end of the decade, the APNs had become the most prominent expression of the Catholic anti-racism movement (Myatt 1995).

At the same time, however, the grand ideological projects of the APNs started to fade by the end of the 1980s. Those who stayed with the movement increasingly concentrated on the development of an internal black pastoral to focus on cultural strategies, such as the celebration of inculturated Masses (Burdick 1998a). In the 1990s, official internal black pastoral groups began to emerge in the church throughout Latin America under the heading of the Pastoral Afro. Partly because of church politics in Bahia, however, such an internal pastoral organization did not appear in Salvador until 1999, when the Centro Arquidiocesano de Articulação da Pastoral Afro (CAAPA) was founded.

Like many relatively recent movements within the Catholic Church ranging from liberation theology to the Catholic Charismatic Renewal, the Pastoral Afro traces its roots to the revolutionary changes in the Catholic Church that took place during Vatican II (Myatt 1995). Staffed primarily by priests of African descent, CAAPA's general aims are to raise black consciousness and self-esteem, to create a dialogue with the Candomblé community, and to reaffirm Afro-Brazilian identity (cf. Burdick 2002, 2004). A CAAPA publication lists the following specific goals.

1. To awaken self-esteem in the black community to improve one's relations with one's self, with others and with society;
2. To provide studies of Afro-Brazilian culture from a perspective of reclaiming it from the historico-cultural process, in search of human dignity;
3. To give value to and respect diverse cultures in their multiple aspects recognizing in them, when they have them, elements and traces of Afro-Brazilian culture;
4. To identify the cultural elements and the proper expressions of African culture in order to develop a liturgical proposal according to the directions of the document Sacrossantum Concillium no. 37;
5. To promote studies and experiences according to the light of the Word of God, aiming at the construction of a society with equality of conditions and opportunities for everyone, independent of ethnicity and gender;
6. To promote educational practices with an emancipatory element for blacks searching for dignity and citizenship. (CAAPA 2001, 10; translation mine)

Although the objectives listed here have political overtones, the first four objectives focus on self-esteem and culture. Only in the last two objectives do phrases such as "equality of conditions and opportunities" and terms such as "emancipation" and "citizenship" emerge. While the Pastoral Afro is considered part of the black movement, its heavier emphasis on identity and culture compared to politics (in the narrow sense of the term) distinguishes it from more ideologically and politically oriented groups like the MNU.

Afro-Brazilian Identity and Mobilization in CAAPA

Dom Gílio

Dom Gílio Felício, the first black auxiliary bishop of Salvador, has been the president of CAAPA since it was founded in 1999. Dom Gílio is a charismatic man who always smiled widely when I spoke with him. His words are deliberate and carefully chosen, and his accent reveals that he is originally from Rio Grande do Sul (a state in the southern part of the country). He arrived in Salvador as a priest under the conservative Cardinal Dom Lucas, who, took a strong stance against Afro-Catholic syncretism. I heard that when Gílio became involved with Afro-Brazilian cultural and political groups such as Ilê Aiyê and the MNU, Dom Lucas moved him to Cruz das Almas in the interior of Bahia, where that kind of politics and activism is largely lacking. It was not until after Dom Lucas left Brazil for Rome that his replacement, Dom Geraldo, asked Dom Gílio to help lead the struggle against racism in the church.

In Dom Gílio's view, the Pastoral Afro movement has several main goals that overlap with those outlined in the CAAPA publication cited above. First, it aims to foster the realization in the Catholic community and in society as a whole that negritude is a gift from God. In fact, the notion of negritude is central to the black movement in the Catholic Church (Myatt 1995). This notion emphasizes that blacks everywhere in the diaspora, independent of religion, "have a cultural background, a cultural and religious origin, that forms a common heritage." Therefore, Dom Gílio explained, the Pastoral Afro seeks to adapt the Catholic liturgy to "the culture, the richness, and even, let us say, the spirituality, the way of life and the way of responding to the transcendent that comes from people of African descent."

Recognizing that different groups have different heritages and different ways of "responding to the transcendent," the Pastoral Afro focuses on cultural and liturgical pluralism. According to Dom Gílio, many people still believe strongly that being Catholic means living the Catholicism that comes from Europe without mixture. In this view, dancing in the African way is a sin against the Catholic religion. Dom Gílio explains that priests in the black movement believe that being faithful to the gospel of Jesus Christ entails respecting the richness of human culture. Catholics should be able to be happy without renouncing their cultural identities.

In this view, there exists a particular cultural identity and way of living that is inherent to people of African descent. Dom Gílio argues, for example, that the *jeito* (way of being or doing) that the black expresses before the transcendental does not change in the context of Catholicism. The Afro-Brazilian asks, "How am I going to dance for Jesus Christ?" Dom Gílio claims that blacks pray with their whole bodies—not just with words, but also with song and dance. (As I discuss later, however, many people are critical of the racial essentialism entailed by the notion of an inherent Afro-Brazilian jeito).

Dom Gílio explains that in the history of Brazil, this jeito, along with language and other customs, was preserved in the Candomblé terreiros while the Catholic Church sought to marginalize and demonize Afro-Brazilian culture. To some extent this marginalization still continues today, but bishops and priests have opened a space in the Mass for atabaques, which until recently were associated with Candomblé and, due to prejudice, the devil. Yet Dom Gílio maintains that when someone plays an atabaque during Mass, he is not worshiping the orixás: "He is playing for Jesus."

Although most people may in fact distinguish between Catholic and Candomblé practice, it is clear that many Bahians are involved with both religions at the same time. Like the brother of the Irmandade do Rosário I interviewed, Dom Gílio argues that this practice of "double belonging" emerged out of a historical process. "History is guilty," he says. He explains that this historical process involved the interpenetration of hidden and explicit religious practices. That is, since Candomblé was practiced clandestinely for so long in conjunction with and in the shadow of Catholicism, the two religions mutually influenced one another.

Today, however, people in the Catholic Church and in Candomblé are seeking a pure Catholicism and a pure Candomblé. Dom Gílio argues that this purity is difficult to achieve because in the minds of many people these religions are "married." Here again the issues of purity and mixture are central to the discourse of the Pastoral Afro. Dom Gílio points out that many Catholics keep up their obligations in Candomblé, and many who are involved in Candomblé maintain their Catholic practices. For these people, one or the other religion is not sufficient on its own, and again this is due to a historical process by which a relationship of dependency developed between the clandestine and the explicit.

At the same time, some of those who practice Candomblé have no other religion. They manage to sustain themselves sufficiently with Candomblé alone, Dom Gílio explains. Likewise, many black Catholics do not participate in Candomblé. Even if syncretism and double belonging are not the ideal, however, Dom Gílio argues that they at least promote something beneficial—the overcoming of intolerance. He points out that many religions aspire to purity, but they are contaminated with the sin of intolerance (this is a thinly veiled reference to evangelical Christianity). When such religions see themselves threatened, they declare holy war. By contrast, syncretism and double belonging lead to a cultural richness, an overcoming of intolerance, and establish a climate favorable to dialogue.

The cultural richness of syncretism is perhaps expressed most clearly in organizations such as the Irmandade do Rosário. With respect to politics, however, Dom Gílio admits that the brotherhood is rather conservative in comparison to CAAPA. Yet he insists that behind the conservatism lies the progressive idea of defending a cultural and spiritual heritage. Many of CAAPA's activities take place in the Rosário church and the members of the brotherhood accept this, although Dom Gílio admits that "sometimes it seems like they need time to fully digest it."

He reminded me, however, that the irmandade is an organization that was founded to help black people, to liberate slaves, and to bury its members with dignity. In this way, the Irmandade do Rosário and Afro-Catholic organizations like it provided a space of citizenship for blacks. In the time of slavery, these organizations were progressive, Dom Gílio argues. To belong to an irmandade was to belong to a group that was confronting the regime of slavery. Afterward, their rituals turned into traditions that sometimes impeded the irmandades from "taking a step forward." Nevertheless, the Irmandade do Rosário has opened its space to the activities of the Pastoral Afro; when CAAPA wants to celebrate an inculturated Mass, they do not have problems getting members of the brotherhood to participate.

To summarize, Dom Gílio's discourse about the Pastoral Afro turns on the theme of affirming and celebrating an inherent Afro-Brazilian identity and way of being. Although as the president of the Pastoral Afro Dom Gílio is centrally concerned with Afro-Bahian culture, as a person from Rio Grande do Sul he is less familiar with Candomblé and Afro-Catholic irmandades than other priests involved in the Pastoral Afro. Other priests in the Pastoral Afro who grew up in Bahia, however, have a much closer relationship with the Candomblé community.

Padre Clóvis

Unlike Dom Gílio, who moved to Bahia only recently and has no personal ties to Candomblé, Padre Clóvis seems to feel very comfortable integrating his views on the Afro-Brazilian "cosmovision" and current Western pedagogical theory into the same conversation. Padre Clóvis is a Jesuit priest who divides his time between working at the progressive Catholic Center for Social Study and Action (CEAS) and a Catholic orphanage and school for street children. Although he is an intellectual, he does not confine himself to the ivory tower; besides working closely with the street children, he is intimately involved in dialogue with the Candomblé community.

Padre Clóvis refers to the dialogue between Catholicism and Candomblé as *macro-ecumenism*, as the term *ecumenism* by itself generally refers to dialogue within the Christian tradition. He explained that the Catholic Church in Bahia has officially shown interest in macro-ecumenism only since Dom Geraldo arrived in 1999. In 2001, for example, the Archdiocese of Salvador called for a day of prayer for peace in response to the U.S. bombing of Afghanistan that included Catholics, Protestants, and candomblecistas. Clóvis told me that this was the first official, public macro-ecumenistic event in Salvador.

CAAPA, of course, was founded with a macro-ecumenical objective. Yet this does not mean that the mainstream church in Brazil has embraced the ideas on inter-religious dialogue; in fact, Clóvis claims that as of 2002 CAAPA was the only official African pastoral organization represented in the National Council of Brazilian Bishops (CNBB). At this point, he explained, the Pastoral Afro is still organizing itself internally and working to convince others within the church of its importance. Furthermore, besides these internal concerns, the Pastoral Afro is also trying to organize groups external to the church like the APNs did. Yet since it is only recently that the movement became official, Clóvis points out that there has not been much time for it to develop a coherent organizational identity.

It is rather striking that although the black movement emerged in Brazil in the late 1970s, the Catholic Church in Brazil did not take measures to officially address racism until the late 1990s. Padre Clóvis pointed to several reasons for the late arrival of the Pastoral Afro within the church. First, because of the widespread poverty and misery in Brazil, the fight for survival comes before the fight for roots, culture, and religion. The second reason is related to the ideology of racial democracy: until recently many simply denied (and some continue to deny) the existence of racism both in the church and in Brazilian society. Furthermore, the Catholic Church has historically been connected with the rich, powerful, and white, and its current concern with social justice and anti-racism is a relatively new development. In addition, because of the church's long-standing association with the elite, many Bahians with whom I spoke view the Pastoral Afro as an effort to co-opt the black movement, as well as popular religious expressions.

Yet Clóvis sees the Pastoral Afro as an important part of the struggle against racism. In his view, the black movement has three important divisions: urban progressive groups such as the MNU, the PT, and the Pastoral Afro; traditional Afro-Brazilian groups in the rural zones (such as the Irmandade da Boa Morte, which I mentioned above); and radical groups like Sem Terra (the landless workers' movement) that are working toward general economic equity and social justice. The views and practices of the Pastoral Afro and traditional Afro-Catholic groups, however, are not always congruent.

Clóvis explained that the sisters of Boa Morte, for example, have a kind of political and racial awareness that differs from that of the university-trained members of the Pastoral Afro and the black movement. Another priest described the difference as that between "living negritude" in everyday practice versus "racial consciousness" as intellectual and political awareness. Clóvis explained that in Brazil the black movement emerged in the cities and has remained primarily an urban phenomenon, so there is often a lack of connection with traditional Afro-Brazilian groups in the rural areas. The concern with affirming a positive Afro-Brazilian identity and raising self-esteem, however, forms a bridge between the concerns of the political activists and the cultural traditionalists.

Afro-Brazilian Identity, Education, and Self-Esteem in CAAPA

Padre Fidele

Padre Fidele is originally from Senegal but has been in Brazil for the past few years working with the Pastoral Afro. He has an office in the CAAPA headquarters in Pelourinho, but he spends most of his time working at a Pastoral Afro center called the Padre Heitor Pastoral Afro Center (CENPAH), named after a late priest who was very active in the black movement. One of the major tasks of CENPAH, which is located in the poor and predominately Afro-Brazilian *bairro* of Sussuarana, is to foster black self-esteem through education. The goal is both to prepare young people for the vestibular (the highly competitive university entrance exam) and to raise Afro-Brazilian cultural awareness. Here Padre Fidele explains.

> Fidele: The Pastoral Afro is a pastoral that, first, tries to work with the self-esteem of blacks. This is the fundamental step for the Pastoral Afro. So, the pastoral wants to try to reconstruct the identity of blacks; we try to collaborate. [We focus on] self-esteem because we see that many blacks do not accept themselves [se assumem], they don't accept themselves as people, they don't like themselves. The black person has

very low self-esteem, he does not value himself. Why? Because, on the one hand, of racial discrimination, and on the other hand, [because] negritude is marked by stigmas. There are many negative stereotypes connected with blacks: his hair is bad, he is stupid. . . . So, as a result many blacks don't accept themselves. Our work is to try to rescue black culture while raising the black's self-esteem. We also work at integrating the black into society, so that the black becomes a full-fledged citizen.

Stephen: How does the Pastoral reconstruct black identity? Through African culture?

F: Through African culture. I see several steps. First, I think that black Brazilians see a mythical Africa because it was always put in their head that their history began with slavery, right? Brazilians have history books that, in general, start the history of Africa beginning with slavery, as if blacks never had a history of freedom, a history of kings and queens. So, the first step is to provide the black Brazilian with the true history of the black starting with Africa, but also [the history] here in Brazil of struggle and resistance. Another thing is to work with the issue of the body: the black's hair is not bad, the black's hair is different from the white's hair. Is the white's hair beautiful? Yes. Is the black's hair beautiful? Yes. These are differences. Often people attribute inferiority to normal differences. So, I think we need to break the mechanisms that attribute inferiority to differences.

Padre Fidele's explanation of the purpose of the Pastoral Afro begins with the concept of individual self-esteem and proceeds to the concept of ethnic valorization. In this way, he makes an explicit link between the politics of culture and the domain of the personal. In this view, cultural affirmation is important not only because different cultures should be respected in themselves, but also because of the negative effect of cultural stigmatization in Afro-Brazilian communities. Thus, the valorization of Afro-Brazilian culture and the rediscovery of African history serve to reconstruct a positive identity to provide the basis for self-esteem. As I discuss below, however, there is less consensus within the Pastoral Afro about the cultural basis of Afro-Brazilian identity than would appear at first glance.

Padre Ferdinando

Padre Ferdinando lives and works at CENPAH in Sussuarana. Unlike the other priests I met who were involved with the Pastoral Afro, Ferdinando is white; he was born in Italy and came to Brazil in 1987. Before moving to Salvador he lived in Fortaleza, where he worked with local offshoots of the GRUCON (which he referred to simply as Consciência Negra or CN) and APN movements. In the 1980s, Padre Ferdinando explained, the APN was involved with enculturation and evangelization while the CN was more interested in providing general aid to the black community. Partly because the CN was associated with liberation theology and leftist ideologies that were waning in influence by the end of the 1980s, the APNs became more popular in the 1990s.

CAAPA was founded in Salvador in 1999, yet Ferdinando, like others with whom I spoke, said the organization is still not well accepted. First of all, he explained that early on, the black movement purged itself of particular religious ties, but most believed that if there were any "authentic" religion for blacks it would be Candomblé. This created an obstacle for organized Catholic participation in the movement. Furthermore, in contrast to the APNs, CAAPA is under the control of the church hierarchy, and this creates suspicion. He pointed out that the problem is many people see the church as an institution that helped keep the slaves subordinated. He argues, for example, that today most people say the irmandades served to preserve Afro-Brazilian culture and so on, but it is clear to him and others that the irmandades were another way to subordinate, co-opt, and divide and conquer people of African descent.

In fact, Ferdinando himself believes that CAAPA was founded largely for political reasons that were only tangentially related to concern about people of African descent. He suggests that the Pastoral Afro in Salvador was formed partly in anticipation of a pan–Latin American conference on racial issues in the Church—the Encontro de Pastoral Afro-Americana (EPA)—that was hosted in Salvador in 2000. According to Ferdinando, the Brazilian bishops were embarrassed that Brazil was the only country in Latin America that lacked a Pastoral Afro and quickly founded one in Salvador.

Despite his reservations about the reasons that CAAPA was founded, Padre Ferdinando is committed to helping people of African descent use the structures and resources that the organization provides. Padre Ferdinando is a psychiatrist whose work at CENPAH focuses on the development of black self-esteem. He divides this objective into two components: raising self-esteem with respect to intellectual capability and with respect to racial identity. Like Padre Fidele, he works with students in CENPAH's pre-vestibular course, where students are made aware of their "poder de estudar" (power to study). Ferdinado maintains that passing the vestibular and going on to the university raises not only individual self-esteem, but also that of the student's family; it also generates social, economic, cultural, and political capital in the black community.

The other side of Padre Ferdinando's work deals with what he refers to as the "de-internalization" of pernicious racial dichotomies. He traces the lack of positive representations of blacks and the idea of black racial inferiority to the ideology of *embranquecimento* or whitening. He disagrees with those who believe that slavery was the most violent crime against blacks, because in that case at least one knew who the enemy was; in the case of whitening, the ideology and the negative representations are internalized by their victims (cf. Fanon 2002). The specific ways that CENPAH conceives of and confronts this ideology are presented in the following excerpt from an issue of the Cadernos de Educação Afro-Brasileira (Afro-Brazilian Educational Workbooks) dealing with a course for teachers titled "Auto-Estima e Identidade Negra: Miscigenação e Ideologia do Branqueamento" (Self-Esteem and Black Identity: Miscegenation and the Ideology of Whitening). The following are the objectives of the course.

1. To be familiar with the importance of valuing Cultural Pluralism, especially with respect to people of African descent, as a cross-cutting theme that permeates all of the disciplines in the process of scholastic and educational process in a Liberating Praxis.

2. To be familiar with the *Culture, History and Traditions of Africa* from the past to the present, as an indispensable recuperation of true ethnic roots.

3. Reformulate the *Self-Esteem*, unmasking the *ideology of whitening* that depresses and discriminates against *Black Identity and Miscegenation*.

4. Denounce, without treaties or concessions, Racism, raising awareness of and reaffirming *Human Rights* for all ethnicities, religions and sexes.

5. Rediscover the *true history of Slavery and Black Resistance in Brazil and America, as well as the unofficial History of Blacks in Brazil*.

6. To be familiar with the *Religions of African Origins* present in Brazil with their historical and cultural heritage of resistance.

7. To promote the enabling (capacitacão) of professors and leaders for the *Intercultural and Interethnic Dialogue* in the Schools and Communities. (CENPAH 2001; translation mine)

This excerpt traces the connections between self-esteem, education, culture ("history," "heritage," "traditions," "identity," "religion"), power ("ideology," "resistance") and politics ("human rights," "dialogue"). It is interesting to note that while item number 4 makes a strong political statement, numbers 5 and 6 associate "resistance" with the cultural domains of "history" and "heritage." In item number 7, by contrast, the counter-ideological strategy promoted for professors and leaders is "Intercultural and Interethnic Dialogue." Thus, although the discourse of the Pastoral Afro is often more politically oppositional than that of Afro-Catholic groups like the Irmandade do Rosário and Boa Morte, at the same time its discourse appears less militant than that of the MNU. In the Pastoral Afro, as I have shown, the focus is more on cultural identity and self-esteem than on overt political action.

Yet as Padre Ferdinando explains, the issues pertaining to the specific form and content of this Afro-Brazilian cultural identity are complicated. Everyone agrees that negative aspects should be eliminated from Afro-Brazilian identity, such as stereotypes, the connotation of inferiority, and so on, but there is little agreement on what should take their place. One option is the aesthetics of Rastafarianism, but Ferdinando points out that not everyone is going to adopt that lifestyle. As for religion, many say that Candomblé is the obvious foundation for a positive identity, yet there are many people who, although they respect African-derived religion, do not want to get involved with it. In the Catholic anti-racism movement, some want to fully inculturate Masses to include African dress, while others do not want to change it at all since Catholicism is ostensibly universal. As a result, the inculturated Masses that we see today are a compromise—the essential Catholic liturgy combined with some Afro-Brazilian elements.

Padre Ferdinando's views about the construction of Afro-Brazilian identity differ significantly from Dom Gílio's notion of an inherently black way of being. In fact, many black Catholics are uncomfortable with what they see as the essentialist tendencies of the black movement within the church (cf. Burdick 2003). Padre Ferdinando's comments therefore hint at what some consider the precarious foundations of the Pastoral Afro's discourse about Afro-Brazilian identity. All culture-based approaches to consciousness raising and mobilization are complicated by the problem of essentialism and the risk of cultural appropriation. In addition, the Pastoral Afro's identity-building efforts take place on the shifting ground of relations between the Catholic Church and the Afro-Brazilian religious community. Thus, many Bahians with whom I spoke are highly critical of the Catholic Church's recent efforts to become involved with the black movement.

Views of the Pastoral Afro in the Candomblé Community

While many Catholics strongly objected to the idea that Catholic priests were "dialoguing" with candomblecistas, some of the most vocal critics of the Pastoral Afro with whom I spoke were members of the Candomblé community.

Here, for example, Angela, a candomblecista, identifies the Catholic Church with the white elite.

> You already know that the Catholic Church is elite, elite, really elite! You don't see blacks in the Catholic Church who are . . . catechists. . . . You don't see black catechists in the church of Vitória, you don't see black catechists in the church of Graça, you don't see black catechists in the church of Santo Antônio da Barra, you don't see black catechists in the church of the Catedral Basílica. Why? It's elite!

Some are also critical of the balancing act that Catholic priests are trying to perform in their attempts to integrate Catholicism and Afro-Brazilian culture. According to Angela,

> So the bishop and the archbishop have to play a game, they have to sit on the fence, with one foot in the water and one on dry land; on the fence, understand? Because when they raise the host they say, "This is the lamb of God." He is not going to say, "This is the lamb of Obatalá, of Orumilá, of Odudua [Yoruba gods]." Is he going to? No! So, I don't even believe in the church of Rosário dos Pretos because while it has drums and even black hymns, when it is time to raise the host and the chalice that he says is the bread and wine of life, he does not say that it is the bread of the black's life using these words: "this is the lamb of Obatalá, or Odudua, or of Olurum." He is not going to! Those that are our gods, they won't do! He is going to say the lamb of God, you understand?

Many people with whom I spoke in the Candomblé community are wary of syncretism. As Angela explained,

> I don't think that water mixes with gas. One never mixes the Catholic Church with Candomblé. Candomblé entered into Catholicism in the first place because of an imposition of the Jesuits when they were here in Brazil.

Miriam, another candomblecista involved with the black movement, explained her suspicion of the Catholic Church.

> Listen, after I began to see myself as a person, as a human being, as a being who can perceive and conceive my own opinions, I had a serious problem with the Catholic Church. Because in the last century the Catholic Church contributed a lot to the genocide of black people. It was that which contributed most to our extermination here [in Salvador]. The

church succeeded, over many years, to hide our religions, the true religion of afro descendentes. Thus, the church began to associate the saints with the orixás. There are some terreiros that make this separation, but there are still others that continue to associate Santa Bárbara with Iansá yet, in reality, this does not exist. Santa Bárbara is Santa Bárbara and Iansá is Iansá, Santo Antônio is Santo Antônio and Ogum is Ogum, Oxalá is Oxalá and Senhor do Bonfim is Senhor do Bonfim. So, if today the church is repenting, this repentance that the pope made does not convince me—I don't accept it. And if today the church wants to work in partnership with the Candomblé terreiros, I am sincerely suspicious. I feel that it is a way for them to try to justify some of what they did for many years. So, in my own opinion, this does not convince me.

The Pastoral Afro often appears to be steering a middle course between the supposedly uncritical syncretism of Afro-Catholic popular religion and the militant opposition to syncretism of many in the Candomblé community. This is particularly evident in the discourse of double belonging through which the Pastoral Afro legitimates its attempts to draw upon the heritage of Candomblé and of Afro-Catholic groups such as the Irmandade do Rosário, while rejecting uncritical syncretic practices at the same time. Yet it is often difficult to see just how double belonging and syncretism differ from one another in practice.[2]

Those candomblecistas I quoted above, who were equally adverse to the ideas of syncretism and double belonging, see the Pastoral Afro as engaged in a precarious and disingenuous strategy of playing both sides. Their opposition is largely due to their persistent view, despite the efforts of the Pastoral Afro to refigure the church as the rescuer of Afro-Brazilian identity, that Roman Catholicism is a white elite religion that has long been complicit in the oppression of blacks and the repression of their religion. From this perspective, candomblecistas should be involved with Candomblé and Candomblé alone. As I explore in the next chapter, in fact, discussions about the relationship between Candomblé and Catholicism have moved to the center of debates about Afro-Brazilian identity.

Candomblé, Afro-Brazilian Culture, and Anti-Racism

Salvador is home to the oldest and most famous Candomblé terreiros in Bahia, including Opô Afonjá, Casa Branca, and Gantois. Many of these terreiros, or their parent terreiros, were founded as early as the nineteenth century. As some of the most respected Afro-Brazilian institutions in the country, they enjoy a prestige in Salvador that is not accorded to Candomblé houses elsewhere in Bahia and Brazil. A number of Bahia's most prominent politicians and entertainers, for example, are patrons of one or the other of Salvador's terreiros.

Compared to the simple terreiros I saw in rural Cachoeira, for example, many of the terreiros I visited in Salvador were remarkably spacious and ornate. Ilé Axé Opô Afonjá, for example, has its own elementary school, and the shrines of the orixás are well-constructed houses rather than mud huts, as they often are in the interior. The terreiro of Pilau de Prata features statues of the orixás to greet visitors as well as exhibits explaining terreiro history, a library, and an archive. In addition to these high-profile terreiros, there are hundreds of smaller Candomblé houses that vary along a wide range of size and practice. Other terreiros I visited were simple and modest, but unlike in Cachoeira, where many Candomblé houses were quietly hidden away on the hilltops, they always seemed to be bustling with a line of people waiting for consultations.

The Candomblé community in Salvador is not monolithic, and strong tensions exist between and within different terreiros. As I discussed earlier, terreiros are generally affiliated with specific nações, or African-derived cultural traditions, such as Nâgo (Yoruba), Angola, or Jejê. Yet the Nâgo influence is dominant in Bahian Candomblé, and Yoruba culture is widely considered to be the original source of Afro-Brazilian religion. Practically all of the Candomblé terms that have found their way into popular culture, for example, are Yoruba. Because of this Nâgo/Yoruba hegemony, members of the Angola and Jejê nações often complain that their terreiros are marginalized and perceived as less authentic. In this way, some argue that this "nâgocentrism" replicates the hierarchical relations of the Brazilian religious in the Candomblé community (cf. Matory 2005).

Another major issue in Salvador concerns modernization versus the maintenance of tradition. For example, in more traditional terreiros, especially in rural Bahia, candomblecistas undergoing initiation are secluded—much like a hundred years ago—in simple mud huts. In many terreiros in Salvador, however, initiates live in modern buildings. Furthermore, some terreiros have shortened the traditional initiation period and others have loosened rules about initiates-in-training holding jobs outside of the terreiro (cf. Johnson 2002, 12).

While these accommodations of modern life may be convenient or even necessary, they expose the terreiros that adopt them to charges of breaking with sacred traditions and replacing them with a "fast-food" model. In this view, terreiros that depart from tradition are less authentic, less legitimate, and produce "half-baked" initiates. Yet many of those who support the "modernization of tradition" are members of the Bahian intelligentsia, who belittle traditionalism as narrow-minded and provincial. Along these lines, Johnson (2002) discusses the feedback loop between public discourses about Candomblé and ritual practice that continually transforms Candomblé.

A related issue that I will examine more closely below is that of syncretism versus re-Africanization and anti-syncretism (Jensen 1999; Prandi 1999). As its name suggests, the re-Africanization movement aims to return to authentic African traditions. An early manifestation of this movement was the introduction of Yoruba schools in Bahia that came to be filled with Candomblé initiates in the 1960s. The more recent anti-syncretism movement is concerned with eliminating Catholic elements from Candomblé practice. The aim of this movement is not so much to revitalize African traditions as to establish Candomblé as a religion in its own right, separate from Catholicism.

Like the re-Africanization movement, however, the anti-syncretism movement is concerned with the negative effects of the commercialization of Candomblé. Candomblé is often featured prominently in tourist advertisements, and Bahia has a worldwide reputation as a powerful center for African-derived religion. People from all over Brazil and from abroad come to Salvador to have a consultation at these terreiros. Many other visitors to Salvador attend less "authentic" Candomblé performances that are arranged by tour guides. While this is a source of income for some, as I discuss below, such commercialization is controversial in the Candomblé community.

Today the practice of Candomblé in Salvador is relatively open compared to the past. Before the 1970s, terreiros were required to register with the police

Figure 6. These statues depicting many of the orixás are located at the Dique de Tororó, a park near the center of Salvador and adjacent to the municipal soccer stadium. Candomblé is a prominent symbol of Bahian identity in many ways.

before performing ceremonies. Today, at least officially, Candomblé terreiros enjoy all of the legal rights of any other religion. One example of this openness is the ubiquity of Candomblé symbols and images throughout the city. At a public park in the center of town (Dique de Tororó), for example, large statues representing the different Candomblé orixás are displayed in the middle of a lake. Smaller versions of each statue are found at different places on a path around the water along with explanations of the characteristics of each orixá and the Catholic saint(s) with which they are identified.

Due in part to this openness, however, to some extent Candomblé has been made banal as it has been incorporated into daily life in Salvador. Shopping malls and apartment buildings are named after Candomblé deities. Candomblé symbols and dances are used in public festivals. In this way and in conjunction with the tourism industry, Candomblé becomes less of a religion and more a part of the local folklore. In addition to the issue of the relationship between Candomblé and Catholicism, this "folklorization" has become a major concern in the Candomblé community in Salvador. In the usage of many candomblecistas, folklorization has a decidedly negative connotation and is associated with trivialization and commodification.

Still another important issue in the Candomblé community is the relationship between Candomblé and the black movement. Some in Salvador believe that this relationship cannot be overstated. According to Angela,

> Without Candomblé, the black movement would not exist, you understand! Because these are the roots that we bring from our ancestors, see? And if you don't have your mind, your self, and your faith, you are no one! You have to have faith in something because, that way you will survive, you will have hope for a better future.

Most terreiros in Salvador, however, do not make such an explicit link between Candomblé and politics. Those who are involved with politics are usually involved individually.

> Stephen: And are there other terreiros and people who don't like to be involved with political things in the black movement?

> Angela: Who don't like to be involved in political things? For example: Casa Branca doesn't involve itself, my terreiro doesn't involve itself. . . . In my terreiro people are not involved in the black movement, you see? Now, I am involved! I support the fight of the blacks, I support it because blacks have to have their space in society. But for you to have your space in society, you have to fight, you have to have, before anything else, you have to have culture, you have to have instruction, you have to have education!

Thus, people's levels of political involvement in the black movement vary within the Candomblé community, and most of those who become politically involved do so individually rather than in the name of their terreiro. This is not to say that political involvement is discouraged, only that it appears not to be the highest priority for most Candomblé initiates (cf. Agier 1998). One terreiro that has attracted much attention for the anti-syncretic statements of its leader, Mãe Stella, is Ilé Axé Opô Afonjá.

Opô Afonjá and Anti-Syncretism

Candomblé terreiros have long been a locus of Afro-Brazilian ethnic affirmation. In the 1980s, many terreiros entered into public discussions about the politics of religious practice. Prominent leaders of Candomblé terreiros in Salvador began to question the traditionally syncretic relationship between Candomblé and Catholicism such as is embodied in Afro-Catholic organizations like Boa Morte and the Irmandade do Rosário.

In 1983 a group of five prominent Candomblé Iyalorixás (female ritual leaders), including Mãe Stella of Opô Afonjá, drafted an anti-syncretic manifesto in which they denounced syncretism as part of the heritage of slavery.

> The Iyas and Babalorixás of Bahia, in accordance with the positions taken in the Second World Conference of the Traditions of the Orixás and Culture from the 17th to the 23rd of July 1983 in this city [Salvador], make it publicly known that after this conference it is clear that our belief is a religion and not a syncretic sect.
>
> We cannot think nor let others think of us as folklore, an animistic sect or a primitive religion, as has always been the case in this country and this city, be it by those who oppose and detract by writing on walls and in articles—"Candomblé is a thing of the Devil," "primitive or syncretic African Practices"; or be it because our ritual clothing is used in public contests, our liturgical symbols are used in tourist advertisements, and even our own houses of worship, our temples, are included in the folklore columns of Bahian newspapers.
>
> During slavery syncretism was necessary for our survival, now its results and public manifestations include Candomblé adepts and priests participating in church washings, going out on processions to mass, etc., which undermines us as a religion and marginalizes Candomblé as something exotic, as folklore and tourism. (Ilé Axé Opô Afonjá 2002; translation mine)

In the first paragraph of this document, the authors declare Candomblé's status as a religion as opposed to a syncretic sect, and they legitimize their pronouncement with reference to the Second World Conference of the Traditions of the Orixás and Culture. Syncretism here is understood pejoratively as something that is not legitimate or sufficient on its own, a meaning that is more commonly deployed in actual religious fields than the ostensibly neutral anthropological usage of the term. In fact, recent commentators such as Droogers (2005; 1989) and Stewart and Shaw (1994) have argued that concepts such as syncretism or popular religion, which entail attendant notions of "religious authenticity," are inherently political.

In the second paragraph of the declaration, the authors distinguish Candomblé from folklore, animism, primitive religion, and things of the devil. The authors refer to the vilification of Candomblé (by evangelicals and conservative Catholics) and denounce those involved with the folklorization and commodification of African-derived religion. In the final paragraph the authors specifically admonish those who participate in Afro-Catholic festivals ("church washings" refers most directly to the "syncretic" Festival of Bonfim discussed below) and activities, since by doing so they undermine Candomblé's status as a religion and marginalize it as "something exotic, as folklore and tourism."

Today this document is kept in a museum at the terreiro Ilé Axé Opô Afonjá. Along with it are the Catholic saints' images that the leader of Opô Afonjá, Mãe Stella, removed from the ritual spaces of the terreiro when the document was drafted. These Catholic items on display at Mãe Stella's terreiro represent an interesting inversion of the displays of Candomblé paraphernalia at Salvador's Afro-Brazilian museum, a prime tourist destination located in the center of the historical district flanked by several of the city's most prominent Catholic churches.

While many people involved with the anti-syncretism movement emphasize their continued respect for Catholicism (at least from a distance), some in the Candomblé community are openly hostile to the church and view it as an exploitative institution of the white elite. No matter how much the church claims to have reformed, Afro-Brazilians are unwilling to overlook its historical complicity with slavery or the fact that priests are overwhelmingly white. In this view, syncretic Afro-Catholic groups such as the Irmandade do Rosário are complicit with the oppressor, and the irmandades of the past were first and foremost instruments of colonial control rather than vehicles for black liberation and resistance. Thus, in contrast to the Irmandade do Rosário's ties to the church and its emphasis on cultural preservation, the discourse of anti-syncretism stresses cultural autonomy.

Other leaders in the Candomblé community, however, are opposed to breaking off relations with the Catholic Church, citing the importance of Afro-Catholic festivals such as Santa Bárbara and São Lazaro in Salvador as well as Boa Morte in Cachoeira (Consorte 1999). The issue of anti-syncretism is complicated by deeply ingrained Afro-Catholic traditions in Bahia. Most terreiros in Bahia are culturally, if not politically,[1] conservative and appear uninterested, at least on an organizational or institutional level, in a political confrontation with the Catholic Church.

Nevertheless, Mãe Stella and those like her stress that cultural innovation and resistance are not inimical to the maintenance of tradition and ancestral values (Theodoro 1999, 282). In this view, however, the tradition of struggling against cultural domination is opposed to and supersedes the tradition of syncretism. Moreover, anti-syncretism is seen as both an affirmation of female authority—an assertion that the mãe de santo no longer has to "ask permission" to practice her religion from the Catholic priest—and of African culture, as expressed in the saying "the refusal of syncretism is an affirmation of liberty" (Gebara 1999, 409; translation mine). In fact, some see the discourse of anti-syncretism as anti-racist in its rejection of white, Western ways of rendering Candomblé. Yet as I explore below, anti-syncretic discourse does not usually address explicit political issues.

Graça

Graça is a filha de santo at Opô Afonjá, a practicing psychologist, and a graduate student in anthropology at the Federal University of Bahia. Like many academically oriented members of the Candomblé community, she is concerned with Afro-Brazilian cultural and political issues. In my first interview with her, I asked her about Opô Afonjá and the re-Africanization movement, and she explained,

> Well, actually, in the terreiro of Axé Opô Afonjá, this concept of re-Africanization is not discussed much because Axé Opô Afonjá is actually similar to a little Africa. Because even the Africans who come from Africa and visit find in Opô Afonjá the things of traditions, rituals, things that no longer exist in Africa and which Opô Afonjá preserved, you see?

The term *re-Africanization* is inappropriate, according to Graça, because Opô Afonjá sees itself as even more authentically African than Yoruba religion as it is practiced in Africa today. Instead, in Opô Afonjá the emphasis is on anti-syncretism.

> The issue of syncretism is very serious there. Mãe Stela does not allow syncretism, she thinks that syncretism is a way of going back to being slaves.
> Mãe Stela explained this very well. She said that Santa Bárbara existed, she was an energy that people sought, and [on the other hand] there is an energy [that exists] as Iansã. Also: the orixá is a living thing, the orixá is nature! Santa Bárbara is dead! . . . So, the energies are completely different. How are you going to worship them in the same way? So she says: you can have a Mass said for Santa Bárbara, but for Iansã you offer an *acarajé*.

Mãe Stella makes a clear categorical distinction between the saints and the orixás and the practices that are appropriate for their worship. At Opô Afonjá, for example, she has eliminated the Mass that traditionally marks the end of the initiation phase into Candomblé. Yet anti-syncretism is not commonly conceived as a political movement, as the following exchange between Graça and me indicates.

Stephen: So, does anti-syncretism have to do directly or indirectly with resistance against discrimination, against . . .

Graça: Against freedom of worship [liberdade de culto].

S: Yes, but beyond that, does the freedom of worship have to do with the freedom of afro descendentes? . . . Are there many people in Opô Afonjá who are involved politically? That is, does anti-syncretism have to do with political involvement as well?

G: No.

S: No?

G: No because, actually, the person who raised the flag of anti-syncretism . . . was Mãe Stela herself, and she always explains it from the religious point of view.

S: Religious . . . but are there people who are involved . . .

G: There are people in the black movement . . . who adopt Mãe Stela's idea. But . . . they don't explain it in terms of energy or from the religious side. They explain it from the political side.

Thus, Opô Afonjá maintains a separation between religion and politics. In addition, as one might expect, the members of the terreire are wary of the Pastoral Afro. As I noted earlier, Dom Gílio of the Pastoral Afro told me that he visited Opô Afonjá and was well received there. Yet Graça speaks of skepticism on the side of Opô Afonjá.

Graça: I saw Dom Gílio, who is a person from the Pastoral Afro who went to Afonjá a few times. But I think that Afonjá, it closes itself to this issue of the Pastoral Afro.

Stephen: Closes itself how?

G: Closes itself. With one eye open and the other closed. This is not anything that was said, but I feel it. . . . It is like this: we treat each other very well, "you can come here, OK? But I am Mãe Stela and you are Dom Gílio!"

In Graça's view, then, the relationship between the Pastoral Afro and Opô Afonjá is less one of dialogue than of cordiality and respect from a distance. When I mentioned the Pastoral Afro to Fabio, another member of Opô Afonjá, he shook his head and said that one cannot be involved in both Catholicism and Candomblé. The next day, however, I ran into Fabio at the festival for Santa Bárbara in Pelourinho. When he saw the puzzlement on my face he simply laughed and said that he views the Mass of Santa Bárbara as something folkloric; in this way, he turns the tables on the folklorization of Candomblé.

In fact, several Bahians with whom I spoke told me that although Mãe Stella prohibits her filhos from attending Mass, they often end up going in secret (just as some evangelicals allegedly go to Candomblé in secret). Furthermore, while many people in the Candomblé community make an explicit distinction between Candomblé and Catholicism, most terreiros in Salvador maintain certain syncretic practices. In fact, Mãe Stella's view is not representative of the whole Candomblé community in Salvador. As Angela explained,

> But to end religious syncretism, today this is complicated because there are the old ones who talk like this: "No, my daughter! Jesus Christ is Senhor do Bonfim, Our Lady of the Conception is Oxum Iemanjá, and Our Lady of Candeias is Oxum". . . . But they have nothing to do with each other!

Furthermore, Consorte (1999, 81) argues that since the advent of the anti-syncretism movement, nothing seems to have changed, and popular Afro-Catholic festivals continue in Salvador as they always have. For many in the Candomblé community, then, Catholicism is an integral part of Candomblé tradition.

In one terreiro that I visited frequently, for example, the filhos de santo talked regularly and openly about attending Mass and paying the priest to say Mass for their deceased family members. The day-to-day activities at this terreiro focused almost completely on healing and not at all on Afro-Brazilian politics. When I told the mãe de santo, Dona Risalva, that my research was about religion and racism, she asked, "How can the orixás, who are black, be racist?" When I explained that I was interested in the ways that religious groups struggle against racism, she seemed uninterested. Nearly every day of the week Risalva had a line of people waiting to see her for consultations that led to healing. Many of her patrons were light-skinned and dressed like members of the middle class.

Thus, Dona Risalva's terreiro did not appear to be an explicit site of Afro-Brazilian identity formation or social struggle. In light of this, and of the prominent role that white elites play in the Candomblé community, it appears that Candomblé constitutes an oppositional culture more in the imagination of black elites than in actual practice.[2] As I have emphasized in this section, although Candomblé often figures centrally in the discourse and imagery of the black movement, Candomblé practice is usually not construed as overtly political in itself. Occasionally, however, especially in the wake of extreme instances of religious conflict, the politics of religious practice come to the foreground.

Religious Intolerance

For many people in the Candomblé community with whom I spoke, expressions of intolerance against Candomblé are the point where religion and racial politics intersect. Here, Miriam tells me about such an incident.

> Miriam: I don't know if you are aware that a month ago in [Beiru] there was [an incident of] discrimination in a Candomblé terreiro called Vila São Roque, into which the Protestants went in and threw acid, sulfur, and other things. They want to defame the Candomblé terreiros and our religion. There was a demonstration at the town hall so that there would be no more discrimination against our religion because it was one of the first [religions]. Since the beginning of the world we have been hearing about the religion of Candomblé, which is the religion of the afro descendentes and deserves respect. Just as all Candomblé terreiros as well as all the adepts of the Candomblé terreiros respect the other religions, we also want the respect of our religion.
>
> Stephen: Does religious intolerance have a lot to do with the issue of racism?
>
> M: Even on the ninth of this month—this month commemorates "Black Awareness Month" in Brazil—in the town hall of Salvador there was a special session about religious intolerance and other consequences where representatives of all the religions were. It was a very good debate! And there was a protest too, on the 20th [of November, Black Consciousness Day], where there was a wing of just religious people. And we were there! The people of the black movement, the people who sympathize with the cause, even if they are not Candomblé adepts, they are there participating in demonstrations of that nature.

The special session on religious intolerance referred to above took place in Salvador's City Hall on November 9, 2001. Present at the meeting, titled "Religious Intolerance and Its Consequences," were representatives of Catholicism, Candomblé, Islam, Zen Buddhism, the International Baha'i Community, the Universal Church of the Kingdom of God (IURD), and the National Council of Christian Churches as well as the Movement Against Religious Intolerance. The meeting was organized not only in response to the various incidents of religious intolerance (namely, attacks against Candomblé terreiros by evangelicals) that had taken place recently in Salvador, but to address the events of September 11.

Although the meeting focused on religious intolerance, many of the speakers also raised the issue of racism. For example, the representative from the International Baha'i Community argued,

I often say that religious intolerance and racism constitute the two worst plagues of humanity. They have caused so much suffering and they still continue to claim their victims. Although racism is not the theme of this meeting, we cannot forget it, because racism has claimed the lives of six million people, simply because someone thought that one race is superior to another.

Here the speaker draws a parallel between religious intolerance and racism without making an explicit connection or accusation. He may have spoken indirectly in order to avoid an overt confrontation with the pastor from the IURD who was present at the meeting. Again, many see the IURD as the most blatant culprit in the vilification of Candomblé.

When his turn came to speak, however, the pastor from the IURD addressed the issue directly and attempted to decouple the issues of religious intolerance and racism.

Everyone has to have the right to think and to say what they think in relation to their religion. That is my opinion. . . . I think that the answer comes when we start to respect human beings. And when we try to connect religiosity to the issue of racism, this is a little difficult. I went to South Africa and I was amazed. I went to Mozambique and I was amazed. In a big worldwide conference against racism in South Africa, I did not see any religious expression. What they were discussing was the discrimination of races. . . . So, what is it that we are seeing? We are seeing the religious issue once again taken and brought into the issue of race so that our discussion is based in love [sic] rather than reason. What is it that we want in the racial issue? Equality. Equality of what? Equality of opportunity, income, schooling, housing. Religion cannot do this. Those who have to do this are the . . . policies that we have been demanding from the government.

In this selection the pastor positions himself, along with the others at the conference, in support of racial equality ("What is it that *we* want in the racial issue? Equality"). Yet his reference to the secular nature of the conference against racism in South Africa and his assertion that government policy, not religion, can provide racial equality frame the struggle against racism as a political rather than a religious issue. Thus, the pastor momentarily shifted the topic of the conference to an interrogation of the relationship between religion and anti-racism and skirted the issue raised by the previous speaker, namely that of the connection between religious intolerance and racism. In response to the pastor's comments, however, the representative from the Candomblé community made an unmistakable but indirect reference to the IURD's antagonism toward African-derived religion and categorically equated religious intolerance with racism.

> I've participated in various seminars with Baptist and Adventist pastors and I have had dialogue with various representatives of Christian religions. However, I have never had the opportunity to be at a table where there is a representative of one of the segments of Christianity that recently has been a rock in the shoe of many practitioners of Candomblé. . . .
>
> For me intolerance really is a synonym for racism. . . . Here in Bahia, here in Brazil, in relation to Candomblé, intolerance is a synonym of racism, and we have to think in other ways and use other measures; we have to change this attitude.

Furthermore, the representative of the Movement Against Religious Intolerance was even more explicit and condemnatory.

> Religious intolerance simply destroys a religion whose adepts it intends to conquer. It perpetuates the notion of the inferiority of Africans and their descendants, a notion that was created by [slave handlers] and colonizers in order to justify the atrocities committed against Africans of the diaspora and of their continent. It adds up to the process of crushing of the self-esteem of black people, against which African, North American, Caribbean, and Brazilian militants come fighting. . . .
>
> The Movement Against Religious Intolerance has the firm conviction that whatever religious proselytization, whatever action with the aim of changing religious belief of another person is violence, is cultural rape. No one, that is no one, has the right to think that they are morally superior, racially or culturally or in whatever way. Whatever attitude in this direction is similar to the Nazis and this is not by mere coincidence.

Here, the relationship between religious intolerance and racism is laid out in the strongest of terms. In the view of the Movement Against Religious Intolerance, religious intolerance is not simply bigotry; it is a detestable expression of a genocidal attitude. From this perspective, religion and politics are inseparable.

Thus, some activists would like to restrict evangelicals' ability to proselytize and to publicly characterize Candomblé as devil worship. This raises at least two important questions, the first of which concerns freedom of religion. Although my sympathies lie squarely with candomblecistas who have been abused and defamed, I cannot overlook the irony of those whose religion was persecuted by the government for so long seeking to restrict others' religious freedom. Yet the fact that some evangelical Christians have aggressively sought to "liberate" people from Candomblé and have even "invaded" terreiros remains a serious problem. Some have clearly passed over the line that separates spreading the gospel and infringing on others' rights guaranteed in the Brazilian constitution.

A second and related concern has to do with accusations of racism. Historically speaking, we can see that at least some of the reasons that Candomblé came to be characterized as diabolical were racist. In general, Christians have tended to demand religious exclusivity and to regard other traditions as insufficient. Moreover, Christians usually depicted the religions of those they conquered and/or enslaved in the New World and Africa as degenerate, if not diabolical. Thus, the idea that Candomblé is devil worship was as much a product of discourses justifying slavery and colonization as it is of conclusions drawn from reading scripture.

Over time, however, Candomblé has become a symbol for evangelicals and others of a wide array of social ills. Many evangelicals see Candomblé as the religion of those who are socially marginal and live in misery. This notion, of course, was prevalent among white elites at the beginning of the twentieth century and thus has a long racist history (Johnson 2002). Black-movement activists and many Candomblé practitioners respond that by fully embracing one's identity and heritage, one can make a better life. Yet does this mean that black evangelicals hate themselves simply because they do not practice Candomblé? In my experience, no. But this does not mean that attacks on Candomblé are not, even if unintentionally, complicit with racist discourses.

Debates about the relationship between religion and racial politics remain highly contentious in Salvador. At the center of these debates are competing views of Afro-Brazilian religion and its relationship to people of African descent, as well as the contested vision of where religion and politics overlap and where they diverge. These issues concern not only those involved with the black movement per se, but the evangelical community as well, which is divided on questions of Afro-Brazilian identity and racial politics.

Afro-Brazilian Culture, Identity Politics, and Activism in Salvador

Despite the contested relationship between culture and politics within Afro-Brazilian communities, Afro-Brazilian cultural and religious practices continue to play a central role in public events, celebrations, and protests. It is against this backdrop that evangelicals and others stake their claims against the entanglement of race, religion, and politics. To a large extent, however, anti-racist initiatives in Bahia have for the most part consisted of the politics of culture. That is, the line between cultural celebration and political action in Bahia is usually blurry, as a look at some of Bahia's many popular festivals illustrates.

Carnaval

Perhaps the second most popular festival in Brazil after Carnaval in Rio, Salvador's Carnaval is known for its emphasis on Afro-Brazilian culture. In this way, the celebration of Carnaval is intertwined with the politics of performing what it means to be Afro-Brazilian. In addition, many Afro-Brazilian Carnaval organizations explicitly link themselves to the black movement. Nevertheless, the manifold ways of celebrating Carnaval are differentiated largely along the lines of race and class. Seen in this context, Bahian Carnaval provides a prime example of the politics of culture.

In 2002 the Afro-Brazilian emphasis of Salvador's Carnaval was even more pronounced than usual. That year, Africa was chosen as the theme of the pre-Lenten celebration. Called "Carnaváfrica," Carnaval 2002 celebrated Salvador's African heritage, as the following newspaper article explains.

Figure 7. "Africa" was the theme of Carnaval 2002, and this display illustrates some of the prominent ways that Africa was imagined during this celebration.

Carnaváfrica brings black beauty to the streets.

To come up with a theme for its 2002 Carnaval, Salvador went to drink from its origins. The so-called Black Rome will assume, in the five days of revelry, all of the colors and rhythms of its African side. Carnaváfrica, which takes place from the 7th to the 12th of February, will spread elements referring to Africa across the stage of the celebration. . . . "The intention is to valorize the African contribution to the culture of Salvador, one of the blackest cities in Brazil, and, at the same time, to show that Africa is much more than just drums. Despite slavery, the African heritage survived and grew roots" said the president of Emtursa, Eliana Dumêt. (*A Tarde*, February 6, 2002; translation mine)

During Carnaváfrica, more time and space was allotted to Afro-Brazilian cultural groups such as *blocos afros* than in most years. Furthermore, for several months around Carnaval season, the historical district was elaborately decorated with African themes and images, as this article explains.

Carnaval/The Historical Center dresses African

The decoration of the Batatinha Circuit during Carnaval 2002 will be inspired by the culture of black Africa. The decorative pieces, which are being made by the sculptor Telma Calheira, will represent tribal masks, animals and jungles. . . . The fact that Pelourinho and the vicinity is the scene of a festival honoring Africa and the African heritage of Bahia has not failed to be [seen as] a historical irony in the afrodescendente community, since the ground of the same place absorbed the blood of the slaves spilled in cruel punishments. The homage arrives a little late, since, as Margareth Menezes says in her song "Alegria da Cidade," despite so much pain that was inflicted on the blacks, they are principally responsible for Salvador's joy. (*Correiro da Bahia*, January 16, 2002; translation mine)

As this newspaper article points out, the irony of honoring Africa in a neighborhood whose name means "the whipping post" is quite poignant. Furthermore, many have commented on the inconsistency of celebrating the African contribution to Bahian culture in the context of the glaring racial inequalities that exist in Bahia today. Nevertheless, the Afro-Brazilian culture has tremendous appeal in Bahia, especially during Carnaval. Even during years when Africa is not the theme, the most popular Carnaval groups are the blocos afros such as Olodum and Ilê Aiyê and the *afoxés* (groups with explicit connections to Afro-Brazilian religion) such as the Filhos de Gandhy. Not incidentally, these are the Carnaval groups that most directly engage issues of Afro-Brazilian identity and anti-racism.

Olodum

Olodum is a popular Afro-Brazilian cultural group and is most often referred to as a bloco afro with reference to its original raison d'être—participation in the yearly Carnaval celebration. Olodum is perhaps best known in Brazil and abroad for its drum corps composed of young Afro-Brazilians, which was featured on Paul Simon's *Rhythm of the Saints* album. Weekly concerts that feature the drum corps make up much of the group's activities during the year. In addition, Olodum incorporates images, language (the group's name is derived from that of a Candomblé god), and musical motifs from African-derived religion.

During Carnaval, Olodum is a central attraction. Yet in addition to its cultural activities, the directors of Olodum see the group as having a political mission. Its Web site refers to Olodum as "an NGO of the Brazilian black movement" that exists "to combat racial discrimination, to stimulate the self-esteem and pride of Afro-Brazilians, and to defend and fight for civil and human rights for marginalized people in Bahia and in Brazil" (Olodum 2003). Like many Afro-Brazilian organizations in Salvador, Olodum blurs the line between culture and politics.

Ilê Aiyê

Ilê Aiyê is another prominent cultural group and bloco afro with political engagements in Salvador. The bloco's name is usually translated from Yoruba as "house of life," and, like Olodum, Ilê Aiyê incorporates Afro-Brazilian religious motifs. According to its Web site, "Ilê Aiyê emerged as an expression of the anguish of groups of blacks searching for cultural self-affirmation. . . . This fact in itself is essentially political, and why not say revolutionary" (Ilê Aiyê 2003; translation mine). What is truly revolutionary about Ilê Aiyê is that it emerged to confront racial inequalities during the military dictatorship, a time when anything that challenged the image of Brazil as a racial democracy was seen as subversive. The following song, for example, was sung at the first appearance of Ilê Aiyê in the Carnaval of 1975.

> "What Bloco is this?"
> I want to know
> It is the black world
> That we came to sing for you

White (person), if you knew
The value that the black has
You would take a bath in pitch
So you would be black too
I'm not going to teach you my hustle [malandragem]
Nor even a little of my philosophy
He who gives light to the blind
Is the white bengala of Santa Luzia
What bloco is this?
I want to know
It is the black world
That we came to sing for you
We are crazy blacks
We are very cool
We have *cabelo duro* ["hard hair," used as a racial insult in other popular
songs, but redeployed with pride in this context]
We are *Black Power*

(Movimento Negro Unificado 1988, 11; translation mine)

Even in contemporary Bahia, these lyrics would be considered confrontational. The mention of "Black Power" (in English) in the last line of the song, a direct reference to a militant racial movement, was something very controversial in the 1970s. In fact, in 1975 Ilê Aiyê was denounced in a newspaper article titled "Racist Bloco, Discordant Note" for imitating North American inflammatory racial discourse and for inciting racial conflict in a country that supposedly had no racial problems (*A Tarde*, February 12, 1975).

Today Ilê Aiyê states that its objective is to preserve, valorize, and promote Afro-Brazilian culture. It is also concerned with black revolts in Brazil that "contributed strongly to the processes of strengthening the ethnic identity and self-esteem of black Brazilians" (Ilê Aiyê 2003; translation mine). Along with Olodum, then, Ilê Aiyê is one of the most prominent cultural institutions involved with the black movement in Bahia.

Filhos de Gandhy

Founded in 1949, the Filhos de Gandhy Carnaval Association is much older than both Olodum and Ilê Aiyê. Inspired by the Indian leader Mahatma Gandhi, a group of stevedores formed the group in the name of nonviolence and peace (Filhos de Gandhy 2003). Unlike many Carnaval groups, the presence of women and alcoholic beverages is prohibited in the parade of the Filhos de Gandhy. In fact, the group is considered an afoxé rather than a bloco because of the Afro-Brazilian instruments it incorporates and due to its explicitly religious emphasis. In addition to Afro-Brazilian religious elements, the members of the Filhos de Gandhy march wearing a white costume (symbolizing peace), including a turban and sandals, which lends an Arabian look to the group.

While these groups are often politically engaged, for a good portion of the year they are primarily focused on the celebration of Carnaval. This is not to say that politics fades into the background during this time; on the contrary, the political message of these groups is broadcast to large numbers of people during Carnaval. In contrast, however, other Afro-Brazilian activists choose to put their efforts into more politically oriented groups rather than culturalist organizing strategies.

The MNU and the PT

Although Salvador is best known as the center of African-derived culture in Brazil, it is also the focus of Afro-Brazilian political activism in the northeast. Many activists in Salvador are affiliated with groups such as the MNU and/or political parties such as the PT. In fact, an informal and precarious connection between the MNU and the PT has existed since the late 1980s (Jones 1995). Most of the activists I met were involved with both MNU and the PT, and many of them worked for a congressman named Luiz Alberto. As I discuss below, cultural celebrations often provide the context for their various campaign initiatives.

One of the relatively few people of African descent in the Brazilian government, Luiz Alberto has been a congressman since 1997 and a member of the PT since 1980. He was also one of the founding members of the MNU and has been a delegate to all of its national conferences. In addition to labor and other PT issues, Luiz Alberto's campaign focuses heavily on problems of concern to people of African descent.

My first contact at Luiz Alberto's office was a man named Ivonei. A thin, dark-skinned man in his late thirties, Ivonei is a member of Luiz Alberto's campaign staff and is also active in the MNU. He began our first interview by explaining to me that the MNU is a national-level organization with the objective of fighting racism in whatever way it manifests itself—in the labor market, in terms of religious intolerance, in gender relations, and so on. He has been involved in the MNU since 1990, and he claims that since then he has seen *consciência* (black awareness) grow. The blocos afros, for example, have helped improve self-esteem and racial awareness among blacks through their celebration of Afro-Brazilian music and aesthetics.

This racial awareness, Ivonei pointed out, was particularly evident on November 20 (which I discuss below), when fifty thousand people gathered in Salvador to commemorate Zumbi of Palmares. Furthermore, he says, recent research has made people more aware of racial inequalities such as wage differences. Finally, the government has officially acknowledged that racism exists, and this has helped to legitimate the MNU's efforts. Nevertheless, he laments, Brazil is still strongly linked to the structures of racism.

Ivonei explained that the MNU faces several main obstacles to mobilization against racism. The first problem is financial; since the movement has never had funding from the Brazilian government or from groups abroad, it must survive on contributions and volunteer labor. Ivonei believes that this lack of funding stems partly from the organization's radical image. He says, however, that the world has changed since the MNU was founded; the dictatorship is over, and in the context of democracy the MNU is now more of a progressive than a radical organization. He points out that because the ideological clash between capitalism and communism is less relevant to politics today, the MNU must change with the times, perhaps by embracing the fabled "third way" and distancing itself from the hard-line Marxism that characterized its discourse in the 1970s and 1980s.

Ivonei also mentioned the problem of Brazil's massive external debt. Debt payments, he explained, represent money that might have been used to help the black community by providing housing or public health improvements. Therefore, he argues, some of the responsibility for alleviating inequalities in Brazil is in the hands of rich countries, the leaders of which should rethink their debt policies.

One of the most frustrating things about racism in Brazil, Ivonei explained, is that it is "invisible" (cordial, de facto) rather than "incidental." As a result, racism in Brazil is often marginalized by the media, which tends to focus on reporting exciting events. He pointed out that every time a racial confrontation occurs in the United States, it is all over the television, but when thousands of people march on Brasilia, this is not covered in the U.S. news. In fact, he believes that the activist community in Brazil is better organized than it appears in the international media.

Although Ivonei is active in the MNU, he does not take part in Candomblé. When I asked about connections between the MNU, the PT, and Candomblé, he replied that the MNU is independent of any political party, religion, or government. Many people who are involved with the MNU are also affiliated with the PT because the PT's progressive political agenda fits well with the objectives of the MNU, but others are members of the Democratic Socialists (PDT) and other leftist parties. As for religion, Ivonei said that the MNU tries to respect Brazil's religious pluralism.

Ivonei affirmed, however, that a certain connection between Candomblé and the MNU has emerged from the MNU's efforts to protect Candomblé from persecution. With respect to the Catholic Church, the MNU is highly critical of what it sees as Catholic complicity in the submission and enslavement of blacks. Nevertheless, Ivonei admitted that groups like the Pastoral Afro might have an important role since they provide blacks in the church with a sense of their own history. Furthermore, although those involved in the MNU or the PT may be critical in theory of religious or culturalist mobilization strategies, activists often take advantage of popular festivals as a way to communicate a political message to large crowds of revelers.

Lavagem do Bonfim

The Lavagem do Bonfim is a traditional syncretic celebration and one of the high points of the calendar of festivals in Salvador. The celebration honors Nosso Senhor do Bonfim (Our Lord of the Good End), the patron of Salvador who is popularly identified with Oxalá in the Candomblé pantheon. On the third Thursday in January, tens of thousands of people gather to make a six-kilometer "pilgrimage" through the streets of the lower city of Salvador. Thousands of people walk from the Igreja da Nossa Senhora da Conceição da Praia to the Igreja do Bonfim to witness a ritual washing of the steps of the church performed by initiates of Candomblé.

In 2002, however, I attended the Lavagem do Bonfim more as a political event than as a religious ceremony. I marched the streets of the lower city with Pedro, a MNU/PT organizer from Cachoeira, and his friends from the PT in Salvador. The event illustrated how political messages are often communicated in the context of popular celebrations in Bahia, frequently making it difficult in practice to draw the line between political and more culture-oriented mobilization strategies.

The day of the Lavagem do Bonfim 2002 I took a bus to the lower city and arrived at the church of Nossa Senhora da Conceição da Praia early in the morning. While I waited for Pedro and his friends I sat down across from the church and watched a group of Baianas arrive, dressed all in white, carrying flowers. Soon men from the Filhos de Gandhy appeared wearing T-shirts calling for peace in response to the recent U.S. bombing of Afghanistan.

Eventually Pedro showed up with his friends and we joined the procession. Two of the young men in our group wore Rastafarian wigs and Luiz Alberto T-shirts as they walked through the crowd on stilts. Other groups represented in the procession included the several Carnaval blocos, political parties, unions, and businesses such as gas stations. As we made our way toward the Igreja do Bonfim we were joined by Luiz Alberto himself.

After less than an hour of marching, we left the procession to join the crowds celebrating on the sidewalk along the pilgrimage route. There we stood and watched the parade go by for hours in the heart of the lower city. In the afternoon someone showed up in a costume with a huge Luiz Alberto puppet head and stood waving at the passersby. Everywhere vendors were selling beer, water, soda, sandwiches, barbecued meat, and snacks while everyone mingled, drank, and danced. To my surprise, we ended up making no effort to see the actual church-washing ceremony. I learned that this is typical, however, and that only a very small percentage of the people are at the church right at the moment that the ceremony takes place. Other than the brief religious ceremonies that most people never saw, the event resembled a giant urban barbecue.

The PT group I was with took full advantage of the huge crowds and sociable atmosphere to do some political promotion and networking. Festivals like the Lavagem do Bonfim are the highlights of the yearly calendar; moreover, what is striking about these celebrations—as opposed, for example, to the home-and-family-oriented holidays that are most important in the United States—is their public nature. Thus, in the Brazilian context, popular festivals are a way to "take the message to the street." Political mobilization is often intertwined with the carnavalesque, such as during the celebration of Black Consciousness Day.

November 20th

The 20th of November is Black Consciousness Day in Brazil. The holiday was instituted in the late 1970s by activists who were critical of the tradition of celebrating the anniversary of the abolition of slavery on May 13th. Many felt that abolition had been simply a formality and that Afro-Brazilians continued in slave-like conditions throughout the twentieth century. Thus, November 20th—the anniversary of the day Zumbi of Palmares died in 1695—was proposed as a more fitting day to celebrate Afro-Brazilian resistance.

In 2001, weeks before November 20th, billboards were posted along Salvador's main highways that read,

BLACK CITY—Salvador, the most African city in Brazil
November 20th, Black Awareness Day

A major focus of the celebration, in addition to the history of the *quilombos* and of black resistance in Brazil, was slavery reparations. Reparations had been one of the major themes of the Third Worldwide Conference Against Racism, Racial Discrimination, Xenophobia, and Related Intolerance earlier that year in Durban, South Africa. The reparations issue was highlighted in educational pamphlets about Black Consciousness Day disseminated by the MNU and Ilê Aiyê.

November 20th was also promoted as a day to reflect on black identity, as can be seen in the following excerpt from a pamphlet published by Movimento Brasil: Outros 500 Resistência Indígena, Negra e Popular (Brazil Movement: Other 500 Indigenous, Black and Popular Resistance).

HE WHO SAYS MESTIÇO SAYS BLACK!

That's right. The history of the mestiço is linked to the history of the "negada" which is the word with which the elites designate blacks and Indians. . . . In fact, during colonization, mestiços were not treated very differently. . . .

Today, however, many mestiços try to pass for white. Or rather, they identify themselves with those who discriminate against them! They deny who raised them and gave them life. . . .

Let us not let ourselves be fooled anymore! The entirety of our being depends on this. On this also depends the dignity of the Brazilian people. We are black, and so what? We are the majority and we are going to govern the country. . . . The turning of the mestiços is the piece that is lacking in the process of national liberation. . . . Viva Zumbi! (2001)

This pamphlet highlights one of the central problems related to Afro-Brazilian mobilization: the fact that many people of African descent identify themselves as mixed or brown, but not as black. As the author points out, however, blacks and *mestiços* are both discriminated against by white elites. Thus, according to the author of the pamphlet, liberation depends on the mestiços recognizing their common interest with all nonwhites.

Black Consciousness Day Celebrations in Salvador

On November 20, 2001, I set out for Campo Grande, an urban neighborhood in the center of Salvador. Parked around the main plaza were several enormous double-decker trucks with stages on top and speakers on their sides, gearing up for the afternoon parade. In the plaza several capoeira groups were performing;

the members of one group were wearing T-shirts that read "Capoeira—Black Identity, Zumbi Lives." Also in the plaza were an array of different political groups flying their banners and handing out pamphlets, including the PT, the Communist Party, and the Democratic Socialists. In addition, a number of interest groups were handing out literature on AIDS and other issues of concern to the black community.

Many people walking around the plaza carried signs or wore T-shirts demanding reparations. Nowhere did I see the obvious use of Candomblé elements or symbols. This would be consistent, however, with a concern with not contributing to the folklorization of Candomblé by displaying it out of context. Yet later that day when I went to observe the Black Consciousness Day celebrations in Pelourinho, I attended a parade that was much more religiously oriented than the mostly political activities that were going on in Campo Grande.

The parade in Pelourinho, which originated in the nearby Afro-Brazilian neighborhood of Liberdade, was made up of different groups following each other through the streets, playing music and dancing. Paraders in some of the groups were carrying Candomblé paraphernalia and dancing in a way similar to what is seen during Candomblé ceremonies. The procession made its way through the cobbled streets of Pelourinho to its destination in front of the Rosário church just as Mass was beginning. The Rosário church was packed, and on each side of the altar sat several priests of African descent, many of them members of the Pastoral Afro who came to celebrate Black Consciousness Day.

The events of Black Consciousness Day reflect some of the complexities and tensions that characterize Afro-Brazilian identity politics in Salvador. While there seems to be consensus among activists about the focal symbols and issues of the celebration—Zumbi, resistance, and identity—there are clear differences in approach. The differences were most striking in the contrasts between the two parades, one politically oriented and the other manifestly religious in its content. As I examine later, some see this apparent split between cultural and political approaches as a hindrance for the black movement.

Indeed, it often seems that Afro-Brazilian organizations cluster into two distinct constellations: one made up of groups concerned with religious or cultural affirmation and the other focused on political mobilization. To some extent, however, most groups in Salvador engage both cultural and political issues. In fact, a number of groups and events in Salvador mediate between two poles of cultural affirmation and political mobilization, including Carnaval groups and popular street festivals. In practice, then, the boundaries between Afro-Brazilian religion, culture, and politics are shifting and permeable. Thus, much of the consciousness raising that targets the Afro-Brazilian "masses" is accomplished through culturally and religiously oriented events such as Black Consciousness Day, Carnaval, and the Lavagem do Bonfim. Again, this practice has led to considerable debate about the value of culturalist versus more explicitly political approaches to mobilization in the black movement. Some have criticized the movement's preoccupation with Afro-Brazilian religious traditions and its supposed lack of ideological coherence. As I discuss in more depth in chapter 6, however, Brazilian activists seem to favor pragmatic and eclectic approaches to consciousness raising over rigid ideological formulations.

Many Catholics, candomblecistas, and evangelicals with whom I spoke argued that the realms of religion and politics should remain separate; others feel that their religious beliefs compel them to be politically engaged. Perhaps the most contentious debate I explored along these lines is that concerning the relationship between religion and racial politics. As I pointed out above, for example, because of its appalling history of complicity in racial domination, many are very suspicious of the Catholic Church's involvement with anti-racism. Many with whom I spoke maintained that because of the intimate connection between religion and Afro-Brazilian identity, the practice of Candomblé is inherently political. From this perspective, separating Candomblé from Catholicism is part of a larger project of asserting the autonomy and dignity of people of African descent. In this view, religious intolerance and racism are often equated. Yet those who are most often faced with charges of religious intolerance—the members of the IURD and other conservative evangelicals—argue that a distinction should be maintained between religion, race, and politics. On the other hand, many progressive evangelicals contend that religion and racial identity should be dissociated but that religion and racial politics are intimately related. In fact, as I examine in the next chapter, alternative and potentially useful approaches to Afro-Brazilian identity and politics are currently emerging in progressive evangelical communities.

5

Alternative Identities, Emergent Politics

It is clear that much discourse about Afro-Brazilian identity centers on Candomblé, even if Candomblé is not an evenly shared practice in Afro-Brazilian communities. The discourses of syncretism, double belonging, and anti-syncretism, for example, all turn on the relationship between Candomblé and Catholicism. Furthermore, relations between communities of candomblecistas and Christians are not understood as mere metaphors for race relations. As I discussed in the last chapter, intolerance against Candomblé has been equated with racism.

Yet the emphasis on Candomblé in representations of Afro-Brazilian identity overlooks the significant religious diversity that one finds in Afro-Brazilian communities. Moreover, involvement in Candomblé is forbidden for the growing number of evangelical Christians in Brazil, who tend to stress their identities as Christians more than any particular ethnic tradition. Accordingly, in this chapter I focus on the distinctive ways in which evangelicals of African descent engage religious discourses and practices as they construct their identities and struggle against racism. I suggest that because of their emphasis on electoral politics and culturally inclusive approaches to mobilization, progressive evangelicals have much to contribute to conversations about the struggle against racism in Brazil.

As I have emphasized throughout this book, the construction of Afro-Brazilian identity in Bahia is intertwined in complex ways with identity politics elsewhere in the African diaspora. Besides the Afro-Brazilian cultural heritage, for example, many Bahians of African descent draw from increasingly globalized discourses and practices as they construct their ethnic identities, including black Protestantism from the United States, the negritude movement from Francophone Africa, Rastafarianism from the Caribbean, and musical styles ranging from reggae to hip-hop (Sansone 2003; Hanchard 1999; Reichmann 1997, 1999a, 1999b; K. Butler 1998b; Carvalho 1993). At the same time, many visitors from Brazil and abroad come to Bahia to experience what is often praised as one of the most authentically African black cultures in the New World, and this cultural tourism tends to focus on local Afro-Brazilian practices such as Candomblé.

Yet the unqualified identification of Bahia and black Bahians with African-derived religion—an association that is reinforced by tourism promoters as well as Afro-Brazilian activists—has become a target of criticism from evangelicals and a controversial issue in the black movement. Evangelicals of African descent often find themselves at odds with the close identification of blackness with Candomblé in Brazilian culture in general and in the black movement in particular. And rightly so: despite the fact that participation in it has sometimes been presented as the sine qua non of black identity, Candomblé is but one aspect of the experience of people of African descent in Brazil. This is not to deny that African-derived religion was central to the maintenance of African ethnic identities during slavery in Brazil, or that after abolition Candomblé played a central role in the formation of an overarching Afro-Brazilian identity (Harding 2000; K. Butler 1998b). Clearly, however, highly racialized representations of Candomblé have frequently played a role in racial ideologies. Like many representations in the racial imagination, they cut both ways. Candomblé, for example, has been imagined both as a "primitive cult" to which Africans inevitably regressed and as the "root religion" of people of African descent in the New World.

In fact, Candomblé is far from an evenly shared practice among Afro-Brazilians. Although the numbers are increasing, only around 2 to 3 percent of the Brazilian population reported being involved with Candomblé in 1995. Furthermore, according to nationwide studies, about half of Candomblé initiates are white (Prandi 1995). Thus, only a minority of Afro-Brazilians are involved with African-derived religion.[1] This, along with the fact that many blacks, especially evangelical Christians, are strongly opposed to such practices suggests that Candomblé's status as a symbol of black identity is a contested issue among Afro-Brazilians (Sansone 2003; D'Adesky 2001; cf. Selka 2003). Activists and academics both within and outside the black movement have argued that the focus on African-derived traditions as the basis for black solidarity is problematic. Critics point out that the emphasis on religious symbols and practices that fail to resonate with significant numbers of Afro-Brazilians alienates potential constituents of the movement (Barcelos 1999; Reichmann 1999a, 1999b; Burdick 1998a, 1998b; K. Butler 1998b; Hanchard 1994).

Even within evangelical Christian communities, people are divided in their attitudes toward traditional Afro-Brazilian practices like Candomblé. As I highlight in the next section, most evangelical Christians are conservative and eschew African-derived religion. Further on, however, I examine how some evangelicals are reaching across religious lines as they mobilize against racism.

Evangelicals in Salvador

As in Brazil as a whole, the majority of non-Catholic Christians in Salvador are affiliated with evangelical denominations, particularly Pentecostal churches. Yet Salvador is home to many "historical," "mainline," or "traditional" Protestant churches ranging from Anglican to Methodist. The earliest of these churches to arrive in Bahia, those of the Anglicans and Lutherans, were founded to serve foreign Protestant communities living in Salvador, while denominations like the Baptists and Methodists arrived later in the nineteenth century as missionary churches (Da Silva 1998). While the immigrant churches tended to remain homogeneously white, the Baptists and the Methodists actively recruited Afro-Brazilians as members.

Today, these traditional mainline Protestant churches, regardless of their origins as immigrant or missionary, are much more likely than their Pentecostal counterparts to take part in ecumenical and anti-racist activities. Yet, again, traditional mainline Protestants make up a very small percentage of the Protestant population (although some churches, particularly Baptist ones, often straddle the fence between traditional Protestantism and Pentecostalism). In general, the more traditionally oriented churches are smaller and tend to keep a low profile in contrast to some of the highly conspicuous Pentecostal churches in the city such as the IURD.

The Igreja Universal Reina de Deus (IURD)

The Universal Church of the Kingdom of God is one of the most popular denominations in Cachoeira and is the fastest growing church in Brazil. Again, this is partly because of its appropriation of elements from Brazilian popular religion. In addition, the IURD owns several radio and television stations through which it spreads its message. This message often focuses on how believers can be freed from poverty, sickness, and relationship problems by ridding themselves of the evil spirits that are believed to cause these misfortunes.

The success of the IURD is also partly attributable to the fact that it holds more worship services each day than any other church in town. Every IURD church holds at least three services a day, and each day has its theme. Monday's theme is prosperity, Tuesday's is cleansing and curing, Wednesday's is the Holy Spirit, Thursday's is the family, Friday's is liberation from evil spirits, Saturday's is love therapy, and Sunday is for praise, adoration, and the holy supper. The IURD's use of the media for "advertising" as well as its uniform schedule of frequent and specialized worship services reflects the marketing/franchising mentality that has helped to drive the denomination's spectacular growth.

As in many evangelical churches, much of the IURD's discourse focuses on evil spirits, which are often identified with the entities of the Candomblé pantheon. Some members of other evangelical churches, however, believe that the IURD is obsessed with the devil and evil spirits. "All they talk about is demons and money," one Bahian complained. A clear example of this focus on demons is the *culto de libertação* (worship for liberation) held on Fridays to rid people of evil spirits.

In the context of the IURD, Afro-Brazilian religion is more than something that is simply used as a negative example in discourses about evangelical identity, as is the case in many Christian churches. During the IURD services, Candomblé spirits regularly become embodied in members of the congregation and are subject to inquisition and exorcism. This dramatizes the transformation of the believer's body and soul upon entering the community of evangelicals in a most striking and tangible way. The literal demonization of Candomblé that is at the heart of this process of defining evangelical identity, however, often leads to heated conflict. As I discussed in the last chapter, in Salvador, where groups of evangelicals have physically attacked Candomblé terreiros, candomblecistas have publicly decried acts of intolerance against their religion and equated such attacks with racism.

One of the most striking religious structures in Salvador is the IURD's "Catedral da Fé" (Cathedral of Faith) located where the main highway that passes through the city intersects with one of its main boulevards. Constructed in 2000 next to Salvador's largest mall and across the street from the interstate bus terminal, the cathedral could hardly be more strategically located for conspicuous visibility. The building's exterior is imposing and the space of the interior vast. It is four stories high, and the floor is covered with a sea of seats as in a giant theater. Adding to the theater effect are the "stage" upon which the altar sits in the front of the cathedral and the box seats that can be reached from the upper floors of the building. Living in Cachoeira, I had become accustomed to Pentecostal churches that were less imposing than even the shabbiest Catholic chapel in town, so I found the Cathedral quite impressive.

Figure 8. The Cathedral of Faith Universal Church of the Kingdom of God. This massive structure, which rivals the largest Catholic churches in Salvador in size, is located in one of the busiest parts of the city across from the main bus station and next to Salvador's largest shopping mall.

The IURD maintains a high profile by the location of its cathedral, its ubiquitous churches, and through its extensive use of radio and television as well. The church owns radio and television stations throughout Brazil (Da Silva 1997), and its television channel in Salvador features daily religious programs including a call-in during which callers can discuss their problems with a pastor and be directed to the nearest Universal church. Many of the problems that people call about are financial and personal (unemployment, difficulties with one's family or spouse, etc.). Yet many others call about what in the United States would be considered medical or psychiatric problems. For example, a common announcement on the IURD's channel lists ten "symptoms" for which people should visit their local church, including 1) nervousness, 2) headaches, 3) insomnia, 4) fear, 5) fainting spells, 6) suicidal thoughts, 7) sicknesses that doctors can't diagnose (or cure), 8) hearing voices, 9) addiction, and 10) depression.

As with other popular religions in Brazil, one of the primary functions of the IURD is to provide help for medical and psychiatric problems, especially for the poor, who have little access to education and modern Western medicine. Many within and outside of Brazil are concerned, however, that the IURD effectively discourages people from seeking proper attention for serious medical and psychiatric conditions. An incident in England involving the death of young Victoria Climbié after she visited the IURD for an exorcism led to an investigation of the church's healing practices (*Guardian*, May 9, 2003; BBC News, December 6, 2001). Although it became clear that the girl died from parental abuse and neglect, many argued that the IURD prevented the girl from receiving the medical attention she needed. Investigators eventually concluded, however, that the IURD made no explicit claims that it could offer miraculous healing and that the pastor of the church actually advised Climbié's great-aunt to take the girl to a doctor. Yet for many Brazilians the connections between the IURD, exorcism, and healing are quite clear.

Soon after moving to Salvador I attended services at an IURD church near my apartment. Although the church was located in Barra, one of the more affluent neighborhoods in Salvador, it was not much larger or better decorated than those I had seen while living in Cachoeira. Some things were different, however: the building was air conditioned, for example, and the stereo speakers on the walls were smaller than the huge stacks of amplifiers I had seen in similar churches in Cachoeira. Most of the congregation was informally dressed, not much differently than the people walking out on the street, although a few were wearing dresses or a shirt and tie. On average, on the days that I visited the church, about a third of the worshipers were women. Furthermore, people were lighter skinned than at other churches I had attended: most appeared *morena clara* (light brown), and only about one person out of five was black or white.

The pastor who conducted the service on my first visit to the church was a stout white man with thick glasses. Unlike the eight attending *obreiros* (assistants), who wore white tops and blue pants or skirts, he sported a colored shirt and tie. At the start of the service a young man piped in on a synthesizer, then the pastor led everyone in a prayer with hands in the air. The pastor led several songs, one of which seemed like a routine from a musical—he danced around the front of the church trading off singing parts with the obreiros while the audience sang "sai, sai, sai, em nome de Jesus!" (leave, leave, leave in the name of Jesus—an exhortation to demons) and waved their hands. The musical performance provided a striking contrast to the somber tone of the Catholic Mass to which I was accustomed.

When the singing ended, each member of the congregation went to the front of the church to have his or her forehead anointed with oil. Afterward the congregants formed a circle around the pews and stood along the walls of the church, hand in hand, with their eyes closed. The pastor and obreiros yelled for evil spirits to leave and prayed that everyone would be "transformed." Many people were speaking in tongues and praying aloud as this was happening; the church was a sea of voices. The pastor and his obreiros approached some of the members of the congregation to lay hands on them. Finally, before sitting down in the pews, the congregants walked in a circle around the church, singing, clapping, and making hand gestures to accompany the songs.

The next item on the agenda was the salt that I had seen piled in bags next to the altar as I entered the church. The pastor explained that he had bought ninety-one kilos of salt (he never explained the significance of the number) to be used to "fight the enemy." During his sermon he made reference to David, who, according to the Bible, defeated his enemies in the Valley of Salt. I assume this was the inspiration for his enterprising idea.

The pastor instructed each person to take a bag of salt home and explained that the salt should be put in food, spread around the house, and even taken to work—anywhere to defeat the enemy. He clarified that while the "enemy" literally refers to the devil, he was also speaking figuratively about one's financial, health, and family problems. The pastor announced that each person who wanted a bag should come up to the front of the church, write his or her name on a sticker, and put the sticker on the bag. He explained that each bag would remain in the church for a week to be prayed over every day and that each person should pick up his or her bag on Friday in exchange for an envelope containing R$13.

After a number of people signed up for a bag of salt, the pastor began his sermon for the evening. His central theme was that religion concerns much more than practices such as the use of magic salt. He warned the congregation that they should not seek God just because he cures and liberates them; instead, one should seek to deliver one's whole life into God's hands. The pastor asked if anyone would like it if someone married them just for their inheritance, and the congregation answered, "No!" He declared that one must serve God, not simply engage in *promessas*, and that there is much more to religion than the promise of prosperity, health, and a blessed family.

The pastor appeared to be preaching directly against the theology of prosperity for which the IURD is infamous. At the end of his sermon he pointed out that there are many people (he mentioned scientists in particular) who do not understand God and therefore do not understand that offerings (like the R$13 for a bag of salt) are not used to enrich the pastor but to build new churches all around the world. The cynicism that the pastor was deploring has a basis in fact, however. The IURD has recently been investigated for fraud and is frequently criticized for its emphasis on money (*New York Post*, July 23, 2000; *Chicago Tribune*, May 17, 2001).

The following week I stopped by the church and talked to one of the pastors about my research. He explained that if I wanted permission to conduct interviews and administer questionnaires at his church, I would have to get it from someone who possessed more authority than he did. He suggested I try visiting the Catedral da Fé, the administrative headquarters of the IURD in Salvador. Later that week I headed to the cathedral with my questionnaires. There I was bounced around among several obreiros, auxiliary pastors, and a receptionist. No one was really sure what to do with me. Finally the receptionist told me I needed to talk to a man in management named Reginaldo. He was packing up for the day so she gave me his number and said to call him for an appointment. I called him the next day, and we agreed to meet the following week.

When I arrived at the cathedral on the day of our appointment the receptionist asked me to sit for a while, then took me up on the elevator to another reception room to wait for Reginaldo. The impression I got from the lobbies and the elevator in the cathedral was that of a massive bureaucratic institution. By the time Reginaldo came to greet me, I felt a bit self-conscious that I was wearing shorts and a short-sleeved shirt because everyone else was dressed rather formally. Moreover, Reginaldo did not seem very enthusiastic at first, which made me even more uncomfortable.

Reginaldo took me into a small cubicle with a table, situated in a huge room that looked like it could have been the center of a thriving business. I gave him one of my cards and a copy of my letter of introduction from the Universidade Federal da Bahia and once again explained my research to him (I had already spoken with him briefly on the phone). I showed him one of the questionnaires; he looked it over while I sat silently. When he finished, he leaned back in his seat and finally became animated. He shared his ideas on race with me. He told me that in his opinion, the biggest racists are the blacks themselves, who, if they applied themselves, could make a better life. Furthermore, he said, racism is absurd in Brazil, especially in Bahia, because no one is 100 percent white (Reginaldo is rather dark-skinned himself). He seemed interested, however, and said he thought the questionnaire was okay. We agreed that I would come back Monday afternoon to get final approval to conduct interviews and administer questionnaires at the IURD.

When I returned on Monday, I could tell by the look on his face that Reginaldo was going to give me bad news. He said that it is prohibited to do studies like this (pointing to the questionnaire) in the church. When I asked for an explanation, he simply repeated, "Because it is prohibited." Realizing that I was not going to get a satisfactory answer, I thanked him for his time and left. The IURD is very wary of the media and of the way they are portrayed by outsiders in general, so Reginaldo's refusal was not completely surprising.

Furthermore, Reginaldo's bosses may have objected to the references to the MNU and Afro-Brazilian culture in the questionnaire. They may have been concerned, not without some justification, that I might attempt to portray the IURD as unsympathetic to the black movement. As an institution, the IURD appears aloof toward racial issues, and, as I have discussed above, its representatives have expressed opposition to mixing religion and racial politics. Clearly, then, the decision-makers at the IURD would have had little interest in allowing the church to be scrutinized by a foreigner studying racism.

My experience at the IURD was the only situation in which I was categorically denied access during my fieldwork. I recall many other occasions when I was repeatedly put off until another day (most often by Candomblé practitioners) or made to jump through endless hoops (at the Catholic Church's archives in Salvador) until I earned someone's sympathy or gave up in frustration. Yet because of its efficient, bureaucratic modus operandi, its overt policy of suspicion toward the media, and its implicit hostility toward my research topic, the IURD shut me out with none of the customary pleasantries.

I was able to speak with a number of pastors and obreiros from the IURD while I was living in Cachoeira, however. Access was much easier for me there because of my friendship with a former obreiro at the IURD and easier still because churches in the interior operate more in terms of personal relationships than those in Salvador. Not surprisingly, all of the pastors and obreiros from the IURD I spoke with in Cachoeira denied that racism was a serious problem in their communities. Despite this lack of explicit concern with racism, the issue of the relationship between the IURD and Afro-Brazilian identity is more complex. On the one hand, the IURD clearly demonizes African-derived religion and culture as it constructs Candomblé as the religion of the devil. On the other hand, as I discuss below, the IURD incorporates elements from Afro-Catholic popular religious culture. Thus, the IURD is thoroughly conversant with the religious worldview of the marginalized Afro-Brazilian. On the whole, however, the IURD's lack of a stance on racism is at odds with the aims of the black movement. By contrast, some evangelical groups in Salvador are fully engaged in the struggle against racism.

The Movimento Evangélico Progressista (MEP)

As I have already pointed out, many activists see Candomblé as a natural basis for a shared Afro-Brazilian ethnoreligious and sociopolitical identity, even if only a minority of people practice it. Evangelical Christians, by contrast—even those involved with the struggle against racism—generally avoid Candomblé even if they are not hostile toward it as a matter of principle. Partly as a result, evangelicals are underrepresented in the mainstream black movement and are sometimes accused of being politically apathetic or even racist. My research on the Progressive Evangelical Movement, however, demonstrates that spaces indeed exist in Brazil in which evangelical Christianity, progressive politics, and racial struggle intersect. Yet this is not to suggest that race is always a primary concern for the MEP. Like other leftist groups in Brazil, it is oriented mostly toward a class-centered critique of the inequitable distribution of resources in Brazil. Racism is, however, a significant issue on its progressive political agenda.

My choice to focus on a politically progressive organization like MEP raises the question of whether MEP's anti-racist stance is grounded more in party politics than religion. Are evangelicals engaging issues of identity and racism in churches that are outside of the progressive fold? In fact, as the black evangelical movement gains national visibility, an expanding array of church groups and grassroots organizations—some with no particular political affiliation—are taking a stand against racism in cities like Rio, São Paulo, and Salvador (Burdick 2005). Against this backdrop, MEP stands out as a national organization in which evangelicals address race and racism as explicitly political questions. In contrast, for example, many local Pentecostal churches are engaging these issues through the performance of evangelical rap and reggae music (Burdick 2006, personal communication).

The MEP was founded in 1990 and today has local groups in most Brazilian states. Although its members make up a small percentage of the evangelical population, they are a vocal minority. Most of the churches affiliated with the MEP are Anglican, Baptist, Lutheran, or Presbyterian, but one-third belong to the Assembléia de Deus (Assembly of God), a Pentecostal denomination. Although the movement is not officially linked with any political organization, members who are involved in politics tend to belong to the left-wing Partido dos Trabalhadores (Workers' Party; PT). In fact, during Lula's campaign for the presidency as the PT candidate, MEP representatives formed the Committee of Evangelicals for Lula (*Folha Online*, October 16, 2002).

In the MEP's definition, similar to that of many evangelical churches, evangelicals are those who accept and proclaim Jesus Christ as their only and sufficient savior. It declares itself to be "conservative and orthodox in theology, affirming the authority of the Bible and the importance of evangelization, conversion, and prayer" (MEP 2001, 4; translation mine). Yet its approach to social issues is rather unorthodox for an evangelical movement. The first principle of its pastoral approach, for example, is resistance against oppression (MEP 2001). The movement emphasizes that Jesus reviled leaders who oppressed their people and called on Christians to be compassionate toward others. Moreover, it stresses that Christians should welcome suffering in the name of justice (MEP 2001). Members point to the scriptural basis for their progressive politics. This kind of biblical interpretation is at odds with the more conservative approaches to politics that are common among evangelicals—particularly Pentecostals—in Brazil.

The intersection of discourses about progressive politics, evangelical Christianity, and racial identity in the movement was apparent in a conference of the Bahian branch held in Salvador during my fieldwork. The conference, the branch's second, took place in a modest two-story Episcopal church a few blocks from the beach in Pituba, one of Salvador's more middle-class neighborhoods. As opposed to the Episcopal churches I had visited in the United States, which are often indistinguishable from Catholic ones, this one was decorated almost as sparsely as most of the Pentecostal churches I had seen in Brazil.

At the front of the room, a table and chairs for the panel of speakers sat below a simple altar. A banner hanging from the table read "Second MEP Meeting"; below that another banner read "Theme: The Presence of Christian Faith in Political and Social Issues." As I waited for the conference to start, I thumbed through some of the pamphlets that I had picked up at the door. One of them mentioned a national MEP meeting in Brasilia in 1999 that had focused on the life and teachings of Martin Luther King Jr. as one of its main themes.

Soon after I arrived, a moderator greeted the audience and introduced the conference panel of three speakers: Elizete Da Silva, a professor of the history of religion from the Federal University of Bahia who wrote her doctoral dissertation on Protestantism in Bahia; Creuza Costa, the director of the Domestic Workers' Union; and Walter Pinheiro, a congressman affiliated with the Workers' Party. Throughout the two-hour meeting that followed, the members of the panel and commentators in the audience emphasized the progressive character of Protestantism, as shown by its historical involvement with democratization and the promotion of literacy and its role in anti-slavery, feminist, and civil rights movements in North America. Several participants cited Martin Luther King Jr. as a shining example of socially engaged Protestantism. At the same time, however, Da Silva stressed the need to create a homegrown Brazilian Protestantism, one separate from that of the missionary churches from the United States. Although the conference centered on the theme of political participation, Pinheiro stressed that the relationship between religion and politics was problematic. Many progressive pastors, quite understandably, in his view, were unwilling to pledge their churches or denominations to specific political parties. In sum, the vision of evangelical identity that emerged from the conference drew heavily upon the historical legacy of Protestant Christianity. With respect to racial issues, participants often referred to the history of black Protestant anti-racism in the United States in particular. Black progressive evangelicals were attempting to construct a politically engaged identity based on the common experiences of blacks throughout the diaspora.

Evangelical Christianity, Politics, and Afro-Brazilian Identity

Politics

Although its members are careful to avoid equating church and party, the MEP is as much a political movement as it is a religious one. As Elizete Da Silva explained,

> MEP is a very recent movement in Brazil and even more recent in Bahia. It is a movement that has, like it says, a progressive, not conservative, characteristic and that has been bringing people together who have a less traditional view of the religion, especially groups linked with the Baptists. Baptists who are more, I would say, not the traditional ones, not Baptists who are fundamentalist, but Baptists who are more liberal.

Here she contrasts the perspective of the MEP, using the Baptist Church of Graça in Salvador as an example, with that of the majority of evangelical churches in Bahia.

> [The Baptist Church of Graça] is a church that is from a line that is much more liberal than the other religions in the Baptist denomination. And the Pentecostals, I would tell you that they always—they have been in Bahia since 1930—they always have had a very veiled political participation. They say that they have nothing to do with politics but, in fact, they end up supporting campaigns of politicians on the right, politicians who

make deals and give things in exchange. . . . The MEP has a small group of Pentecostals that participate; there are even people who are connected with a congressman who is from the Socialist Party. The truth is that this is very rare. The more traditional people of the Pentecostal church did not vote for him [the Socialist], they did not vote for PT, because they said that they [the Socialists and the PT] were involved in oppositional politics. And why? Because the Pentecostals as well as the traditional Baptists work in a very fundamentalist line. Well, you must remember a biblical text called Romans 13 that says that all authority comes from God and all evangelicals must obey these authorities. So, he [the evangelical] takes this text literally. That is exactly what I am saying; they take a fundamentalist reading of that text. So, most of Protestantism, the Baptists as well as the Pentecostals, and the more conservative Presbyterians as well, march in this direction. So, that federal deputy [the Socialist] really is a rare thing. It is for that reason that he is not well seen in the Assembly of God, which is the group with which he is associated.

Thus, progressive evangelicals are often marginalized even in their own churches. As Creuza Costa explained,

There are people [Pentecostals] who participate [in progressive politics] and when the leadership of the church or, rather, the head pastor finds out, he expels the person from being a member of that church. There are cases of people who were expelled from the church for participating in a political movement. . . . Often I felt the resistance of others to being in a movement that seeks social rights, because the majority of evangelical people think that we have to be concerned only with the spiritual life, to think only about the spiritual life after death.

When I asked, "Even people from the Baptist Church?" she answered,

Yes, including people from the Baptist Church. Now, the Baptist Church is better than the Pentecostals. The Pentecostals are the worst when it comes to level of political consciousness in society; they are very alienated. And, often the big leaders . . . they end up alienating people, telling them which candidates they should vote for—the pastor's candidate—without political discussion . . . and without discussing the candidate's project. So, they are interested in electing the candidate who is going to give things to them or their church, not to society or to the community as a whole independent of religious creed.

Pentecostals are not apolitical, Creuza and Elizete argue, even though they are often portrayed that way. On the contrary, they tend to vote for conservative candidates at the request of their pastor without critically considering whom they are supporting. Moreover, Creuza complains about the lack of Pentecostal involvement in the Domestic Workers' Union and says that Pentecostals, who generally do not participate in strikes, reap the benefits of the union's efforts without paying their dues. By contrast, MEP members are often involved in public activities and demonstrations: "On November 20, Black Awareness Day, we participated with banners, MEP participated in the November 20th protest march with banners. . . . On the first of May, Workers' Day, we also participated in the Workers' Day march, and we participated in other events." She argues that for the evangelical not to be engaged in the world is willful avoidance of reality.

> When a woman is discriminated against in the labor market, the evangelical woman is also discriminated against. When the black person is discriminated against in society, the black evangelical is also discriminated against. So, there is no point for us to keep thinking "I am evangelical so everything is OK and great!" This is not true. We have to keep our feet on the ground. Jesus Christ was not alienated, Jesus Christ did not alienate anyone; he gave people the option to choose. The biggest revolutionary on earth was Jesus Christ, the biggest revolutionary!

Although progressive evangelical discourse focuses on the conservative political climate that prevails among Pentecostals, a Pentecostal left wing is emerging (Cleary and Stewart-Gambino 1997; Freston 1994). As I mentioned above, a large number of MEP members is affiliated with the Assembly of God, and progressive evangelicals who belong to this denomination include the former national president of the MEP. In addition, one of the most noted Afro-Brazilian affiliates of the MEP, the PT politician Benedita Da Silva, is Pentecostal as well (Silva, Benjamin et al. 1997). As one Pentecostal MEP member put it, "Jesus was a leftist." Thus, although the image of the conservative Pentecostal is frequently invoked as a contrastive figure in constructions of progressive evangelical identity, Pentecostals are by no means politically homogeneous.

Religion and Afro-Brazilian Identity

Besides its politics, another characteristic that distinguishes the MEP from other evangelical groups is its stance toward other religions. Here, for example,

Creuza comments on the attitude of progressive evangelicals toward Catholicism and Candomblé.

> After becoming an adult one defines oneself as being evangelical by professing faith in Christianity and in Christ as one's only savior. But we respect people who are in the Catholic Church, in Candomblé, and we respect because the Bible itself says "not with force nor with violence." Each person knows the way they want to follow, is that not true?

I followed up by asking her about the association between the MNU and Candomblé, pointing out that for many evangelicals it was an obstacle that the MNU is run by people involved in Candomblé. She replied,

> For me it is not [an obstacle] because I have my mind made up. I respect my brothers there, my black brothers of the MNU. I am also involved with the MNU; I am also black independent of being evangelical, Catholic, or involved with Candomblé. What unites us is race. Religion can unite us, but we can respect one another and live together and discuss the issues that interest and have to do with us, each one respecting the religion of the other.

Clearly, then, although Creuza respects Candomblé, she does not base her identity as a person of African descent on it.

> There are people who say that Afro-Brazilian identity . . . is your hair, it is your physical characteristics, all that; and people argue that it is religion also. But I am Afro-Brazilian, and I don't profess Candomblé as my religion. Here's the thing: do you think that in Africa everyone was involved with Candomblé? Not only now, but since then, 500 years ago when blacks were brought across the Atlantic here to Brazil, even then, do you think that the only religion that existed was Candomblé? I believe that there were other religions, because Africa is a continent and in that continent there were other languages, diverse languages. So, if there were diverse languages and diverse customs, there were also other religions and other festivals. And so? How do you explain this? For example, I heard that there in the United States the majority of African Americans are evangelical.
>
> So do people stop being people of African descent because they have another religion, because they are not of Candomblé? I don't stop being of African descent because I am not of Candomblé. I am evangelical, and I continue to be of African descent, black, of African descent. My sisters

and my friend are Catholics who continue to be of African descent. My relative who is an atheist, she also continues to be of African descent.

Creuza offers a cogent critique of the naturalized relation between being black and involvement in Candomblé. In my discussions with her she presented a view of racial identity based in shared descent and the experience of racism rather than in particular religious or cultural traditions. Yet as we will see, Christian scripture plays a central role in the formulation of the progressive evangelical approach to racial politics.

Again, progressive evangelicals—in contrast to many progressive Catholics, for instance—maintain a clear distinction between respect for and involvement in other religions such as Candomblé. At the same time, however, the MEP promotes an ecumenical approach to interfaith relations. This tolerant approach differs markedly from that of most evangelicals in Bahia. Between 2000 and 2002, the media reported several cases in which Pentecostals physically attacked Candomblé terreiros. Furthermore, during its television and radio broadcasts, the Universal Church of the Kingdom of God—one of the most influential evangelical organizations in Brazil—routinely denounces Candomblé as devil worship. Elizete explains,

But that missionary Protestantism, especially the Pentecostalism of the Universal Church of the Kingdom of God, they condemn, even demonize the Afro religions. It seems to me that they thrive on this demonization, in the sense that the converts, the people, the newly converted must abandon all the practices of Candomblé because that is of the devil. And when a mãe de santo or a pai de santo or a filho de santo involved in Candomblé converts, this is a great celebration.

MEP and Black Identity

MEP offers a space within evangelical Christianity in which progressive political discourse is possible and black identities can be affirmed. Yet some maintain that this space has largely been carved out by exceptional people drawing on discourses exterior to evangelical Christianity. As Elizete argues,

People [evangelicals] who call themselves black, who assume their negritude, who affirm that they are of African descent, they learned this outside of the church. Creuza did not learn to be black in the Baptist church. She learned it in the black movement, she learned it in the Domestic Workers' Union, she learned this in the Workers' Party, which has a strong group that works on this issue of minorities, of identity. And Benedita [Da

Silva] also, who is a black woman who took practically the same path that Creuza is taking today, she was part of the popular movement, then she was a candidate, became an alderman, then a deputy, a senator, and now, the vice governor of Rio. In fact, I think that the evangelical churches still don't give the contribution that they should give for initiatives against racial discrimination. Why don't they? Because historically Protestantism in Brazil, as in the United States also, the white in Protestantism always rejected the world of the afrodescendente.

This does not mean that there is nothing in the Protestant tradition for people of African descent to claim, just that these are not the things that evangelicals in Brazil generally emphasize: "I was there in the Protestant church, my father is a Protestant pastor, and I only heard about Martin Luther King when I entered the university. You know why? Because all the missionaries who came here were white and were not interested in talking about the black church, much less Martin Luther King." Today, progressive evangelicals look to Martin Luther King Jr. as an example to follow. Yet Elizete does not favor a wholesale importation of North American Protestantism.

I think that the MEP and the progressive movements have to move away from the foreign influences that are malevolent, those that are bad, be-cause, for me, a part of this conservatism of Brazilian Protestantism is a North American heritage, of North American fundamentalists. . . . So, in this sense, I think that one has to move away [form North American influences] in the sense of taking what is good, but the discriminatory practice, the conservative practices, I would even say racist [practices] of the American missionaries—one needs to leave this behind. What is good, we learn, what is not good, we leave there. So, in this sense . . . I am not xenophobic.

Thus, an Afro-Brazilian identity is possible in the context of Protestantism, and this is what the MEP is working toward: "Protestants don't need to look for other sources of identity; within Protestantism itself they could get their own sources and could make a re-reading of Brazilian reality." Yet such a rereading of Brazilian reality from the perspective of black progressive evangelicals is just beginning to emerge.

The Baptist Church of the Ministry of Liberation

While many of those who attended the MEP conference belong to the predom-inately middle-class Baptist Church of Graça, others are members of smaller, more grassroots congregations in poorer areas. The church that Creuza attends, for example—the Baptist Church of the Ministry of Liberation—is located in the poverty-stricken bairro of Mata Escura on the outskirts of Salvador. As Creuza points out with respect to the name of the church,

When they say "liberation," this is not liberation of the soul or the spirit, no! It is liberation from alienation, from oppression, from all these things. And it is a church that has a progressive view. . . . This liberation is not spiritual, no! It is the liberation of you liberating your brother who isn't aware, and because he is not aware he doesn't know how to vote; because he isn't aware he does not know the importance of studying and he does not fight for better conditions. So, it is this liberation that we're talking about, you see? Liberation from oppression of gender, race, citizens, understand?

The building in which the church is located is very small and somewhat dilapidated and would be very easy for a first-time visitor to miss since, aside from a modest sign, it is not well marked. The bairro, which many consider a favela, is clearly urban but has the unfinished, run-down feel of the poor towns in the interior of Bahia. When I visited the church for the first time, I immediately noticed the lack of space; there was barely room for fifty people to sit down. José, the pastor, was born in the *sertão* (arid backlands) region in the interior of Bahia, where most people are of indigenous and Portuguese descent; in fact, José appears more *índio* (native Brazilian) than black. Two of the first objects I noticed in the church, however, were a tambourine and an African-style drum that are sometimes played during services. This is something that until then I had thought was unheard of in evangelical worship.

On my first visit to the church I asked José to contrast the perspective of his church with that of more conservative Pentecostal churches.

The visions of those churches, there are many. . . . [The conservative Pentecostal churches] only see the spiritual side. We believe that man is spiritual and that it is important that he learn about spiritual life, but, beyond this, we are material . . . and we need to take part in the political and social reality. So, we don't go around preaching that when we die we have to go to heaven; we have to act here and now. To transform the system, this is a biblical view, because Jesus had this view. Our view of Jesus also differentiates us a little from our brothers. Conservative theology has, as its principle, accept Jesus, accept Jesus: enter into a religious group and this group closes itself to the rest of the world. Our religion is not that way. There they continually pray, calling to God, conforming to death while still alive: "He who dies will be in heaven." We do not believe in this way; we also believe that there is a spiritual life that needs to be developed, but meanwhile we have to act and transform. Jesus did this by transforming society with his Word, liberating men from oppression from suffering, from discrimination, racism, from oppression, and when there is oppression there is injustice, and we hope that God liberates us.

In contrast to that of the majority of evangelical church members, José's perspective is based on a progressive reading of the Bible, including the prophets of the Old Testament: "If you look, they [Isaiah and Jeremiah] revolted against an unjust system! They were rising up against . . . their prophecy was against injustice and needs to be interpreted with respect to blacks. Liberty, independence; the Jewish people at that time were oppressed by external things and oppressed by their own people."

The week after my first interview with José, I returned to the church to attend Sunday services. The service began with hymn singing—all common evangelical songs sung in the typical evangelical style—that is, enthusiastically, accompanied by hand clapping and other gestures. About fifteen adults, most of them dark-skinned, attended, and the congregation was split evenly between men and women. After the hymns, José read from the gospel. His selection was a narrative from the fifth chapter of the Gospel of John, which tells of Jesus healing a sick man. In the sermon that followed José explained that the man whose story was told in the gospel was a beggar without the use of his legs who was trying to make his way to a healing pool. He was left behind in the dust, however, by all sorts of people who were able to walk. The people who passed him by—powerful men, politicians, and the like—thought of the beggar as trash to be thrown away (José dramatized this by crumpling up a piece of paper).

Jesus, however, saw the beggar's worth as a human being. José maintained that what was wrong with the man was really in his mind. Even if the beggar had a physical birth defect, José argued, his problem was that he believed people when they said that he was worthless and that his defect was a reflection of sin. José suggested that the problem with his legs was psychosomatic, and it was not until Jesus looked into his eyes and said, "Your faith has healed you, get up" that he could walk.

This was a sermon quite different from any that I had heard in other evangelical churches, as the pastor's discussion of the beggar's place in society was replete with references to social inequalities. Furthermore, José demystified the curing of the man's illness, which is a sharp turn away from the emphasis on spiritual healing not only in evangelical churches but also in popular Brazilian religion in general. As another example, José cited the story of a man who had been exorcized of a demon in a Pentecostal church—but he maintained that the name of the demon was 51 (a popular brand of sugarcane rum).

The Baptist Church of the Ministry of Liberation is rare even among Salvador's progressive evangelical churches in its explicit incorporation of the discourse of liberation theology and in the use of African-style drums during its services. Yet while the progressive current represented by this church is relatively marginal, progressive evangelical institutions exist above the church level. In addition to the Bahian branch of the MEP and its affiliated churches, Salvador is home to a progressive evangelical seminary, O Instituto de Educação Teólogico da Bahia (the Institute of Theological Education of Bahia; ITEBA).

O Instituto de Educação Teólogico da Bahia

ITEBA is an evangelical postgraduate institution that trains progressive evangelical leaders. Its teachings are based in liberation theology and focus on issues of race, gender, poverty, and social justice in particular. Marlene, the current director of ITEBA, who was a Baptist missionary for twenty years, explained the school's vision.

> Here our perspective, and those churches connected with ITEBA, [from] which our students come to study, is a perspective of liberation theology. To liberate the human being as a whole, not just, as in the perspective of the Pentecostal churches where the human being is alienated from the world where he lives, you see, where people are suffering, suffering from racism and all types of violence, racial as well as . . . gender violence.

In Brazil, liberation theology is most often associated with the Catholic Church, and in fact many people are surprised to hear that evangelicals are involved with it. Yet, like many North American blacks, Marlene contends that liberation theology began in black Protestant churches.

> Liberation theology in Latin America began in the evangelical churches. It started with Ruben Alves and other theologians of liberation. After, the Catholic Church joined in. It is not a Catholic thing. Many of the Catholic theologians became famous, that's how this idea started that it was a Catholic thing. We can see that historically, this started with men and women from evangelical churches, from Presbyterian and Methodist churches.

Marlene explains that ITEBA does not simply emphasize liberation theology in its generic form, which focuses mainly on class relations.

> Here, we don't just deal with liberation theology. We also teach theologies that are relevant to gender and race—liberation theology only addressed class. So, we are looking for a theology for our daily lives as black women, not something imported.

Furthermore, she explains,

> My own private vision of God is that of black feminist theology; here at ITEBA we also work with this line of theology. This is where blacks want to be visible in theology, not a theology that comes from abroad, a European theology, or white American [theology]. We are fighting as Latin Americans and Bahians, including against racism in our own churches.

ITEBA's approach is ecumenical as well. Classes are even offered on the theology of African and African-derived religions, which are taught by an anthropologist.

Evangelical Christians and the Black Movement

Clearly, the figure of the reactionary and intolerant evangelical is a stereotype that fails to account for diversity within evangelical communities. In fact, a distinctively black evangelical identity and approach to anti-racism is emerging in Brazil.[2] Moreover, many believe that the black movement is broad and inclusive enough to encompass Christian groups such as the Catholic Pastoral Afro as well as progressive evangelicals.

Most would agree with the assertion that evangelicals are not uniformly conservative or indifferent to racism and other issues affecting people of African descent. It would be more contentious to argue that black evangelicals are no less racially conscious than their counterparts in Catholic and Candomblé communities, but in my analysis of the questionnaires I administered to Bahians concerning racial issues, I found no significant differences between evangelical respondents in general—even excluding members of the MEP—and others in their answers to questions about racism as a social problem (Selka 2003). Significant differences did exist, however, in the ways people answered questions about their attitudes toward and participation in Afro-Brazilian culture.

Not surprisingly, for example, evangelicals reported that they avoided Afro-Brazilian practices such as Candomblé. Thus, in my research on anti-racism in Bahia, I found that the most significant differences between evangelicals and candomblecistas were less a matter of awareness of racism than of attitudes toward Candomblé and other traditional Afro-Brazilian practices. This unexpected finding suggests that evangelicals are indeed among the "lost constituency" of the black movement (Burdick 1998a, 1998b). In fact, many believe that the movement should be inclusive enough to encompass progressive Christian and African-derived religious groups alike.

Yet this is a complicated issue. As progressive evangelicals' constant efforts to distinguish themselves politically from Pentecostals suggest, most evangelicals in Brazil are conservative. In reality, institutions concerned with progressive activism and alternative black identities are still nascent in Brazilian evangelical communities. Thus, so far the movement has had a limited impact on the evangelical community and on Brazilian society as a whole. A look at voting patterns confirms that progressively oriented evangelicals form a relatively marginal group. Studies of political party affiliation, for example, indicate that evangelical Christians account for approximately 29 percent of the membership of the conservative Partido da Frente Liberal (Liberal Front Party; PFL) and around 10 percent of the membership of the progressive PT (Soong 2004). Again, evangelicals make up 15 percent of the population, so we find that nearly twice as many members of the PFL and one-third fewer members of the PT are evangelical than we would expect if evangelicals were represented in these parties in the same proportion as they are in the population in general. Yet, although this reveals a considerable tendency toward conservatism, it also indicates that nearly three million evangelicals—a substantial number—vote for PT candidates, not to mention those who support the number of other progressive parties in Brazil.

At least in terms of electoral politics, then, the progressive evangelical vote is by no means negligible. Accordingly, recent studies have taken note of progressive evangelical initiatives and questioned the monolithic image of the conservative evangelical (Burdick 1998a, 1998b, 1999; Freston 1994; Garrard-Burnett and Stoll 1993; Myatt 1995). Yet the fact that the fastest-growing evangelical denominations in Brazil today (such as the Universal Church of the Kingdom of God and other neo-Pentecostal churches) are staunchly conservative and openly hostile toward Candomblé has not helped the MEP's efforts to recast evangelical politics and carve out a space for evangelicals in the mainstream anti-racist movement. Setting aside the question of whether it is fair or accurate for Afro-Brazilian activists to view all evangelicals as adversaries or to dismiss them as lost causes at best, it is clear that such attitudes effectively limit evangelicals' participation in the black movement (cf. Burdick 1998a).

Furthermore, the marginal position that progressive evangelicals occupy in the arena of Afro-Brazilian identity politics reflects ambivalent attitudes toward Christianity in the transnational cultural economy of the African diaspora. While progressive evangelicals are highly critical of white North American missionaries in Brazil, for example, references to black Protestantism in the United States are a prominent feature of progressive evangelical discourse. North American black Protestants who visit Bahia, however, are generally more interested in African-derived culture than in dialogue with the local Brazilian Protestant community. Notions of recovering or reclaiming one's identity through African-derived cultural traditions are central not only to the discourse of the black movement but to the promotional language of transnational cultural tourism as well. This powerful discourse forms the backdrop against which black evangelicals construct their identities.

In addition to these issues of ethnic identity, the project of constructing alternative black identities in evangelical communities is complicated by other factors. As I have already pointed out, a major obstacle for progressive evangelicals concerned with social justice is that many outside of the MEP equate evangelical Christianity with conservatism. Although progressive evangelical discourse draws connections between the Protestant tradition and emancipatory causes such as feminism and the abolition movement, many Bahians and American cultural tourists alike connect these very things not with evangelical Christianity but with Candomblé.

An advantage of this progressive evangelical approach to mobilization, however, is that it moves away from a narrow focus on particular ethnoreligious identities toward a more culturally inclusive perspective. The approach I have discussed here shares the political focus of anti-racist organizations like the MNU while departing from the emphasis on particular cultural affirmations that characterizes most African-derived and Catholic religious groups associated with the black movement. As a basis for mobilization, of course, evangelical Christianity lacks Candomblé's naturalized connection with blackness; yet the evangelical movement has grown very rapidly at the grassroots level among people of African descent. This problem brings us back to basic questions about the connections among religion, ethnic identity formation, and social mobilization. Accordingly, in the final chapter I turn to a focused discussion of the complex and contested ways that religion is enmeshed with the politics of Afro-Brazilian identity.

6

The Politics of Afro-Brazilian Identity

Throughout this book I have highlighted the complex relationship between religion and Afro-Brazilian identity. I have shown that although Candomblé is often invoked as an emblem of Afro-Brazilian identity, the connection between Candomblé and blackness is far from simple or straightforward. Moreover, I have emphasized that Christian responses to questions of black identity are varied and often conflicting. While many Catholic and evangelical Christians stress their identities as Christians more than any particular ethnic identity, the Pastoral Afro in the Catholic Church and similar initiatives in evangelical communities attempt to embrace black ways of being Christian. In fact, many Afro-Brazilians are active in both Candomblé and Christian communities, and the relationship between Candomblé and Christianity is characterized by many parallel and overlapping representations and practices.

I have also brought attention to the uneven politicization of Afro-Brazilian religion, culture, and identity, an issue that I explore in more depth in this chapter. Those who are outside of the fold of the black movement in Bahia, for example, generally do not frame the practice of Candomblé in terms of the construction of a politically engaged identity. Nevertheless, as I explored in the chapters on Cachoeira in particular, even when the practice of Candomblé is not explicitly politicized it is often indexed to questions of social marginality and respectability. Often, the everyday practice of Afro-Brazilian religion seems to enact an implicit and embodied resistance to white domination. It is this idea of resistance—along with a certain aura of authenticity—that the urban black movement draws upon and places in the foreground of its representations of Candomblé.

Granting that Afro-Brazilian identity and racial politics are characterized by multiplicity and complexity, what are some of the recurring themes that make some generalizations possible? At the absolute least, in what ways can we see that the various identities and approaches that I have examined here respond to a common (historical, political, religious) backdrop? As I will explore in this chapter, any attempt at defining an Afro-Brazilian identity must engage the discourse of mestiçagem, which tends to undermine the foundations for strong black identities and confrontational approaches to racial politics. As a result, Afro-Brazilian religious and cultural practices are never fully racialized. That is, since the idea of race itself is in question in Brazil, the notion that one practice or another could belong to a particular racial group is suspect in a society that largely defines itself in terms of mixture. If the use of Candomblé as an ethnic emblem is a contested issue, then the idea of a black Christianity is even more controversial, as one might expect. Moreover, these questions of identity are enmeshed with questions of political mobilization. In other words, all of the approaches to combating racism that I have discussed here must grapple with the fact that in Brazil, the idea that people of African descent share a common identity, let alone a common sociopolitical agenda, is often represented as a foreign concept.

In this final chapter I attempt to address these issues by integrating three major themes that run throughout this book, beginning with the relationship between religion and identity. First, I review my findings and arguments about Candomblé, Christianity, and Afro-Brazilian identity in particular and offer some suggestions about the relationship between religion and identity formation in general. Next, drawing on theoretical approaches to understanding the connections between collective identities and power relations, I address my findings concerning the relationship between Afro-Brazilian ethnoreligious identity and everyday politics of race in Bahia. Finally, I turn to macropolitical questions concerning the politics of identity and the black movement in Brazil. I engage recent perspectives on identity-based social movements that shed light on ongoing debates about Afro-Brazilian sociopolitical mobilization.

Religion and Identity

In this book I have emphasized that the connections between Candomblé and Afro-Brazilian identity are more tenuous and the links between Christianity and Afro-Brazilian identity closer than one would expect from reviewing the literature on these issues. Most of the candomblecistas with whom I spoke in Bahia discussed their practice primarily in terms of spiritual and practical, as opposed to ethnic or political, motivations. Nevertheless, as I have explored in previous chapters and as I will examine in more depth in the following pages, religious practice occupies the sizeable middle ground between the political and the non-political for many Afro-Brazilians.

Christian engagements with questions of Afro-Brazilian identity and anti-racism are as complex and interesting as those of candomblecistas. In the past few decades, the theology of inculturation has opened the door to a wide array of ethnic affirmations in the Catholic Church. As I have examined here, many evangelicals, who have often been stereotyped as hostile toward local cultural identities, have followed suit. Some of my colleagues, however, insist that evangelical anti-racists must have picked up the discourse of the black movement outside of the predominantly conservative evangelical community. They are probably right in most cases. Yet a consistent focus of concern in the anthropology of religion has been the ways in which actors rework religious discourses and practices for their own purposes—including, most classically, in the context of syncretic re-interpretation—and the case of progressive anti-racist evangelicals in Bahia provides an excellent illustration of this process.

As I have shown, questions of Afro-Brazilian identity, especially in Bahia, where Candomblé is frequently equated with blackness, are often indexed to religion. To some extent, as I address in this chapter, this may be partly due to the fact that Afro-Brazilian identity is viewed as something cultural rather than racial. Nevertheless, we can also see that religion has been central to social and identity movements in many contexts, including most obviously the civil rights movement in the United States. Religious practice forms a primary means of maintaining identity in many diasporas (Kokot, Tölölyan et al. 2004), which raises the question: what is distinctive about this relationship between religion and collective identity?

Religious Practice and Technologies of the Self

As we see among Irish Catholics, Hindu Tamils, and Tibetan Buddhists, religion and ethnic identity are often intimately linked. Yet this particularizing tendency works alongside a drive toward global, universal identities that seem to erode particular ethnic identities, as many argue evangelical Christianity does. In all of these cases, however, we can see that religion directly engages questions of identity.

The relationship between any particular religion and ethnic identity is discursively constructed; there is no inherent relationship between Candomblé and Afro-Brazilian identity, for example. Yet religious practice in general lends itself to the formation of deeply felt identities. Although anthropologists have often discussed religion in terms of meaning and belief, practice is at least as important, if not more fundamental, to religious experience (cf. Durkheim 1995; Asad 1993; Bell 1992, 1997). Emile Durkheim famously argued that the main purpose of religion is to bring members of a society together to foster social solidarity; in this view, the beliefs that justify such practices are secondary elaborations. Talad Asad (1993) contends that the emphasis on religious belief among Western scholars is an artifact of Protestant Christianity, which elevates discourse above practical and embodied understandings performed through ritual. Following thinkers like Durkheim and Asad, I argue that what makes religion important for identity formation is not so much the explicit beliefs that it includes but its use of practices that are oriented toward the construction or transformation of the self.

Asad (1993), for example, examines the construction of selves through rituals and disciplinary procedures in religious communities. In Asad's view, rituals are better approached not as figurative or symbolic phenomena to be decoded but as embodied practices that organize activities aimed at the development of a particular kind of self. In this way, Asad attempts "to go beyond deciphering symbolic meanings" (1993, 106) to focus on religion and ritual practices as a continuous process of social subjection that takes place in the context of structured communities.

Drawing upon Michel Foucault's (1999, 1995) ideas about governmentality, Asad focuses two interdependent types of power processes at work in religious communities: repressive processes by which one is disciplined from without (transitive techniques of power) and those processes in which a self aims to create the will to obey (intransitive technologies of the self). He points out that transitive disciplinary practices (procedures of observation, punishment, and evaluation) commonly work in tandem with intransitive technologies of the self that mobilize subjects' hearts and minds in the process of creating disciplined selves. This often entails the development of certain types of self-awareness in conjunction with procedures for modifying one's thinking and behavior.

In Candomblé communities, for example, adepts are subject to a long and arduous period of initiation in which they are separated from the everyday world.

> In the course of initiation, the old personality is broken, annihilated, in order to be substituted by another. The new self knows nothing of the world in which he/she must live from then on, so it is necessary to relearn everything. . . . [Thus, the new personality must] reintegrate into ordinary society and retake his/her place in a carnal family [as opposed to the spiritual family of Candomblé]. (Bastide 1958, 56; translation mine)

Initiation practices explicitly aim at a transformation that is referred to as a kind of rebirth into a community. Similar language is used to describe those who accept Jesus in the evangelical Christian context. In addition, during Candomblé festas initiates literally incorporate the deities to whom they are devoted, and Pentecostals who manifest the gifts of the Holy Spirit are understood as the conduits of something other than their everyday selves. These rituals and practices of embodiment take place in the context of structures of authority and according to certain standards of "apt performance" (Asad 1993). Those who begin new lives and acquire new identities through religion do so not simply though symbolic entry into the imagined community of Christians, but by submitting themselves to disciplinary practices and the scrutiny of others.

The combination of transitive and intransitive techniques of power, which forms a type of "governmentality" that Foucault refers to as "pastorship," was a process central to all the religious groups I studied. In Foucault's usage, pastorship designates "power techniques oriented towards individuals and intended to rule them in a continuous and permanent way," which he refers to as an "individualizing power" in contrast to the centralizing power of the state (1999, 136).

The notion of pastorship draws on the metaphor of the pastor as a shepherd whose duty it is to wield power over his flock by gathering, guiding, and watching over them in order to ensure their salvation. The shepherd must know each individual sheep, and Foucault argues that it is through this individualizing knowledge that pastoral power is manifested (1999). In Candomblé terreiros and smaller evangelical churches, religious leaders are usually familiar with the personal details of followers' lives. In Catholic churches, such details are often revealed through the practice of confession. Pastoral power refers to the ways that such personal knowledge of the religious adept—knowledge of pivotal crises, distinctive characteristics, and the texture of a person's life—is mobilized in the construction and maintenance of a religious identity.

Although one can easily imagine contexts in which there is continuous firsthand contact between those in authority and those they administer (e.g., prisons, classrooms, boot camp), what is distinctive about pastoral power is that it seeks to know the individual in order to use the knowledge acquired to further his or her subjection (to power) and subjectification (construction as a subject). In addition, at least ideally, this process of pastoral subjection is not only continuous but lifelong—that is, it persists not simply for a specific period of time or only until a limited purpose is fulfilled. Thus, while conversion and initiation ceremonies are often dramatic, they mark only the first stage in the formation of the religious self.

In other words, one's identity as a Christian or as a candomblecista is not finalized by rites of passage; it must be sustained and developed through ongoing procedures of subjection. Processes that are basic to the everyday work of religious subjection include learning to make appropriate bodily gestures and facial expressions during religious ceremonies, acquiring the proper prosody and quality of voice for speaking and singing in the church or terreiro, and internalizing the structures of feeling shared by members of one's religious community. As Thomas Csordas (1994) points out, another important means by which subjects come to embody a religious habitus is participation in healing practices, which are central to the religious field in Bahia.

Such processes and procedures are guided by others in the community who, largely through the apt performance of religious practices, are already well sutured to their identities. In this way, members of a religious community maintain a level of surveillance over each other that aids in the production of apt performances and guards against lapses of discipline. Moreover, as Judith Butler (1990) suggests in her discussions of performativity, the repetition of rituals and other acts, including the kinds of bodily practices enacted in religious contexts, lends normative status to the identities that are thereby constructed. These identities come to appear as issuing from an interior essence even though they originate in public practice and social discourse.

A more generalized but equally powerful form of surveillance is the relentless observation, not only of outward behavior but of internal states, by an omniscient presence—such as one's conscience, an imagined other, or the divine gaze. As I examined above, for example, many evangelicals felt that it was pointless to sin or violate church doctrine in secret because God is constantly watching. The theme of an all-knowing divine being who vigilantly keeps account of one's thoughts and deeds recurs constantly in scripture, sermons, and everyday discourse. Thus, the inability of humans to escape the divine gaze, even in our private thoughts, is a key element of Christian discipline.

In a similar way, candomblecistas, most of whom consider themselves to be Christian, often refer to an omniscient entity who watches over human beings. Moreover, in the cosmology of Candomblé, the world is populated by a host of gods and spirits who are not simply recording our thoughts and deeds for a future day of judgment. Santos and ancestral spirits, for example, are seen as disembodied others who mete out rewards and punishments in the here and now.

Accordingly, in Candomblé and in popular Bahian religion in general, success and misfortune in this world are frequently attributed to supernatural agents. Thus, believers' desires and frustrations are often mobilized in the service of their religious subjection. Conversion and initiation, for example, are commonly associated with personal gain or relief from suffering. Consequently, dramatic conversion and initiation stories are often central to people's narratives of their religious identities.

Yet as I have examined in this section, routine procedures of subjection and constant surveillance are as instrumental as conversion and initiation rituals in shaping religious selves. Again, it is also important to emphasize the active role that agents play in this process of subjection. As subjects' attachments to their religious identities deepen, for example, they learn to narrate themselves in a way that marshals the material of their life histories in the service of the ongoing construction of an identity as a Christian or candomblecista.

Paradoxical as it may sound, many people find processes of subjection to be empowering. That is, using religious symbols and practices, social actors are often able to reposition themselves with respect to their lives and the social world. Thus, religion should be recognized as a powerful means of identity construction and self-discipline, and not simply as a source of social control or as a means by which the social order is inscribed onto subjects (Csordas 1994; Asad 1993; Comaroff 1985). The question remains, however: what kinds of identities do people form and enact in particular religious settings? I have generalized about how religious practice relates to the construction and maintenance of self-identity, but as I will discuss below, the extent to and ways in which such religious identities are enmeshed with ethnoracial identities varies widely.

Religion, Ethnicity, and Race

The construction of one's identity is not just a personal matter; it is most often a collective undertaking. Especially for members of marginalized groups, questions of identity are closely intertwined with questions of power. In fact, as I have shown in the preceding pages, the very act of calling oneself black in Brazil can be construed as a political statement. Accordingly, affirming a black identity in Brazil is not simply a demand for rights and equality; it is a demand to be recognized and accepted as black and to organize politically on that basis. As I explore in this section, such demands circulate in what can be called political economies of representation, in which individual and collective actors struggle over what it means to be a candomblecista, a Christian, or an Afro-Brazilian.

Ethnic Politics

Discussions of the origins of ethnicity and ethnic politics have tended to center on the debate between essentialist (primordialist) and constructivist (instrumentalist) perspectives (Comaroff 1996; Pieterse 1996). Although primordialist discourses remain powerful in everyday life and in the language of nationalism, most anthropologists agree that the notion that ethnic or cultural characteristics are inherent to a group of people is without merit. Thus, ethnicity is widely viewed as consisting of ongoing processes of construction, and the identification and investigation of these processes has become a major anthropological preoccupation.

Ethnicity has become increasingly salient in today's world as people's allegiances have shifted from nationalism to identities associated with units smaller or larger than the nation, including ethnic, religious, and special interest groups. Broadly speaking, this shift has taken place as a result of the retreat of the nation-state due to globalization, the decline of Cold War grand ideologies, and widespread democratization (Pieterse 1996). It is clear from a quick perusal of the daily news that ethnic loyalties have replaced nationalism and secular ideologies as a main source of identity in many places in the world. Moreover, such identities have proliferated despite, and often as, an explicit challenge to supposed trends toward global cultural homogenization (cf. Castells 1997).

Again, like all identities, ethnicity is defined relationally, through oppositions. Furthermore, ethnic oppositions often originate in struggles over unequal access to power and resources (Wilmsen and McAllister 1996). In addition, ethnic identities often originate outside the groups to which they are attributed, as ethnic labels are often imposed onto subordinate groups by dominant ones. Edwin Wilmsen writes,

> Thus, ethnic politics is the politics of marginality. Indeed, ethnicity appears to come into being most frequently in just such instances when individuals are persuaded of a need to confirm a collective sense of identity in the face of threatening economic, political, or other social forces. But ethnic politics are by their very definition attributes of marginality and relative weakness. . . . Ethnicity, then, is a relational concept, one in which the dominant are able to define the subordinant. (Wilmsen and McAllister 1996, 4–5; cf. Pieterse 1996, 33)

Yet the situation in Brazil is more complicated than this description. For one thing, Brazilians have generally avoided attributing membership in the same ethnic or racial group to all people of African descent. While blacks and morenos share an equally marginal economic, political, and social position in Brazilian society, they are often represented as distinct kinds of people with different life chances. In effect, this approach maintains white supremacy while inhibiting solidarity among nonwhites at the same time.

As I have pointed out above, the fact that the majority of people of African descent in the country do not identify as black is a basic problem for mobilization along racial lines in Brazil. Although bipolar distinctions between white and black or nonwhite are commonly employed by researchers and activists, other systems with many more mediating terms are used in official and popular practice. Thus, racial classification is an issue of central importance in the black movement.

In an effort to encourage the Brazilian public to adopt a dichotomous racial classification system, for example, in 1991 activists launched a campaign urging people of African descent to identify themselves as *negro* (the preferred term for people of African descent for those in the black movement) on the national census (Nobles 1995). Although such efforts have had little impact on the ways that people identify themselves on the census, racial discrimination and affirmative action have moved into the sphere of public debate since the early 1990s.[1]

The practice of researchers and activists in Brazil lumping people of African descent into one category while supposedly ignoring the terms they use to refer to themselves, however, has been a source of criticism, including charges of Yankee imperialism and racism from Brazilians and Europeans as well (Guimarães 2001). In their 1999 article, for example, Bourdieu and Wacquant claim that the black/white dichotomy is irrelevant in Brazil. Taking Hanchard's (1994) work on the black movement in Rio as a case in point, they argue that the position that Brazilian social reality is "black and white" stems from an American intellectual imperialism that aims to impose its own racial conflicts onto other cultures. In response, however, French (2000) defended Hanchard's analysis and the distinction between white and nonwhite by referring to decades of research on racism and racial inequalities in Brazil by Americans and Brazilians alike. As I discuss below, however, the divergence between popular versus activist and academic discourses about racial identity complicates mobilization efforts in the black movement.

While the topic of racial identity is particularly contentious in Brazil, discourses about Brazil's African heritage have long been central to representations of Brazilian national identity. Most recently, this heritage has been recognized as a major draw for tourists. Thus, at least since the 1930s, negative representations of blackness have coexisted with romanticized appropriations. This further complicates the picture vis-à-vis Wilmsen's description of ethnic politics. Today, Afro-Brazilian identity is affirmed and celebrated in the context of black cultural and activist organizations, but also through state initiatives and the tourism industry. Afro-Brazilian ethnic politics remains one of marginality, but in a sense it is no longer a politics of marginalization. That is, Afro-Brazilian identity politics largely concerns the appropriation of marginality in an unbalanced economy of representation. As John Comaroff points out, "the conditions that give rise to a social identity are not necessarily the same as those that sustain it" (1996, 166). If Afro-Brazilian identity emerged in response to the marginalization of people of African descent, then today it is sustained largely because many expressions of it—including Candomblé most prominently—have been integrated into popular representations of Bahian identity.

The Racialization of Religion

So how do the connections I have described between religion, identity, and politics play out in practice? In Bahia, ethnoracial struggles are often intertwined with struggles between religious groups. Historically, the status hierarchies that are reflected in the realm of ethnic and racial relations have been replicated in the differential amounts of material and symbolic capital that accrue to different religions in Brazil. Throughout this book I have explored the various and often conflicting ways that Candomblé, Catholicism, and evangelical Christianity are represented from different positions in the religious arena. In religiously pluralistic societies such as Brazil, the various religious groups and institutions that constitute the religious arena often have unbalanced relationships with one another in terms of power and prestige. Catholic Christianity was the official religion in Brazil for most of its history, for example, and the relationship between Candomblé and Catholicism in Brazil is intimately intertwined with conquest and racism.

Yet these relationships that shape the religious arena are complex and shifting. The Catholic Church in Brazil has passed through alternating periods of relative tolerance and severe repression of African-derived religion. In fact, if one examined any period in the history of the church in Brazil one would most likely find it internally divided in its attitudes toward Candomblé. My impression is that among Catholics in Bahia today there is a prevailing climate of relative tolerance (at a distance). That is not to deny that many Catholics remain strenuously opposed to Candomblé, but today it is evangelical Christianity, not the Catholic Church, that is most often cast as the archenemy of Candomblé.

In fact, Candomblé has become highly visible in Bahia over the past several decades. This development is certainly related to the increasing appropriation and commodification of Afro-Brazilian culture. For better or worse, Candomblé has been integrated into representations of Bahian identity to such an extent that one can no longer simply lament that Candomblé is a marginalized and denigrated religion (Johnson 2002). Candomblé is presented to tourists, for example, as central to the Bahian way of life. In fact, what makes the study of the politics of cultural (and religious) identity so fascinating is that it often encompasses simultaneous but contradictory processes of marginalization, affirmation, and appropriation.

From a long-run perspective, however, it would be incorrect to deny the unequal relationship between Candomblé and Catholicism and the relative marginality of Candomblé in the religious field. As Pierre Bourdieu contends, religious practitioners work from better or worse positions in a complex and shifting field of relations. Bourdieu's concept of "field" designates certain kinds of social spaces, conceived of as arenas of struggle over legitimation, that are constituted by shifting configurations of positions related to each other in terms of domination, subordination, homology, and so forth. These relations are based on types and amount of "capital" (in the case of the religious field, this capital is symbolic) that are currency in the field in question (Swartz 1997; Bourdieu and Wacquant 1992). Those in the dominant positions in such fields are able to control the distribution of capital and establish what gets counted as "orthodox," in contrast to what is illegitimate or "heterodox."

Even as we acknowledge that the inequalities that characterize relations between particular religious and ethnic groups in Bahia are historically contingent, we should recognize that they are relatively persistent. In Bahia's religious field, for example, Catholic, Candomblé, and evangelical groups engage each other in conflicts over legitimacy as they compete for members. These conflicts often take the form of struggles over classification in which each religion reduces the others into its own terms: In evangelical discourse Candomblé santos are demons and Catholics are idolaters; in Catholic discourse Candomblé is a cult and evangelicals are fanatical heretics; in Candomblé discourse Catholics are self-serving elites and evangelicals intolerant zealots. Furthermore, such struggles are equally salient within these religious groups as between them: Catholic conservatives oppose Afro-Catholic irmandades and the Pastoral Afro; progressive evangelicals oppose conservative Pentecostals; anti-syncretists in the Candomblé oppose those who seek to preserve and deepen the connection between Candomblé and Catholicism.

Again, these oppositional discourses often pivot on claims about orthodoxy versus heterodoxy, purity versus mixture, and superiority versus inferiority. As I have explored in this book, these discourses are deployed in varying ways from different positions in Bahia's religious field, however, so that the results of particular struggles over legitimacy and prestige are hardly predetermined. Anti-syncretic Candomblé leaders have challenged Catholic hegemony, for example, and as Paul Johnson (2002) argues, over the course of the twentieth century Candomblé has moved from "tumor to trophy." As I discuss in more depth below, however, to the extent that these uses of Candomblé are the result of appropriation, they end up reproducing unequal relations of power between groups.

Moreover, many Bahians continue to view conservative Catholicism as the religion of the white elite and Candomblé as the religion of the black *marginal* (someone who is outside of respectable society). Even when Candomblé is affirmed as an emblem of Bahian identity, this is often seen as an act of appropriation that implies asymmetrical relations of power. In a general way, then, certain hierarchies that structure the religious and ethnic fields persist in the midst of struggle. In addition, discourses about religion often overlap with discourses about ethnicity and race. As a result, religious and ethnic metaphors used in discourses about racial politics are often homologous. Just as religious syncretism is a central trope in the ideology of racial democracy, the argument that Brazil is largely a mixed-race nation is often deployed to trump oppositional racial discourses.

Nevertheless, Candomblé remains a key ethnic emblem for many Afro-Brazilians. Bourdieu, following Max Weber, argues that religion serves to consecrate, legitimize, and naturalize a way of life and characteristics of a group or class (1991, 14). From this perspective, Candomblé grounds Afro-Brazilian identity in a sort of embodied ideology (as many would argue Catholicism has done for the privileges of white elites). The close connection that many Bahians of African descent feel between religion and race is expressed in perhaps its clearest form in the equation of religious intolerance against Candomblé with racism.

Yet religion does not always have a direct, affirmative connection with an ethnic or racial group. Although Candomblé is often represented as a "black religion," about half of candomblecistas are white (Prandi 1995). Furthermore, unlike in the United States, self-consciously black Christian churches are uncommon in Brazil—although they are on the rise (Burdick 2005). Religion can just as well serve to gloss or equalize ethnic differences as to construct ethnic identities, and particular religious groups can engage the issue of ethnic identity in a variety of ways. In fact, as I discuss below, religion is often a force for differentiation rather than solidarity among people of African descent in Bahia.

What exists in Bahia and Brazil in general is a set of overlapping but often competing classificatory practices with respect to religion and race alike.

These alternative views reflect competing classificatory claims, and such assertions about the relationship between religions parallel and often articulate with claims about black identity (cf. Matory 2005). For example, the claim that Candomblé and Catholicism are categorically separate religions articulates with the position that oppositional black and white racial identities exist in Brazil. Both of these claims go against the grain of dominant, commonsense classificatory practice in Brazil.

Bourdieu argues that such struggles over classification are central to social conflicts.

> Principles of division, inextricably logical and sociological, function within and for the purposes of the struggle between social groups; in producing concepts, they produce groups, the very groups which produce the principles and the groups against which they are produced. What is at stake in the struggles about the meaning of the social world is power over the classificatory schemes and systems which are the basis of the representations of the groups and therefore of their mobilization and demobilization.(1984, 479)

Bourdieu does not simply argue that conflict is enacted through struggles over the valence of how things are classified, positively or negatively. He also contends that the struggles involve the effort to define the struggling groups themselves. The first case is seen most explicitly in the black movement's fight against dominant racial classifications and religious representations. While the ultimate goal of the movement may be to equalize the life chances of blacks and whites, a primary focus has been overcoming the representations that naturalize and justify inequality and injustice. Thus, consciousness raising largely aims at making people of African descent aware of the negative dispositions that they may have internalized toward their "own people" and their "ancestral religion." In the second case, however, the issue is the existence of the struggling group itself; without this, there is no mobilization.

Thus, the black movement focuses not only on positive images, but on resisting dominant schemes of classification that deny the opposition between black and white in the first place. That is, the black movement engages what Jean Comaroff calls "signifying practices," or forms of human action that, rather than simply reproducing the social order, have the potential to reshape it. Through signifying practice, subjects interact reciprocally with their external environments and in the process "construct themselves as social beings" (1985, 6). This perspective focuses on how social actors mobilize the resources available to them to exert control over the processes through which they are defined. In the context of the black movement in Brazil, such efforts often involve explicit criticism of racist representations and practices. In most other contexts in Bahia, however, such struggles are more tacit and ambiguous. This is where the concept of signifying practices is particularly useful.

According to Jean Comaroff, signifying practices (such as the Afro-Catholic festivals) "may serve both to consolidate existing hegemonies . . . and to give shape to resistance and reform" (1985, 5–6). This is because social actors can never completely overcome the "complex interdependence of domination and resistance, change and perpetuation" (1985, 252, 260). Accordingly, the simple distinction between accommodation and resistance is not always helpful for understanding colonial and post-colonial religious practice. As Andrew Apter writes,

> The Catholicism of Vodun, Candomblé, and Santería was not an ecumenical screen, hiding the worship of African deities from persecution. It was the religion of the masters, revised, transformed, and appropriated by slaves to harness its power within their universes of discourse. In this way the slaves took possession of Catholicism and thereby repossessed themselves as active spiritual subjects. (2005, 178)

Along these lines, Michel de Certeau (1984) has explored the ways in which people use, and in the process remake, what has often been assumed they consume or perform passively, such as media representations or religious practices. De Certeau acknowledges that social practice is constrained by power relations, yet he emphasizes how what he calls "everyday creativity" is enacted through the tactics of "antidiscipline." Although the spaces that ordinary people inhabit (school, work, even homes) are shaped or produced largely by forces beyond their control, actors transform such spaces as they consume them. De Certeau invokes the metaphor of a renter who remakes the room she occupies; while the building is owned by a powerful other, the renter manages to make it her own. Similarly, in his discussion of reading, de Certeau stresses that readers are not passive consumers: readers, like renters, "know how to insinuate their countless differences into the dominant text" (1984, xxii).

This aptly describes the politics of everyday religious practice in Bahia. In addition, much of what I have discussed in this book, however, represents a kind of politics grounded in more open forms of resistance in which differences are not simply insinuated but become the organizing principles of strategies and discursive practices that directly challenge the status quo. This kind of politics, namely the politics of identity enacted in social movements, takes place largely in the public sphere, often using confrontational means. Nevertheless, as I examine in more depth below, the politics of Afro-Brazilian identity often blurs the line between the "micropolitics" of everyday practice and "macropolitical" movements such as those I turn to now.

Identity and Social Mobilization

Clearly, issues of identity are as central to the Brazilian black movement as demands for inclusion and equality. In fact, issues of identity and social mobilization are the focus of both Hanchard's (1994) and Burdick's (1998a) groundbreaking studies of the black movement. As I discussed above and examine in more depth below, Hanchard argues that the movement's emphasis on "culturalism" has diverted energy and attention from political action. Burdick is less critical of the focus on culture per se than of the fact that the representations of black identity that the black movement deploys fail to resonate with significant numbers of Afro-Brazilians. Although I tend to agree with the specific critiques both authors raise, I suggest that recent perspectives on identity-based social movements yield a more encompassing view of the black movement than is offered by Hanchard's or Burdick's analyses. As I discuss in this section, pivotal aspects of identity-based approaches include the understanding that the concern with identity is not simply an expedient means for social mobilization, but stems from a fundamental need for recognition; the interests (political, economic) of a given group are not given, but constructed through discursive practice; and social movements are not unitary entities analogous to persons to which clear agendas and motivations can be ascribed, but complex and shifting networks of discourse and practice that we can often speak of as coherent only by privileging some actors in the movement over others.

Emancipatory and Life Politics

The study of identity has long been central to the social sciences, yet it is an especially important topic today. Anthony Giddens explains that in the late modern world, self-identity

> becomes a reflexively organized endeavor. The reflexive project of the self, which consists in the sustaining of coherent, yet continuously revised, biographical narratives, takes place in the context of multiple choice filtered through abstract systems. . . . Individuals are forced to negotiate lifestyle choices among a diversity of options. (1991, 5)

Today, Afro-Brazilian identity is less something unconsciously acquired by people living in ethnically and socially homogeneous communities (in fact, it is doubtful that such communities ever actually existed) than a lifestyle option that is increasingly mediated through popular culture and other competing and contested representations—including those originating in the religious nexus of practice. Moreover, with the advent of identity-based social movements such as the black movement, personal choices about one's identity become eminently political. In Bahia, individual choices about how to construct one's ethnic identity, which are enacted in spaces defined by power struggle, implicate actors in the wider context of ethnic and racial politics.

The construction of Afro-Brazilian identity in Bahia is intertwined with identity politics elsewhere in the African diaspora in complex ways. Besides the Afro-Brazilian cultural heritage, for example, many Bahians of African descent draw from increasingly globalized discourses and practices as they construct their ethnic identities, including black Protestantism from the United States, the negritude movement from Francophone Africa, Rastafarianism from the Caribbean, and musical styles ranging from reggae to hip-hop (Yúdice 2003; Sansone 2003; Hanchard 1999; Reichmann 1999a, 1999b; K. Butler 1998b; Carvalho 1993). At the same time, many visitors from Brazil and abroad come to Bahia to experience what is often praised as one of the most authentically African black cultures in the New World, and this cultural tourism tends to focus on local Afro-Brazilian practices such as Candomblé.

Giddens' work has been very influential on thinking about processes of identity formation in the late modern world. Giddens' writing about post-traditional self-identity distinguishes between two types of reflexive, public politics of the self: emancipatory politics and life politics. The first term refers to "a generic outlook concerned above all with liberating individuals and groups from constraints that adversely affect their life chances" (1991, 210). Following the enlightenment ideal, it focuses on ending exploitation, inequality, and oppression. Such emancipatory struggles are often expressed through direct action or electoral politics in the political field.

While emancipatory politics concerns life chances, Giddens defines life politics as "a politics of lifestyle" (1991, 214). He explains that

life politics concerns political issues which flow from processes of self-actualization in post-traditional contexts, where globalising influences intrude deeply into the reflexive project of the self, and conversely where processes of self-realization influence global strategies. (1991, 214)

In the context of life politics, the personal is political. As I discussed above, from this perspective the religious groups to which one chooses to belong and the term that one uses to describe one's racial identity are manifestly political decisions. Thus, life politics is often enacted in fields of cultural production, and it mobilizes primarily on the basis of identity (religious, ethnic, sexual) rather than in terms of political ideology.

Considered broadly, Brazil's black movement encompasses both of these types of politics. Yet it is clear that different Afro-Brazilian groups place varying emphasis on emancipation and lifestyle. The MNU, for example, is primarily concerned with political strategies for overcoming exploitation, inequality, and oppression, while the blocos afros are based in the celebration of the Afro-Brazilian cultural heritage.

Giddens' distinction between emancipatory and life politics reflects many of the differences that others have cited to contrast modern and postmodern approaches to politics. Takis Fotopoulos, for example, describes postmodern politics as turning away from "general social, political, and economic issues toward concerns with culture and identity" (2002, 78). Furthermore, Fotopoulos points out that while many emancipatory social movements have emphasized a universalist and anti-systemic approach to human liberation, postmodern identity politics generally appears anti-universalist and reform oriented.

The historical shift from one to the other can be seen in the MNU's backing away from hard-line Marxism toward a more mainstream approach that includes at least indirect involvement in electoral politics. I have shown that in Salvador an informal yet discernible connection exists between the MNU and the PT, a party that was considered quite radical in the 1980s but has since moved closer to the political center. During the same time period, the Catholic black movement's emphasis on radical liberation theology was gradually displaced by an approach based on inculturated Masses, vestibular preparation courses, and building self-esteem.

Many are critical of this shift and see it as undermining any substantial challenges to hegemonic systems of domination. Fotopoulos maintains that

> today's "identity" movements, despite the radical critique they raise against specific hierarchical structures (like those based on gender, race, sexual repression and repression of minorities), never advanced any comprehensive political project for systemic change—their fragmented nature does not allow such a program anyway—but instead promoted cultural and personal identity issues. (2002, 79)

Furthermore, Fotopoulos argues that the focus on lifestyle and spirituality has shifted away from politics, rational analysis, and instrumental action.

Similarly, many activists and academics have noted that the black movement's emphasis on African origins and traditions as the basis for black solidarity is problematic (Sansone 2003; Barcelos 1999; Reichmann 1999b; K. Butler 1998a; Hanchard 1994). As I noted above, Rebecca Reichmann (1999b) contends that the problem of cultural essentialism in the construction of the negro as a political identity has not yet been explicitly confronted. The attempt to rally support around a reified image of Afro-Brazilianness presents a number of difficulties, not the least of which is the general lack of participation in the black movement among evangelical Christians who tend to avoid the Afro-Brazilian cultural and religious milieu.

This poses a problem for mobilization, since evangelicals are the fastest-growing religious group in Brazil today (Burdick 1999, 1998a, 1998b; Freston 1994). As I have shown in this book, evangelical Christianity is by no means intrinsically opposed to anti-racist initiatives. Not only do many people of African descent find personal validation and empowerment in evangelical churches, but those involved with the progressive evangelical movement also are actively struggling against racism. Furthermore, evangelicals' responses to my questionnaire indicated that, not surprisingly, they were less likely than members of other religious groups to participate in traditional Afro-Brazilian culture and religion, to see these as a way to fight against racism, and to believe that in order to be truly black a person should be involved in African-derived traditions (Selka 2003). Yet evangelicals' responses to questions about racism as a personal and social problem were generally not significantly different from the responses of members of other religious groups. This corroborates the contention that the widest gulf between many evangelicals and the black movement is cultural rather than ideological.

The appropriation and folklorization of Afro-Brazilian traditions poses another problem for mobilization. Although the white intellectual elite has long shown a romanticizing or patronizing interest in Afro-Brazilian culture and religion, in more recent years Brazil as a nation appears to be placing greater emphasis on Afro-Brazilian traditions in popular culture and in its constructions of Brazilian national identity. In the religious arena, for example, Candomblé has been used strategically "by the government to obscure issues of race and promote the image of racial democracy by using the religion's fusion of Catholic and African elements as a social metaphor" (K. Butler 1998a, 40). Similarly, in the context of what García Canclini calls "tranquillizing hybridization" (1989), Candomblé has become a folk symbol of a racially democratic state (Matory 2005).

While African culture has been integrated into representations of Brazilianness at least since the 1930s, the process of appropriation escalated in the 1960s and 1970s, when the Brazilian government began to integrate Afro-Brazilian culture into an image of national culture that could be "marketed by Bahia's developing tourist industry" (Teles dos Santos 1998, 123; cf. Sansone 2003). Especially in Bahia, postcards, tourism posters, and Web sites often feature local women in traditional clothing selling typical Bahian food, local men doing capoeira, and colorful scenes from popular Afro-Catholic festivals.

In Pelourinho, the historic and tourist center of Salvador, one can have a picture taken with one of the many Bahian women strolling the town square in traditional costumes, take capoeira lessons from a local master, or even see a "folkloric" Candomblé ceremony (an explicit "performance" in which no one really becomes possessed). Not only have Afro-Brazilian religious symbols been widely appropriated, but cultural groups like Olodum have been co-opted as well (Bacelar 2001). Moreover, elite white politicians have increased their popular appeal by linking themselves to Afro-Brazilian culture (McCallum 1996, 220).

It is important to recognize the unequal relations of power that are revealed in these acts of appropriation. Many point out that white elites in business and government are the primary beneficiaries of Afro-Brazilian cultural production in Bahia. Furthermore, from a religious perspective, many in the Candomblé community charge that the folklorization of African religion for tourists constitutes sacrilege; mock Masses are not performed in the streets of Rome, for example.

Moreover, activists are concerned that to the extent that Afro-Brazilian culture is appropriated, commodified, and folklorized, its power as an organizing principle may be undermined. David Covin (1996) points out that while culture is central to the black movement, MNU publications often warn of the dangers of co-optation and cultural exploitation. Many are concerned that depictions of Afro-Brazilian cultural practices on tourism posters, shopping centers named after Candomblé deities, and traditional performances at state-sponsored festivals may detract from the use of Afro-Brazilian culture as a vehicle for social mobilization and criticism. Livio Sansone contends, for example, that Afro-Brazilians he worked with in Bahia "tended to see the practice of black culture as an escape rather than as a detonator, as a way to elude racism rather than as a way to fight it in organized ranks" (2003, 100). Thus, some suggest that "constructing and celebrating a distinctive cultural identity may be an impediment to political mobilization aimed at racial discrimination" (Fredrickson 2001, 17).

Michael Hanchard (1994) addresses these problems in his discussion of culturalism, which refers to discourses and practices that reify, objectify, and commodify culture while neglecting the fact that cultural production is deeply political. In this view, activists who rely on Afro-Brazilian culture as the basis for racial mobilization may end up undermining their own efforts. As Reichmann argues, the black movement often "reproduces the reification that the dominant culture imposes on black symbols" (1999a, 163). Thus, activists must face a Gramscian dilemma—that is, that both the radical and nationalistic uses of culture emerge from the same source: the recognition of Brazil's African roots (Hanchard 1994).

In fact, the Gramscian approach provides a valuable critique of Giddens' conception of identity/life politics. While Giddens addresses lifestyle practices as vehicles for personal and political agency, his approach neglects to focus on the extent to which the personal and the cultural are shaped by power relations in the first place. Lifestyles, like ideologies, are produced and consumed in fields of power, and, in Gramsci's view, hegemony entails the control of cultural production. From this perspective, vehicles of expression and resistance are often already infused with hegemonic views and practices or are swiftly appropriated and re-articulated for hegemonic purposes.

Yet the picture is still more complicated. The recent work of Matory (2005) and Johnson (2002), however, complicates any simple dichotomy between pure or authentic African or African-derived religion on the one hand versus its appropriation on the other. That is, these authors stress that practitioners deploy discourses of Africanity and purity in strategic ways; furthermore, they stress that the integration of Candomblé into the public sphere has not been a wholly negative development for Candomblé communities.

This raises some important questions: to what extent has the fact that Candomblé has "gone public" (Johnson 2002, 154) had an impact on the ways in which people make use of Afro-Brazilian culture? Does the Gramscian critique of the appropriation of culture rely on too sharp a distinction between authentic culture and its appropriation? How does the commodification of Candomblé relate to its use in campaigns for anti-racist mobilization?

In fact, George Yúdice argues that the practice of culture is often "located at the intersection of economic and social justice agendas" (2003, 17). He contends that in the contemporary world, culture is increasingly seen as a resource to be managed rather than either an autonomous realm of expression or a field of struggle. Thus,

> when culture is touted as a resource, it departs from the Gramscian premise that culture is a terrain of struggle and shifts strategy to processes of management. Compatible with neoliberal reconversions of civil society, culture as resource is seen as a way of providing social welfare and quality of life in the context of diminishing public resources and the withdrawal of the state from guarantees of the good life. (2003, 279)

In this view, culture is not a residual category or an edifice distinct from what "really matters"—politics, the market, and so on; rather, culture *does* something (Yúdice 2003). Today, culture is frequently found at the center of projects that aim at economic and social amelioration—that is, culture is called upon to solve problems. Thus, NGOs capitalize on culture at the same time that the forces of the neo-liberal order such as consumerism and tourism are targeting culture. Nevertheless, Yúdice contends that this does not obviate the NGOs' use of culture as a tool of empowerment: "NGOs and international agencies like UNESCO . . . despite promoting the instrumentalization of culture, nevertheless also promote social justice" (2003, 156). Furthermore, with respect to Afro-Brazilians in particular, he argues,

> Given the importance of representations of blacks and mulattos and their cultural practices in the struggles to define Brazilianness, the challenge to racial common sense must focus on the social and economic status of nonwhites and on how the "consensus culture" has symbolized such practices as samba, pagode (a neighborhood gathering where samba is played), capoeira (an Afro-Brazilian martial arts dance form brought by slaves from Angola), candomblé and umbanda (Afro-Brazilian religions), and so on. (2003, 113)

New Social Movements

While many have expressed valid concerns about identity politics and culture-oriented mobilization strategies, others are more welcoming of the emergence of identity-based social movements. Anthony Appiah, for example, makes a compelling case for the importance of identity in the struggle against racism.

> If one is to be Black in a society that is racist then one has to deal constantly with assaults on one's dignity. In this context, insisting on the

right to live a dignified life will not be enough. It will not even be enough to require being treated with equal dignity despite being Black, for that will require a concession that being Black counts naturally or to some degree against one's dignity. And so one will end up asking to be respected as a Black. (1994, 161)

Identity-based "new social movements" (NSMs) are especially appealing in comparison to the ideological rigidity of many emancipatory movements that subordinate gender, sexual, and racial identities to class relations. In Brazil, of course, the reduction of racial inequalities to class differences is integral to the hegemonic discourse of racial democracy. NSMs represent a post-ideological and pragmatic approach to social mobilization that takes seriously identities that were formerly considered only secondary or merely personal. These movements share an emphasis on

self-reflexivity regarding the construction of social identities, the centrality of the body as a location for political discourse, the emphasis on changing personal relations as a method for revising social relations, the expansion of the political arena into previously "private" areas, the critique of imme-diatist . . . theories of revolution and the preference for transformational models of social change, and the supposed expressiveness rather than instrumentality of new movements. (Sturgeon 1995, 44–45)

In addition to referring to ostensibly new social phenomena, the term *new social movements* indicates an emerging approach to the analysis of contemporary social movements that shifts attention to questions of identity (Melucci, Keane et al. 1989; Touraine 1988; Laclau and Mouffe 1985). Earlier perspectives focused on a given movement's strategic effectiveness in relation to its tangible goals, particularly its success or failure at gaining a "(larger) share of the distributional pie" (Mayer and Roth 1995, 299). In contrast, the NSM perspective focuses less on strategic effectiveness and resource mobilization than on identity construction (cf. Cohen 1985). From this perspective, "the collective search for identity is a central aspect of movement formation" (Laraña, Johnston, and Gusfield 1994, 10). NSM theory assumes that "the pursuit of collective identity flows from an intrinsic need for an integrated and continuous social self, a self that is thwarted and assaulted in modern society" (Laraña, Johnston, and Gusfield 1994, 11). This description is similar to what Charles Taylor refers to as the politics of recognition, in which issues of collective identity, particularly the survival and affirmation of minority and/or threatened identities, enters into the sphere of public policy debates (Yúdice 2003; Taylor and Gutmann 1994). This type of politics disrupts the traditional opposition between individual rights and collective (national) obligations, just as it makes it difficult to understand such NSMs in straightforward, instrumental terms.

Like Fotopoulos, authors Laraña, Johnston, and Gusfield (1994) stress that NSMs are concerned primarily with cultural and symbolic issues rather than inequitable economic structures. Such movements are usually based on diffuse identities and statuses rather than class and generally oppose the unifying and totalizing ideologies of working-class and Marxist movements. Indeed, NSM theorists emphasize the ways in which "class interests" are discursively constructed (Laclau and Mouffe 1985). NSMs "exhibit a pluralism of ideas and values, and they tend to have a pragmatic orientation and search for institutional reforms that enlarge the systems of members' participation in decision making" (Laraña, Johnston, and Gusfield 1994, 6–7). In this way they differ in their organizational structure from the centralized bureaucracies of traditional political parties, as NSMs tend to be scattered and decentralized. Some argue, however, that this tendency of NSMs to organize themselves into "decentralized affinity groups" (Sturgeon 1995, 36) reflects the fusion of theory and practice—that is, the effort to create democratic, pluralistic, and inclusive movements.

This perspective focuses largely on the politics of the everyday. Melucci, Keane et al. (1989), for example, argue that a weakness of previous approaches is that they neglect to attend to the sort of "identity work" that goes on in "submerged networks" during latency periods between crises and public confrontation. Instead of unified empirical objects, social movements are the "combinatory effects of forms of action impacting upon different levels of a social system" (Chesters and Welsh 2005, 191).

Although much of the literature on NSMs focuses on Europe and North America, this kind of social mobilization clearly is not limited to the global north (Alvarez, Dagnino, and Escobar 1998). Today, as Escobar and Alvarez (1992) point out, Latin American social and political space is inhabited by a diverse array of identity-centered movements. In Brazil, for example, identity-based groups, such as those that make up the black movement, have been flourishing since the return of democracy to Brazil in the 1980s (Winant 1994).

The MEP, for example, advances a progressive, reformist agenda that, at least in Bahia, is largely oriented toward the concerns of people of African descent. Yet the members of MEP share not only certain political views and a concern with social justice, but their identities as evangelicals as well. In addition, black members of MEP attempt to build their identities as people of African descent on the foundations of evangelical Christianity. Again, by contrast, many members of the mainstream black movement look to Candomblé for the ethnic basis of their identities. Thus, while the black movement as a whole may "exhibit a pluralism of ideas and values" (Laraña, Johnston, and Gusfield 1994, 6), considerable tension exists within it between different visions of Afro-Brazilian identity.

Identities and Movements

[G]roup identity seems to work only—or, at least, work best—when it is seen by its members as natural, as "real." Pan-Africanism, black solidarity, can be an important force with real political benefits, but it doesn't work without its attendant mystifications. . . . [Y]ou cannot build alliances without mystifications and mythologies. (Appiah 1995, 106)

Many commentators who applaud the rise of identity-based social movements also admit that the strategies that have characterized NSMs are problematic. On the one hand, many have criticized the tendency toward essentialism in a large number of identity-based movements. As I discussed above, for example, some contend that combating supremacist ideologies with positive representations of blackness can replicate the same essentialist premises as dominant racial discourses. Along these lines, Cornel West (1994, 72) laments that black responses to racism have tended to represent blacks as "just like whites" or as a homogeneous group. Both of these positions mirror nonwhite discourses about blacks, the first by reflecting assimilationist discourses and the second by obliterating differences between blacks. West argues that for people of African descent struggling against racism today, the main objectives should not simply be to "produce positive images of homogeneous communities" (1994, 74) or to contest stereotypes. Rather, he argues,

black cultural workers must constitute and sustain discursive and institutional networks that deconstruct earlier modern Black strategies for identity-formation . . . and construct more multi-valent and multi-dimensional responses that articulate the complexity and diversity of Black practices in the modern and postmodern world. (1994, 74)

In this context, one's rejection of, disidentification with, and refusal to perform normative identities (e.g., woman, black) constitutes a potent form of resistance (J. Butler 1994).

Recent thinking about identity politics and social mobilization has steered away from naive essentialism while affirming the importance of inclusive forms of identity in the building of social movements. This turning away from essentialism is in fact a sign of the times, as one of the hallmarks of postmodernity is a heightened awareness of the mediated nature and lack of foundations for identity. As Lauren Langman and Valerie Scatamburlo point out,

> Postmodern insights have astutely criticized essentialism—a presumed existence of inherent forms of selfhood—and have noted that subjects are historical products created in and through a variety of ideologically based discursive and disciplinary practices. (1996, 130)

Thus, postmodernity consists of "unstable subjectivities, fragmented selves, decentered identities" (Reinarman 1995, 100). While Giddens argued that the narrating subject can make a stable whole out of fragments, many challenge the very idea that an abiding, coherent self is possible—and others question whether this is even desirable. Zygmunt Bauman declares, for example, that "if the *modern* 'problem of identity' was how to construct an identity and keep it solid and stable, the *postmodern* 'problem of identity' is primarily how to avoid fixation and keep the options open" (Bauman 1996, 18). This emphasis on flexibility and contingency is reflected in the pragmatic and often eclectic character of NSMs.

On the other hand, some kind of foundation, imaginary or not, arguably remains a necessary prerequisite for an effective social movement. As Appiah (1995) argues, anti-foundationalist accounts of ethnic identity often fail to address ethnicity as a potent organizing principle rather than something simply to be deconstructed. Furthermore, Castells (1997) points out that most contemporary identity projects are based in some form of communal resistance, often against the forces of globalization. Empirically, then, identity politics has become central to a broad spectrum of movements despite—or perhaps in response to—postmodern anti-foundationalism.

With this in mind, as Steven Seidman and Linda Nicholson ask, "How do we generate ways of understanding identity as central to personal and group formation while avoiding essentialism?" (1995, 21). This is the key question. Many analysts, of course, argue that "strategic essentialisms" (Spivak 1988) are necessary for collective political action. Along these lines, Judith Butler (1994) proposes a pragmatic approach to identities, one that welcomes multiplicity and regards foundations as contestable assumptions. This approach does not preclude the deployment of identity terms but recognizes them as sites of "permanent openness and resignifiability" on the ever-shifting "ungrounded ground" of identity politics (1994, 166). This stresses the contingency and multiplicity of identities even as they present themselves as stable. This ironic stance toward identity—simultaneously affirming and relativizing it—constitutes a form of double consciousness.[2]

The relevance of these perspectives to the situation of the black movement in Brazil is a complicated issue. Without a doubt, the admonishments of Seidman, Spivak, Judith Butler, and West against "unreconstructed" essentialism are instructive. As I have discussed above, many have criticized mobilization efforts based on essentialized images of ethnoreligious identity. Along these lines, for example, Sansone argues that black identity in Bahia

> emphasizes some of the dilemmas of Brazilian race relations. It shows a weak feeling of black community together with a strong and rich black culture, which at times enjoys plenty of official recognition, although the participation in black culture cannot be necessarily associated with strong identification with black identity. It also shows that black identity crystallizes only episodically or during ritual moments (mainly, Carnival, candomblé rites, playing capoeira, samba, drum sessions). (2003, 104)

Thus, the traditional Afro-Brazilian practices that the black movement draws upon are highly context-specific, often exclusionary, and not especially conducive to racial identification. As Sansone (2003) argues, contrary to what one might expect, participation in Candomblé in general is not very well correlated with racial consciousness. In fact, in his research, he found that people who reported having positive feelings about Candomblé were more likely to say there is no racial discrimination in Brazil than those who are indifferent to Candomblé or reject it completely.

Similarly, Jacques D'Adesky argues that "Afro-Brazilian religions do not constitute factors of solidarity necessary for blacks. They are symbolic expressions that are positive for some, indifferent for others and negative for a certain number of people" (2001, 160; translation mine). In addition, my analysis of my questionnaire data suggested that respondents involved with Candomblé were not significantly more concerned about racism than respondents involved with other religious groups (Selka 2003).

Perhaps part of the explanation for this, Sansone (2003) suggests, is that a new black identity is emerging among young Bahians today, one that is based more in color consciousness and modern consumption than in traditional culture and religion. This new kind of black identity has been shaped by the influence of discourses about race from abroad, including the United States. While many lament this turn away from Afro-Brazilian traditions, others see this emerging color consciousness as a positive step in the direction of a viable anti-racism movement.

Critics point out that on the whole, however, the black movement has failed to produce mass mobilization against racism in Brazil (Fredrickson 2001; Burdick 1998a). Some claim that this is largely because the movement is dominated by affluent, middle-class blacks with relatively light skin (Nishida 2003; Bacelar 2001; Safa 1998; Burdick 1992). Similarly, I found that among my questionnaire respondents, those who claimed to be most involved with Afro-Brazilian culture and the struggle against racism tended to be better educated and have higher incomes than those who claimed to be less involved (Selka 2003). As a result, the language and objectives of the black movement are often maladjusted to the daily lives of its intended audience, who are largely poor, uneducated, and concerned mostly with material needs (Myatt 1995). Along these lines, Sansone points out that the "black community" of religious practitioners, intellectuals, and producers of traditional food and music who make up the black movement represents "just a small part of black social and cultural life in Salvador" (2003, 75).

As I have examined throughout this chapter, various observers trace the black movement's failure to mobilize significant numbers of Afro-Brazilians to its elite leadership, its overemphasis on a reified ethnoreligious identity, its ideological incoherence, and an overall lack of unity. In this way, critical discourses about the black movement tend to portray it as neglecting questions of ideology and focusing too closely on narrowly defined identities. To be sure, in the 1980s and 1990s many groups in the movement moved away from rigid ideological stances toward more pragmatic and reform-oriented approaches. As I discuss below, however, this lack of a unitary ideology is not simply a strategic oversight.

Moreover, the emphasis on identity in the black movement is a tricky issue. Without a doubt, the critiques of naive essentialism and of exclusionary identities I have discussed here are largely valid. In a society where the majority of people of African descent do not see themselves as part of the constituency of the black movement, however, the construction of some kind of crosscutting Afro-Brazilian identity is essential. In the context of the civil rights movement in the United States, by contrast, the contours of a relatively stable black identity were assumed at the outset, even if blacks differed in their religious affiliations and in their degrees of political radicalization.

Seen from this perspective, the fact that most people of African descent do not strongly identify as black nor view the social inequalities they may experience in terms of racism is as much of a hurdle to racial mobilization in Brazil as essentialism (although these issues are intertwined). Thus, many—myself included—are reluctant to blame the movement's "failure" wholly on strategic shortcomings. In this view, the focus on identity in the black movement and its politically fragmented nature largely results from the difficulty of organizing an anti-racist movement in the context of the hegemonic discourses that deny both race and racism (cf. Reichmann 1999a, 1999b; Guimarães 1995). Accordingly, activists must convince large numbers of people to identify themselves as black and, at the same time, cast a wide enough political net so as not to alienate potential constituents.

At this point one might well wonder, if it is important to avoid alienation, why activists do not focus their message on the common historical experiences and diminished life chances that people of African descent in Brazil share rather than on contested ethnic identities and exclusionary cultural traditions. Again, as I have pointed out throughout this book, part of the reason, at least historically, is that dominant ideologies deny the existence of racial oppositions and reduce racial inequalities to class differences. This is changing to some extent as race and racism move into the sphere of public debate; furthermore, Brazilians were never passive dupes of this ideology in the first place. But the fact that the discourse of racial democracy so permeated Brazilian society made it difficult to mount a sustained critique of racism.[3]

Another issue is the lack of resources to build a political movement independent of the diffuse Afro-Brazilian cultural institutions that have traditionally been the center of Afro-Brazilian struggles. That is, Brazilian activists and others I spoke with in Bahia pointed out that resources are scarce in the black community and among the organizations that constitute the black movement. One of these scarce resources is education, the lack of which makes consciousness raising difficult. Unfortunately, educational programs are limited by the lack of strong, national, well-funded Afro-Brazilian institutions.

Some activists I spoke with were involved with the MNU in the 1970s and 1980s and left the movement because of their frustration over what they saw as its lack of effectiveness due to severely limited resources. They concluded that they could be much more effective working in flawed but established and well-funded institutions like the Catholic Church and the Bahian government. In the context of scarce resources, then, activists in Bahia must take a pragmatic view of mobilization and consciousness raising. In this view, to the extent that folklorization and commodification valorize black culture and bring it into public spaces, these processes have some benefits.

In addition to its widespread poverty, Brazil's relatively recent return to participatory democracy and the persistence of deeply entrenched patron-client politics have made it difficult for strong, unified social movements to emerge. Yet such explanations for the decentralized and fragmented character of the black movement are only partial. From the NSMs' perspective, for example, the movement's diffuse network of alliances and culture-based mobilization strategies are not particular to the Brazilian situation, but are a general feature of global identity politics as they have emerged over the past several decades (Fotopoulos 2002; Langman and Scatamburlo 1996; Laraña, Johnston, and Gusfield 1994).

Moreover, some have a wider vision of the black movement in which its disparate parts fit together. From this perspective, the movement is a constellation of diverse groups that aspire to the general purpose of struggling against racism. Padre Clóvis, a Catholic priest active in the Pastoral Afro movement, for example, explained that the black movement is composed of three prongs: urban progressive groups such as the MNU, the PT, and the Pastoral Afro; traditional Afro-Brazilian irmandades and other organizations in the rural zones; and radical groups like the Movimento Sem Terra (the landless workers' movement) that are working toward general economic equity and social justice (cf. Nascimento and Nascimento 2001; D'Adesky 2001). In fact, progressive activists are turning to traditional organizations as sources of popular authenticity while traditional organizations are leaning on progressive groups for support in a modernizing political system in which traditional patron-client politics are increasingly subject to criticism.

Furthermore, although only a relatively small number of Bahians directly participate in the production and performance of traditional Afro-Brazilian culture, popular Afro-Catholic festivals and Candomblé terreiros can be seen as major spaces of self-representation for black Brazilians (D'Adesky 2001). And while young Bahians today may be less directly involved with traditional Afro-Brazilian practices, Sansone points out that many people involved in the black movement are rediscovering Candomblé "under a new ethnic light" (2003, 99). That is, many younger activists are using Candomblé "diacritically more as a symbol of blackness than for its religious and healing properties" (2003, 99).

Despite the fact that traditional Afro-Brazilian culture is constantly subject to appropriation, irmandades and terreiros have long been bases of Afro-Brazilian power (Fontaine 1985). More recently, however, progressive evangelicals have been struggling to carve out a space of activism and self-representation that is founded on Protestant traditions—including participatory democracy and the battle for civil rights—rather than on any specific ethnic heritage. Evangelicals have long been the bane of Candomblé practitioners and progressive activists, however, and thus it may take some time before they integrate into the mainstream black movement. The evangelical focus on citizenship, however, is crucial. Current progressive discourses of democracy, which focus on the extension of the notion of citizenship from political to social and civil dimensions, form a link between grassroots mobilization and governmental structures (Yúdice 2003). Such a revitalized notion of citizenship will certainly play a central role in the future of identity-based movements in Brazil.

From the perspective that I have outlined here, the categorical separation between culture and politics appears to be of limited utility for analyzing the Brazilian black movement. This distinction suggests that political interests are objectively given instead of constructed through discourse, which is questionable, and that political identities are self-evident, which overlooks the complex identity work that is accomplished in spaces of cultural practice. Simply stated, without preparatory identity work, one would not hear the "call" to assume one's identity and to mobilize on the basis of it. Furthermore, I have also indicated the limits of an approach that begins with the premise that the black movement voices a particular "call" that resonates or fails to resonate with potential constituents of the black movement. To borrow a metaphor from Paul Gilroy (2002), studying the black movement is like listening to jazz; the listener has to be attentive to the variety of voices and calls that often seem to head in their own directions, but are always playing off and referring back to one another so that what emerges is a kind of "ordered disorder."

Representing Multiplicity and Complexity

Throughout this book I have emphasized multiple and often competing views of what it means to be Afro-Brazilian. To a certain extent this multiplicity is something new that has resulted from relatively recent changes in Brazil, including the return to democracy, increasing consumerism, growing religious pluralism, and the intensification of connections to other parts of the African diaspora through transnational media. Yet I do not mean to set the multiplicity of Afro-Brazilian identities today against some supposedly unitary and hermetically sealed identity in the past (cf. Matory 2005). In fact, my emphasis on multiplicity has as much to do with relatively recent shifts in the social sciences as it does with changes in Brazilian society.

In the 1980s, anthropologists and others in the human sciences began to criticize the essentialist or romanticized representations of the other presented in many ethnographies (Clifford and Marcus 1986; Marcus and Fischer 1986; cf. Said 1978). More recently, we have seen another shift that some have called the "complexity turn" (Urry 2005). Often drawing on metaphors from chaos theory, approaches concerned with complexity focus on forms of order that remain on "the edge of chaos" (Urry 2005, 1). In this view, identities are unstable and "characterized by multiple possibilities" (2005, 5).

The notion of diaspora—which is particularly useful for approaching sites of practice characterized by multiplicity, boundary crossings, and classificatory struggles—is directly relevant here. In contrast to the concept of culture, the term *diaspora* foregrounds heterogeneity, unboundedness, dislocation, and hybridity (Kokot, Tölölyan et al. 2004). As we have seen, this describes not only the picture that emerges when we juxtapose communities of people of African descent in different parts of the world, but also the complexity within the local nexus of practice that makes up the African diaspora. What African and African-diasporic cultures have in common is not so much their origins in some primordial Africa, but rather their complex connections to each other that are better understood through the metaphor of rhizomes than that of roots of a tree (Deleuze and Guattari 1977, 1987). It is critical to stress, however, that certain common points of reference—practices, places, and so on—often persist in the midst of flux, even if their significance is constantly shifting. These points of reference make collective identification possible, including the construction of ethnic and racial identities.

The central question that emerges when we look at social life from this perspective is this: how does order and coherence emerge out of multiplicity and contestation? Much of early anthropological thinking stressed how culture was patterned and integrated. Accordingly, many early ethnographies attempted to show how cultural practices functioned within a coherent whole. Later, particularly after the 1960s, assumptions about coherence and consensus faded into the background as many anthropologists shifted their focus to contestation and conflict.[4] Today, others are exploring approaches that go beyond the dichotomy between order and disorder; these approaches focus on forms of "orderly disorder" and "thin coherence" that emerge in the midst of conflict and contestation. William Sewell (1999), for example, maintains that we can view cultures as "thinly coherent" to the extent that they consist of networks of oppositions and distinctions, but he argues that these networks do not constitute orderly systems of elements with inherent or stable meanings. Sewell's argument is consistent with the deconstructionist emphasis on culture as the interplay of distinctions, yet his approach implies that some form of coherence, even if it is illusive, is what makes social life possible.

These themes run through NSMs and diasporic perspectives. These approaches emphasize the contested and emergent nature of identities but stress that something emerges—nexus of affinities, submerged networks, webs of "weak ties"—that allows for some kind of intersubjective reciprocity of perspectives, even if it is fragile, episodic, and shifting (Edelman 2001; Alvarez, Dagnino, and Escobar 1998). My argument with respect to the black movement, for example, has not been that Afro-Brazilian identities are so varied and contested as to render futile any kind of consensus building, but that questions of identity are never settled and that this very indeterminacy drives the movement forward.

Clearly, coherent identities are important from the standpoint of political mobilization. That is, those who are involved in social struggles know that the fact that communities are imagined or identities are constructed is beside the point. Some form of representation is needed, and therefore the crucial question becomes, who is in control of the production of representations, and what kind of communities and identities do we want to imagine? In this reflexive moment, ideas about what constitutes authenticity become much more varied and contested. This is particularly evident in debates over black identities in the New World, their relationship to Africa and the diaspora, and what is distinctive about the black experience.

Candomblé remains at the center of many representations of Afro-Brazilian identity, but it is important to take seriously alternative identities that are emerging in Brazil. Classificatory struggles concerning the connection between religion and race in Brazil, for example, form the context in which black evangelicals are constructing their identities and, in some cases, new approaches to racial politics. It remains to be seen what will become of the evangelical approach to anti-racism, but there is good reason to believe that it will be influential; Burdick, for example, points out that the evangelical black movement "speaks the language of one of the largest, broadest and best-organized segments of the Brazilian population" (2005, 313).

The challenge that all this presents to theory is similar to that which it presents to mobilization efforts: how do we represent complexity in useful and compelling ways? A diasporic perspective is particularly helpful in this regard, as it pushes us not simply to an alternative between the specificity of local black identities and the wider processes that shape them, but to realize how these mutually constitute one another. In this way, a diasporic perspective allows us to attend to the "production of locality" (Appadurai 1996; cf. Hardt and Negri 2000). Local Afro-Brazilian religious practices have become key transnational figures that impact the ways that people of African descent think about their past, and in turn, the ways that Afro-Brazilian religion has been represented by activists, tourists, and politicians have profoundly transformed it. Borrowing another metaphor from Paul Gilroy, we might think of irmandades, terreiros, and churches not as enclosed sites of identity formation, but as a crossroads where different practices and processes intersect: forms of remembering, forces of appropriation, claims to authenticity, spiritual longings, desire for justice, tales of suffering, and hopes for deliverance.

Notes

Chapter 2

1. The hegemony of Yoruba traditions—sometimes referred to as "nâgocentrism"—is a controversial issue in Bahian Candomblé communities. See Matory (2005) for an interesting discussion of the history of this issue.

2. Droogers (1989) and Stewart and Shaw (1994) contend that because concepts such as syncretism or popular religion pivot on claims of religious authenticity and legitimacy, the very use of these terms is contentious and politically charged. Moreover, they stress that the popular appropriation of "official" religion suggested by these terms can partly be understood as a form of resistance against religious authority.

3. Examples of this research include Skidmore's (1993) classic study of the history of racial ideologies, Hanchard's (1994, 1999) and Reichmann's (1999a, 1999b, 1997) research on racial politics, Butler's (1998a) examination of post-abolition Afro-Brazilian identity formation and political struggle, Lovell and Wood's (1998) statistical analysis of inequalities between whites and nonwhites, Sheriff's (2001) ethnography of speaking about race and racism in Rio, Guimarães's (1999) and d'Adesky's (2001) works on contemporary racism and anti-racism, and Telles's (2004) broad and authoritative treatment of race in contemporary Brazil. Especially relevant to the study of religion and identity politics are Burdick's (1993, 1998a) research on religion and the black consciousness movement, Braga's (1995) and Harding's (2000) work on the role of Candomblé in Afro-Brazilian resistance and identity formation, Crook and Johnson's (1999) volume on Afro-Brazilian mobilization, Kraay's (1998) volume on Afro-Brazilian culture and politics in Bahia, and Sansone's (2003) recent book on black identity in Salvador.

Chapter 3

1. Some have employed the term *industrial paternalism* to describe the persistence of patron-client logics within the process of Bahia's industrialization. For a general discussion of paternalism and patronage, see Abercrombie and Hill 1976.

2. The notion of double belonging affirms that many people are involved with both Candomblé and Catholicism but denies that these are truly "mixed" or "confused." This

is not to say this clarifies the issue, however. In fact, the language that emerges around the intersection of Candomblé and Catholicism is marked by its indeterminacy. Different agents make use of the "strategic ambiguity" of discourses of syncretism for varying ends.

Chapter 4

1. Actually, on at least one of the rare occasions that Candomblé terreiros came together to mobilize politically it was for conservative purposes. According to one newspaper article ("A Guerra das Atabaques" [The War of the Drums] *Istoé Independente Online*, May 30, 2001), when the arch-conservative Bahian senator, Antônio Carlos Magalhães, was resigning from the senate, 80 percent of the Candomblé terreiros in Salvador joined together to publicly support him. In fact, the National Confederation of Afro-Brazilian Religions pressured terreiros to participate under the threat of penalties—hence the byline ("Terreiros de candomblé da Bahia são forçados a trabalhar por Antônio Carlos Magalhães. Quem resiste sofre ameaças" ["Candomblé terreiros of Bahia are forced to work for Antônio Carlos Magalhães. Those that resist suffer threats"]).

2. See Agier's (2000) discussion of the black elite in Salvador. Agier contends that for the black elite (Afro-Brazilians who are members of the middle to upper classes in terms of education and income), the most traditionally African practices are at the center of Afro-Brazilian cultural affirmations (e.g., Ilê Aiyé), while those practices that are impure (e.g., syncretic) or which are positioned on the border between black and white social and cultural spaces (e.g., Olodum) are viewed as marginal. Thus, the black elite is largely anti-syncretic, as deploying discourses of purity is often a way to make claims concerning legitimacy.

Chapter 5

1. See Chapter 3, note 2, on participation in Candomblé.

2. John Burdick (2005), for example, has identified no fewer than thirty Protestant groups "dedicated expressly to fighting racism and building a strong black identity" (316) that have emerged in Brazil since 1995.

Chapter 6

1. In fact, in the last ten years, the issue of racial discrimination has moved up on the agendas of government administrations and political parties. In 1996, the Brazilian government hosted International Conference on Diversity, Multiculturalism, and Affirmative Action, during which Fernando Henrique Cardoso became the first president of Brazil to officially recognize these concepts and the problem of racial inequality in Brazil (Reichmann 1999b). Lula's Workers' Party (PT) and his current administration have committed themselves to combating racism ("Brazil's Black and White Poll," *BBC*

News, October 6, 2002; "Brazil Vows Better Care to Blacks," *Brazzil*, August 1, 2004). Laws against discrimination and racial slurs have been on the books since the late 1980s, and today affirmative actions policies are being debated and even implemented in places (Heringer 1999; Sell 2002; Siss 2003; Berbardino and Galdino 2004; Telles 2004; Htun 2005). Yet enforcement of these laws is problematic, and affirmative action policies are controversial in a country where racial identities are not taken for granted as part of everyday common sense (Guimarães 1999).

2. Richard Rorty (1989) suggests that one can maintain an ironic stance with respect to the language that one uses to narrate oneself; that is, one can simultaneously embrace one's identity and affirm its contingency. This ironic stance might be seen as a form of double consciousness. See also Alexander Nehamas's *Nietzsche, Life as Literature* (1985), as well as Martin Heidegger's (1962) notion of resolve.

3. The American Dream myth provides a useful analogy. This myth, typified in "rags-to-riches" stories á la Horatio Alger, promises that the United States is a meritocracy and that social inequalities stem from differences in individual ability, motivation, and so on, rather than from class differentiation or domination. This makes it difficult to critique the class system without being excluded from mainstream political debates as an extremist. Yet there is some basis to the myth: in some ways, class is not nearly as explicitly important in everyday interactions as it is in Europe and Latin America (although one could argue that in the United States' context class is simply euphemized in terms of lifestyle options based on consumption, such as "NASCAR dad" and "yuppie"). At the same time, the United States has the largest income equality of any industrialized nation in the world. Some have argued that the American poor are duped by the allure of the American Dream, but it is clear that Americans are aware of social distinctions along the lines of class, even if this awareness is not usually articulated in dichotomous terms. Many poor voters living in rural America, for example, supported George W. Bush—a privileged scion of the American upper class whose approach to economic policy is oriented toward the wealthy—in 2000 and 2004. Many commentators on the left complained that these Americans were voting against their class interests. Yet class indeed figured prominently into the Republican campaigns, which drew upon popular resentment against the "Northeastern liberal elite" represented by Gore (who is actually from Tennessee, of course) and Kerry.

4. This is not to suggest that all anthropologists before this time ignored contestation and conflict. In particular, Edmund Leach (1954), Max Gluckman (1959), and Victor Turner (1974) emphasized culture as a realm of struggle as well as consensus.

References

Abercrombie, Nicholas, and Stephen Hill. 1976. "Paternalism and Patronage." *British Journal of Sociology* 27 (4): 413–29.

Adriance, Madeleine. 1986. *Opting for the Poor: Brazilian Catholicism in Transition.* Kansas City, Mo.: Sheed and Ward.

Agier, Michel. 1998. "Between Affliction and Politics: A Case Study of Bahian Candomblé." In *Afro-Brazilian Culture and Politics: Bahia, 1790s to 1990s,* ed. Hendrik Kraay. 134–57. Armonk, N.Y.: M. E. Sharpe.

———. 2000. *Anthropologie du Carnaval: La Ville, la Fête et l'Afrique Bahia.* Marseille: Parenthèses.

Alvarez, Sonia, Ernesto Dagnino, and Arturo Escobar, eds. 1998. *Culture of Politics, Politics of Culture: Revisioning Latin American Social Movements.* Boulder, Colo.: Westview Press.

Alves Velho, Yvonne Maggie. 1977. *Guerra de Orixá.* Rio de Janeiro: Zahar Editores.

Anderson, Benedict. 1983. *Imagined Communities: Reflections on the Origin and Spread of Nationalism.* New York: Verso.

Andrews, George Reid. 1991. *Blacks and Whites in São Paulo, Brazil 1888–1988.* Madison: University of Wisconsin Press.

Appadurai, Arjun. 1996. *Modernity at Large: Cultural Dimensions of Globalization.* Minneapolis: University of Minnesota Press.

Appiah, Kwame Anthony. 1994. "Identity, Authenticity, Survival: Multicultural Societies and Social Reproduction." In *Multiculturalism,* ed. Amy Gutmann. 149–64. Princeton, N.J.: Princeton University Press.

———. 1995. "African Identities." In *Social Postmodernism: Beyond Identity Politics,* ed. Linda Nicholson and Steven Seidman. New York: Cambridge University Press, 103–15.

Apter, Andrew. 2005. "Herskovit's Heritage: Rethinking Syncretism in the African Diaspora." In *Syncretism in Religion: A Reader,* ed. Anita Maria Leopold and Jeppe Sinding Jensen. New York: Routledge, 160–84.

Asad, Talal. 1993. *Genealogies of Religion: Discipline and Reasons of Power in Christianity and Islam.* Baltimore: Johns Hopkins University Press.

Azevedo, Marcello de Carvalho. 1987. *Basic Ecclesial Communities in Brazil: The Challenge of a New Way of Being Church.* Washington, D.C.: Georgetown University Press.

Bacelar, Jeferson. 2001. *A Hierarquia das Raças: Negros e Brancos Em Salvador.* Rio de Janeiro: Pallas.

Barcelos, Luiz Claudio. 1999. "Struggling in Paradise: Racial Mobilization and the Contemporary Black Movement in Brazil." In *From Indifference to Inequality: Race in Contemporary Brazil*, ed. Rebecca Reichmann. 155–66. University Park: Pennsylvania State University Press.

Bastide, Roger. 1958. *O Candomblé da Bahia*. São Paulo: Editora Schwarcz Ltda.

———. 1978. *The African Religions of Brazil: Toward a Sociology of the Interpenetration of Civilizations*. Baltimore: Johns Hopkins University Press.

Bauman, Zigmunt. 1996. "From Pilgrim to Tourist—or a Short History of Identity." In *Questions and Cultural Identity*, edited by Stuart Hall and Paul du Guy. 18–36. Thousand Oaks, Calif.: Sage Productions.

Bell, Catherine M. 1992. *Ritual Theory, Ritual Practice*. New York: Oxford University Press.

———. 1997. *Ritual Perspectives and Dimensions*. New York: Oxford University Press.

Berbardino, Joaze, and Daniela Galdino. 2004. *Levando a Raça a Sério: Ação Afirmativa e a Universidade*. Rio de Janeiro: DP&A, Laboratório de Políticas Públicas.

Berryman, Phillip. 1995. *Religion in the Megacity: Catholic and Protestant Portraits from Latin America*. Maryknoll, N.Y.: Orbis Books.

Birman, Patrícia. 1995. *Fazer Estilo Criando Gêneros: Possessão e Diferenças de Gênero Em Terreiros de Umbanda e Candomblé No Rio de Janeiro*. Rio de Janeiro: Dumará Distribuidora de Publicações Ltda.

Bourdieu, Pierre. 1984. *Distinction: A Social Critique of the Judgment of Taste*. Cambridge, Mass.: Harvard University Press.

———. 1991. "Genesis and Structure of the Religious Field." In *Religious Institutions*, ed. Craig Calhoun. 1–44. Greenwich, Conn.: JAI Press.

Bourdieu, Pierre, and L.J.D. Wacquant. 1992. *An Invitation to Reflexive Sociology*. Cambridge: Polity Press.

———. 1999. "On the Cunning of Imperialist Reason." *Theory, Culture and Society* 16 (1): 41–58.

Bowser, Benjamin, ed. 1995. *Racism and Anti-Racism in World Perspective*. Sage Series on Race and Ethnic Relations. Thousand Oaks, Calif.: Sage Publications.

Braga, Júlio. 1995. *Na Gamela do Feitiço: Repressão e Resistência nos Candomblés da Bahia*. Salvador: Editora da Universidade Federal da Bahia.

Brown, Diana DeGroat. 1986. *Umbanda: Religion and Politics in Urban Brazil*. Ann Arbor, Mich.: UMI Research Press.

———. 1999. "Power, Invention, and the Politics of Race: Umbanda Past and Future." In *Black Brazil: Culture, Identity, and Social Mobilization*, ed. Larry Crook and Randal Johnson. 213–36. Los Angeles: UCLA Latin American Studies Center Publications.

Bruneau, Thomas C. 1982. *The Church in Brazil: The Politics of Religion*. Austin: University of Texas Press.

Burdick, John. 1992. "Brazil's Black Consciousness Movement." *NACLA Report on the Americas* 25 (4) (February): 23–27.

———. 1993. *Looking for God in Brazil*. Berkeley: University of California Press.

———. 1998a. *Blessed Anastacia: Women, Race, and Popular Christianity in Brazil*. New York: Routledge.

———. 1998b. "The Lost Constituency of Brazil's Black Consciousness Movements." *Latin American Perspectives* 25 (1) (January): 136–55.

———. 1999. "What is the Color of the Holy Spirit? Pentecostalism and Black Identity in Brazil." *Latin American Research Review* 34 (2): 109–33.

———. 2002. "Negra and Mestiça: Emergent Racial Meanings in Brazil's Black Pastoral." *Luso-Brazilian Review* 39 (1): 95–101.

———. 2003. "The Afro-Catholic Liturgy and the Dance of Eurocentrism in Brazil." In *Race, Nation, and Religion in the Americas*, ed. Henry Goldschmidt and Elizabeth McAlister. 111–32. New York: Oxford University Press.

———. 2004. *Legacies of Liberation: The Progressive Catholic Church in Brazil at the Start of a New Millenium*. Burlington, Vt.: Ashgate.

———. 2005. "Why Is the Evangelical Black Movement Growing in Brazil?" *Journal of Latin American Studies* 37 (2): 311–32.

Burns, E. Bradford. 1980. *A History of Brazil*. New York: Columbia University Press.

Butler, Judith. 1990. *Gender Trouble: Feminism and the Subversion of Identity*. New York: Routledge.

———. 1994. "Contingent Foundations: Feminism and the Question of 'Postmodernism.'" In *The Postmodern Turn: New Perspectives in Social Theory*, ed. Steven Seidman. 153–70. Cambridge, Mass.: Cambridge University Press.

Butler, Kim D. 1998a. *Freedoms Given, Freedoms Won: Afro-Brazilians in Post-Abolition São Paulo and Salvador*. New Brunswick, N.J.: Rutgers University Press.

———. 1998b. "Afterword: *Ginga Baiana*—The Politics of Race, Class, Culture and Power in Salvador, Bahia." In *Afro-Brazilian Culture and Politics: Bahia, 1790s to 1990s*, ed. Hendrik Kraay. 158–75. Armonk, N.Y.: M. E. Sharp.

CAAPA. 2001. *A Pastoral Aro e Os Afrodescendentes*. Salvador: CAAPA (Centro Arquidiocesano de Articulação da Pastoral Afro Mons. Saduc).

Campos, Leonildo Silveira. 1996. "Why Historical Churches Are Declining and Pentecostal Churches Are Growing in Brazil: A Sociological Perspective." In *In the Power of the Spirit*, ed. Benjamin Gutierrez and Dennis A. Smith. 65–94. Drexel Hill, Pa.: Skipjack Press.

Campos Machado, Maria das Dores. 1996. *Carimáticos e Pentecostais: Asesão Religiosa Na Esfera Familar*. São Paulo: ANPOCS.

Canclini, Néstor García. 1989. *Hybrid Cultures: Strategies for Entering and Leaving Modernity*. Minneapolis: University of Minnesota Press.

Carneiro, Edison. 1991. *Candomblés Da Bahia*. Rio de Janeiro: Civilização Brasileira.

Carrette, Jeremy. 1999a. *Foucault and Religion: Spiritual Corporality and Political Spirituality*. New York: Routledge.

———. 1999b. *Religion and Culture: Michel Foucault*. New York: Routledge.

Carvalho, José Jorge de. 1993. *Black Music of All Colors: The Construction of Black Ethnicity in Ritual and Popular Genres of Afro-Brazilian Music*. Brasília, D.F.: Universidade de Brasília, Instituto de Ciências Humanas, Departamento de Antropologia.

Castells, Manuel. 1997. *The Power of Identity*. Malden, Mass.: Blackwell Publishers.

CENPAH. 2001. "Auto-Estima e Identidade Negra: Miscigenação e Ideologia do Branqueamento. Cadernos de Educação Afro-Brasileira." Sussuarana, Bahia: CENPAH (Centro de Pastoral Afro Pe. Heitor).

Chesnut, R. Andrew. 1997. *Born Again in Brazil: The Pentecostal Boom and the Pathogens of Poverty.* New Brunswick, N.J.: Rutgers University Press.

Chesters, Graeme, and Ian Welsh. 2005. "Complexity and Social Movement(s): Process and Emergence in Planetary Action Systems." *Theory, Culture and Society* 22 (5): 187–211.

Churchill, Ward. 1996. *From a Native Son: Selected Essays in Indigenism, 1985–1995.* Boston: South End Press.

Clawson, David L. 1984. "Religious Allegiance and Development in Latin America." *Journal of Interamerican Studies and World Affairs* 26: 499–524.

Cleary, David. 1999. *Race, Nationalism and Social Theory in Brazil: Rethinking Gilberto Freyre.* Oxford: Oxford University Press.

Cleary, Edward L., and Hannah Stewart-Gambino. 1997. *Power, Politics, and Pentecostals in Latin America.* Boulder, Colo.: Westview Press.

Clifford, James, and George E. Marcus. 1986. *Writing Culture: The Poetics and Politics of Ethnography. A School of American Research Advanced Seminar.* Berkeley: University of California Press.

Cohen, Jean. 1985. "Strategy or Identity: New Theoretical Paradigms and Contemporary Social Movements." *Social Research* 52 (4): 663–716.

Comaroff, Jean. 1985. *Body of Power, Spirit of Resistance: The Culture and Power of a South African People.* Chicago: University of Chicago Press.

Comaroff, John L. 1996. "Ethnicity, Nationalism, and the Politics of Difference in an Age of Revolution." In *The Politics of Difference: Ethnic Premises in a World of Power,* ed. Edwin N. Wilmsen and Patrick McAllister. 162–84. Chicago: University of Chicago Press.

Conrad, Robert. 1983. *Children of God's Fire: A Documentary History of Black Slavery in Brazil.* Princeton, N.J.: Princeton University Press.

Consorte, Josildeth Gomes. 1999. "Em Torno de Um Manifesto de Ialorixás Contra o Sincretismo." In *Faces Da Tradição Afro-Brasileira: Religiosidade, Sincretismo, Anti-Syncretismo, Reafricanizaçá, Práticas Terapêuticas, Etnobotânica e Comida,* ed. Carlos Caroso and Jeferson Bacelar. 71–92. Salvador: Pallas.

Contins, Maria. 1992. *Narrativas Pentecostais: Estudos Antropológicos de Grupos de Pentecostais Negros Nos Estados Unidos.* Rio de Janeiro: Centro Interdisciplinar de Estudos Culturais.

Costa, Esdras Borges. 1979. "Protestantism, Modernization and Cultural Change in Brazil." Ph.D. dissertation, University of California, Berkeley.

Covin, David. 1996. "The Role of Culture in Brazil's Unified Black Movement, Bahia in 1992." *Journal of Black Studies* 27 (1) (September): 39–55.

Crook, Larry, and Randal Johnson. 1999. *Black Brazil: Culture, Identity, and Social Mobilization.* Los Angeles: Latin American Center Publications, University of California, Los Angeles.

Csordas, Thomas J. 1994. *The Sacred Self: A Cultural Phenomenology of Charismatic Healing.* Berkeley: University of California Press.

Curry, Donald Edward. 1969. "Lusiada: An Anthropological Study of the Growth of Protestantism in Brazil." Ph.D. dissertation, Columbia University.

D'Adesky, Jacques. 2001. *Racismos e Anti-Racismos No Brasil.* Rio de Janeiro: Pallas.

Da Silva, Elizete. 1997. *Religião, Identidade Brasileira e Globalização. IV Conferência da BRA-SA.* Washington, D.C., November.

———. 1998. "Cidadãos de Outra Pátria: Anglicanos e Batistas na Bahia." Ph.D. dissertation, Universidade de São Paulo, Departamento de História.

de Certeau, Michel. 1984. *The Practice of Everyday Life.* Berkeley: University of California Press.

Degler, Carl. 1971. *Neither Black Nor White: Slavery and Race Relations in Brazil and the United States.* New York: Macmillan.

Deleuze, Gilles, and Félix Guattari. 1977. *Anti-Oedipus: Capitalism and Schizophrenia.* New York: Viking Press.

———. 1987. *A Thousand Plateaus: Capitalism and Schizophrenia.* Minneapolis: University of Minnesota Press.

Droogers, Andre. 1989. "Syncretism: The Problem of Definition, the Definition of the Problem." In *Dialogue and Syncretism: An Interdisciplinary Approach,* ed. J. Gort et al. 7–28. Grand Rapids, Mich.: William B. Eerdsmans.

———. 2005. "Syncretism, Power, Play." In *Syncretism in Religion: A Reader,* ed. Anita Maria Leopold and Jeppe Sinding Jensen. 217–36. New York: Routledge.

Durkheim, Emile. 1995. *The Elementary Forms of Religious Life.* Glencoe, Ill.: Free Press.

Edelman, Marc. 2001. "Social Movements: Changing Paradigms and Forms of Politics." *Annual Review of Anthropology* 30: 285–317.

Escobar, Arturo, and Sonia E. Alvarez. 1992. *The Making of Social Movements in Latin America: Identity, Strategy, and Democracy.* Boulder, Colo.: Westview Press.

Fanon, Frantz. 2002. *The Wretched of the Earth.* London: Penguin.

Farra, Robert Martin. 1960. "Protestantism in Brazil: A Study of the Activities and Results of the Protestant Foreign Missionary Movement in the United States of Brazil." Thesis, University of Nebraska.

Fernandes, Florestan. 1969. *The Negro in Brazilian Society.* New York: Columbia University Press.

Filhos de Gandhy. 2003. "Como Naceu." Cri'Artes Brasil Ltda. <www.filhosdegandhy.cjb.net> (accessed August 8, 2003).

Fontaine, Pierre-Michel. 1985. *Race, Class, and Power in Brazil.* Berkeley and Los Angeles: University of California Press.

Forman, Shepard. 1975. *The Brazilian Peasantry.* New York: Columbia University Press.

Fotopoulos, Takis. 2002. "Transitional Strategies and the Inclusive Democracy Project." *Alternatives: The Turkish Journal of International Relations* 1 (1) (Spring): 72–119.

Foucault, Michel. 1995. *Discipline and Punish: The Birth of the Prison.* New York: Vintage Books.

———. 1999. "Pastoral Power and Political Reason." In *Religion and Culture: Michel Foucault,* ed. Jeremy R. Carrette. 135–53. New York: Routledge.

Frase, Ronald Glen. 1975. "A Sociological Analysis of the Development of Brazilian Protestantism: A Study in Culture Change." Ph.D. dissertation, Princeton Theological Seminary.

Fredrickson, George M. 2001. "Race and Racism in Historical Perspective: Comparing the United States, South Africa, and Brazil." In *Beyond Racism: Race and Inequality in Bra-*

zil, South Africa, and the United States, ed. Charles Hamilton and Lynn Huntley. 1–28. Boulder, Colo.: Lynne Rienner Publishers.

French, John D. 2000. "The Missteps of Anti-Imperialist Reason." *Theory, Culture and Society* 17 (1): 107–28.

Freston, Paul. 1994. *Evangélicos Na Política Brasileira: História Ambígua e Desafio Ético*. Curitiba: Encontrão Editora.

Freyre, Gilberto. 1945. *Brazil: An Interpretation*. New York: Knopf.

———. 1956. *The Masters and the Slaves: A Study in the Development of Brazilian Civilization*. New York: Knopf.

———. 1959. *New World in the Tropics*. New York: Knopf.

Garrard-Burnett, Virginia, and David Stoll. 1993. *Rethinking Protestantism in Latin America*. Philadelphia: Temple University Press.

Gebara, Ivone. 1999. "A Recusa Do Sincretismo Como Afirmação da Liberdade." In *Faraimará—O Caçador Traz Alegria: Mãe Stella, 60 Anos de Iniciação*, ed. Cléo e Martins and Raul Lody. 404–12. Rio de Janeiro: Pallas.

Giddens, Anthony. 1991. *Modernity and Self-Identity: Self and Society in the Late Modern Age*. Stanford, Calif.: Stanford University Press.

Gilroy, Paul. 2002. *The Black Atlantic: Modernity and Double Consciousness*. Cambridge, Mass.: Harvard University Press.

Gluckman, Max. 1959. *Custom and Conflict in Africa*. Glencoe, Ill.: Free Press.

Guimarães, Antonio Sergio Alfredo. 1995. "Racism and Anti-Racism in Brazil: A Postmodern Perspective." In *Racism and Anti-Racism in World Perspective*, ed. Benjamin P. Bowser. 208–26. Thousand Oaks, Calif.: Sage Publications.

———. 1999. *Racismo e Anti-Racismo no Brasil*. São Paulo: Editora 34.

———. 2001. "The Misadventures of Nonracialism in Brazil." In *Beyond Racism: Race and Inequality in Brazil, South Africa, and the United States*, ed. Charles V. Hamilton and Lynn Huntley. 157–86. Boulder, Colo.: Lynne Rienner Publishers.

Hanchard, Michael. 1994. *Orpheus and Power: The Movimento Negro of Rio de Janeiro and São Paulo, Brazil, 1945–1988*. Princeton, N.J.: Princeton University Press.

———. 1999. *Racial Politics in Contemporary Brazil*. Durham, N.C.: Duke University Press.

———. 2003. "Acts of Misrecognition: Transnational Black Politics, Anti-Imperialism and the Ethnocentrisms of Pierre Bourdieu and Loïc Wacquant." *Theory, Culture and Society* 20 (4): 5–29.

Harding, Rachel E. 2000. *Candomblé and Alternative Spaces of Blackness*. Bloomington: Indiana University Press.

Hardt, Michael, and Antonio Negri. 2000. *Empire*. Cambridge, Mass.: Harvard University Press.

Harrell, S. P. 1997. "The Racism and Life Experience Scales." Unpublished instrument.

Hasenbalg, Carlos Alfredo. 1979. *Discriminação e Desigualdades Raciais No Brasil*. Rio de Janeiro: Graal.

———. 1984. *Race Relations in Modern Brazil*. Albuquerque: The Latin American Institute, University of New Mexico.

———. 1986. *Race and Socioeconomic Inequalities in Brazil*. Rio de Janeiro: Instituto Universitario de Pesquisas do Rio de Janeiro.

Hasenbalg, Carlos, and Nelson do Valle Silva. 1988. *Estrutura Social, Mobilidade e Raça*. São Paulo: Vertice.

Heidegger, Martin. 1962. *Being and Time*. New York: Harper.

Heringer, Rosana. 1999. *A Cor da Desigualdade: Desigualdades Raciais no Mercado de Trabalho e Ação Afirmativa no Brasil*. Rio de Janeiro: IERE.

Herskovits, Melville J. 1941. *The Myth of the Negro Past*. Boston: Beacon Press.

Hess, David J. 1985. "Hierarchy, Heterodoxy and the Construction of Brazilian Religious Therapies." In *The Brazilian Puzzle: Culture on the Borderlands of the Western World*, ed. David J. Hess and Roberto A. DaMatta. 180–208. New York: Columbia University Press.

Hoffnagel, Judith C. 1980. "Pentecostalism: A Revolutionary or Conservative Movement?" In *Perspectives on Pentecostalism: Case Studies from the Caribbean and Latin America*, ed. Stephen D. Glazier. 111–23. Washington, D.C.: University Press of America.

Htun, Mala. 2005. "From 'Racial Democracy' to Affirmative Action: Changing State Policy on Race in Brazil." *Latin American Research Review* 39 (1): 60–89.

Hutchinson, Harry W. 1952. "Race Relations in a Rural Community in the Bahian Recôncavo." In *Race and Class in Rural Brazil*, ed. Charles Wagley. 16–46. New York: Colombia University Press.

IBGE (Instituto Brasileiro de Geographia e Estatística). 2005. Electronic database, <www.ibge.gov.br> (accessed July 29).

Ilê Aiyê. 2003. "História." <www.ileaiye.com.bt/historia.htm> (accessed October 31, 2003).

Ilé Axé Opô Afonjá. 2002. "Iansã Não É Santa Barbara." <www.geocities.com/Athens/Acropolis/1322/page4.html> (accessed February 25, 2003).

Ireland, Rowan. 1991. *Kingdoms Come: Religion and Politics in Brazil*. Pittsburgh: University of Pittsburgh Press.

James, Preston, and C. W. Minkel. 1986. *Latin America*. New York: John Wiley and Sons.

Jensen, Tina Gudrun. 1999. "Discourses on Afro-Brazilian Religion: From De-Africanization to Re-Africanization." In *Latin American Religion in Motion*, ed. Christian Smith and Joshua Prokopy. 275–94. New York: Routledge.

Johnson, Paul C. 2002. *Secrets, Gossip, and Gods: The Transformation of Brazilian Candomblé*. Oxford: Oxford University Press.

Jones, Kimberly Faith. 1995. "A Luta Continua. Afro-Brazilian Mobilization within the Context of Racial Democracy: O Movimento Negro, 1978–1994." Ph.D. dissertation, University of California, Los Angeles.

Kiddy, Elizabeth W. 1998. "Brotherhoods of Our Lady of the Rosary of the Blacks: Community and Devotion in Minas Gerais, Brazil." Ph.D. dissertation, University of New Mexico.

———. 2005. *Blacks of the Rosary: Memory and History in Minas Gerais, Brazil*. University Park: Pennsylvania State University Press.

Kokot, Waltraud, Khachig Tölölyan et al. 2004. *Diaspora, Identity, and Religion: New Directions in Theory and Research*. New York: Routledge.

Kraay, Hendrick. 1998. *Afro-Brazilian Culture and Politics: Bahia, 1790s to 1990s*. Latin American Realities. Armonk, N.Y.: M. E. Sharpe.

Laclau, Ernesto, and Chantal Mouffe. 1985. *Hegemony and Socialist Strategy: Towards a Radical Democratic Politics*. London: Verso.

Langman, Lauren, and Valerie Scatamburlo. 1996. "The Self Strikes Back: Identity Politics in the Postmodern Age." In *Alienation, Ethnicity, and Postmodernism*, ed. Felix Geyer. 127–48. Westport, Conn.: Greenwood Press.

Laraña, Enrique, Hank Johnston, and Joseph Gusfield. 1994. *New Social Movements: From Ideology to Identity*. Philadelphia: Temple University Press.

Leach, Edmund. 1954. *Political Systems of Highland Burma: A Study of Kachin Social Structure*. Cambridge, Mass.: Harvard University Press.

Lovell, Peggy, and Charles H. Wood. 1998. "Skin Color, Racial Identity, and Life Chances in Brazil." *Latin American Perspectives* 25 (3) (May): 90–109.

Maggie, Yvonne. 1992. *Medo Do Feitiço: Relações Entre Magia e Poder No Brasil*. Rio de Janeiro: Arquivo Nacional.

Manning, Frank E. 1980. "Pentecostalism: Christianity and Reputation." In *Perspectives on Pentecostalism: Case Studies From the Caribbean and Latin America*, ed. Stephen D. Glazier. Washington, D.C.: University Press of America, 177–187.

Marcus, George E., and Michael M. J. Fischer. 1986. *Anthropology as Culture Critique: An Experimental Moment in the Human Sciences*. Chicago: University of Chicago Press.

Margolies, Luise. 1980. "The Paradoxical Growth of Pentecostalism." In *Perspectives on Pentecostalism: Case Studies from the Caribbean and Latin America*, ed. Stephen D. Glazier. 1–5. Washington, D.C.: University Press of America.

Martin, David. 1991. *Tongues of Fire: The Explosion of Protestantism in Latin America*. Cambridge, Mass.: Basil Blackwell.

Marzal, Manuel M. 1993. "Transplanted Spanish Catholicism." In *South and Meso-American Native Spirituality: From the Cult of the Feathered Serpent to the Theology of Liberation*, ed. Gary H. Gossen, in collaboration with Miguel Leon-Portilla. 140–72. New York: Crossroad.

Matory, James Lorand. 2005. *Black Atlantic Religion: Tradition, Transnationalism, and Matriarchy in the Afro-Brazilian Candomblé*. Princeton, N.J.: Princeton University Press.

Mayer, Margit, and Roland Roth. 1995. "New Social Movements and the Transformation to Post Fordist Society." In *Cultural Politics and Social Movements*, ed. Marcy Darnovsky and Barbara Epstein. 299–319. Philadelphia: Temple University Press.

McCallum, Cecilia. 1996. "Resisting Brazil: Perspectives on Local Nationalisms in Salvador da Bahia." *Ethnos* 61:3–4.

McGregor, Pedro. 1966. *The Moon and Two Mountains: The Myths, Ritual and Magic of Brazilian Spiritism*. London: Souvenir Press.

Melucci, Alberto, John Keane et al. 1989. *Nomads of the Present: Social Movements and Individual Needs in Contemporary Society*. Philadelphia: Temple University Press.

MEP. 2001. *MEP: Movimento Evangélico Progressista*. Pamphlet. Salvador, Bahia: Cartilha.

Mintz, Sidney Wilfred, and Richard Price. 1992. *The Birth of African-American Culture: An Anthropological Perspective*. Boston: Beacon Press.

Moura, Clóvis. 1981. *Os Quilombos e a Rebelião Negra*. São Paulo: Brasiliense.

———. 1986. *Quilombos, Resistência Ao Escravismo*. São Paulo: Editora Atica.

Movimento Brasil: Outros 500 Resistência Indigena, Negra e Popular. 2001. "Quem Diz Mestiço, Diz Negro!" Leaflet. Salvador, Bahia.

Movimento Negro Unificado. 1988. *1978–1988: 10 Anos de Luta Contra o Racismo*. São Paulo: Confraria do Livro.

Mulvey, Patricia. 1980. "Black Brothers and Sisters: Membership in the Black Lay Brotherhoods of Colonial Brazil." *Luso-Brazilian Review* 17 (2) (Winter): 253–79.

———. 1982. "Slave Confraternities in Brazil: Their Role in Colonial Society." *The Americas* 39 (1) (July): 39–68.

Myatt, Alan Doyle. 1995. "Religion and Racial Identity in the Movimento Negro of the Roman Catholic Church in Brazil." Ph.D. dissertation, Iliff School and the University of Denver (Colorado Seminary).

Nascimento, Abias do, and Elisa Larkin Nascimento. 2001. "Dance of Deception: A Reading of Race Relations in Brazil." In *Beyond Racism: Race and Inequality in Brazil, South Africa, and the United States*, ed. Charles V. Hamilton and Lynn Huntley. 105–56. Boulder, Colo.: Lynne Rienner Publishers.

Nason, James D. 1997. "Native American Intellectual Property Rights: Issues in the Control of Esoteric Knowledge." In *Borrowed Power: Essays on Cultural Appropriation*, ed. Bruce Ziff and Pratima V. Rao. 237–54. New Brunswick, N.J.: Rutgers University Press.

Nehamas, Alexander. 1985. *Nietzsche, Life as Literature*. Cambridge, Mass.: Harvard University Press.

Nina Rodrigues, Raymundo. 1935. *O Animismo Fetichista dos Negros Bahianos*. Rio de Janeiro: Civilização Brasileira.

Nishida, Mieko. 1991. "Gender, Ethnicity, and Kinship in the Urban African Diaspora: Salvador, Brazil, 1808–1888." Ph.D. dissertation, Johns Hopkins University.

———. 2003. *Slavery and Identity: Ethnicity, Gender and Race in Salvador, Brazil, 1808–1888*. Bloomington and Indianapolis: Indiana University Press.

Nobles, Melissa. 1995. "Responding with Good Sense": The Politics of Race and Censuses in Contemporary Brazil." Ph.D. dissertation, Yale University.

Novaes, Regina, and Maria da Graca Floriano. 1985. *O Negro Evangélico*. Rio de Janeiro: Instituto de Estudos de Religião.

Olodum. 2003. Grupo Cultural Olodum. <www.uol.com.br/olodum/indexgrupocultural. htm> (accessed July 13, 2003).

Phinney, J. 1992. "The Multigroup Ethnic Identity Measure: A New Scale for Use with Adolescents and Youth Adults from Diverse Groups." *Journal of Adolescent Research* 7: 156–76.

Pieterse, Jan Nederveen. 1996. "Varieties of Ethnic Politics and Ethnicity Discourse." In *The Politics of Difference: Ethnic Premises in a World of Power*, ed. Edwin N. Wilmsen and Patrick McAllister. 25–44. Chicago: University of Chicago Press.

Portelli, Hugues. 1974. *Gramsci et la Question Religieuse*. Paris: Anthropos.

Prandi, Reginaldo. 1995. "Raça e Religião." *Novo Estudos* 42: 113–29.

———. 1999. "Referências Socias das Religiões Afro-Brasileiras: Sincretismo, Branqueamento, Africanização." In *Faces Da Tradição Afro-Brasileira: Religiosidade, Sincretismo, Anti-Sincretismo, Reafricanização, Práticas Terapêuticas, Ethnobotânica e Comida*, ed. Carlos Caroso and Jeferson Bacelar. 93–112. Salvador: Pallas.

Ramos, Arthur. 1940. *O Negro Brasileiro*. São Paulo: Companhia Editora Nacional.

———. 1942. *A Aculturação Negra Do Brasil*. São Paulo: Companhia Editora Nacional.

Read, William. 1965. *New Patterns of Church Growth in Brazil*. Grand Rapids, Mich.: William B. Eerdmans.

Reichmann, Rebecca. 1997. *Equality and Difference: Identity Politics in Brazil.* Santa Cruz: University of California at Santa Cruz, Chicano/Latino Research Center.

———. 1999a. *Brazil: Equality, Difference and Identity Politics.* Oxford: Berg.

———. 1999b. *Race in Contemporary Brazil: From Indifference to Inequality.* University Park: Pennsylvania State University Press.

Reinarman, Craig. 1995. "The Twelve-Step Movement and Advanced Capitalist Culture: The Politics of Self-Control in Postmodernity." In *Cultural Politics and Social Movements,* ed. Marcy Darnovsky and Barbara Epstein. 90–109. Philadelphia: Temple University Press.

Reis, Joao Jose. 1993. *Slave Rebellion in Brazil.* Trans. Arthur Brakel. Baltimore: Johns Hopkins University Press.

Rolim, Francisco Cartaxo. 1985. *Pentecostais No Brasil: Uma Interpretação Sócio-Religiosa.* Petrópolis: Editora Vozes Ltda.

Rorty, Richard. 1989. *Contingency, Irony, and Solidarity.* Cambridge: Cambridge University Press.

Safa, Helen. 1998. "Introduction." *Latin American Perspectives* 25(3) (May): 3–20.

Said, Edward W. 1978. *Orientalism.* New York: Pantheon Books.

Sansone, Livio. 2003. *Blackness without Ethnicity: Constructing Race in Brazil.* New York: Palgrave MacMillan.

Santos, Thereza. 1999. "My Conscience, My Struggle." In *Racial Politics in Contemporary Brazil,* ed. Michael Hanchard. 188–99. Durham, N.C.: Duke University Press.

Schwartz, Stuart B. 1985. *Sugar Plantations in the Formation of Brazilian Society: Bahia, 1550–1835.* New York: Cambridge University Press.

———. 1991. *Slaves, Peasants, and Rebels: Reconsidering Brazilian Slavery.* Chicago: University of Illinois Press.

Seidman, Steven, and Linda J. Nicholson. 1995. *Social Postmodernism: Beyond Identity Politics.* Cambridge, Mass.: Cambridge University Press.

Selka, Stephen L. 2003. "Religion and the Politics of Ethnic Identity in Bahia, Brazil." Ph.D. dissertation, University at Albany, State University of New York.

Sell, Sandro Cesar. 2002. *Ação Afirmativa e Democracia Racial: Uma Introdução ao Debate no Brasil.* Florianópolis, Brasil: Fundação Boiteux.

Sewell, William, Jr. 1999. "The Concept(s) of Culture." In *Beyond the Cultural Turn,* ed. Victoria E. Bonnel and Lynn Hunt. 35–61. Berkeley: University of California Press.

Sheriff, Robin E. 2001. *Dreaming Equality: Color, Race, and Racism in Urban Brazil.* New Brunswick, N.J.: Rutgers University Press.

Silva, Benedita da, Medea Benjamin et al. 1997. *Benedita da Silva: An Afro-Brazilian Woman's Story of Politics and Love.* Oakland, Calif.: Institute for Food and Development Policy.

Silva, Nelson do Valle. 1985. "The High Cost of Not Being White in Brazil." In *Race, Class, and Power in Brazil,* ed. Pierre-Michel Fontaine. 42–55. Los Angeles: University of California, Los Angeles, Center for Afro-American Studies.

Simpson, George E. 1978. *Black Religions in the New World.* New York: Columbia University Press.

Siss, Ahyas. 2003. *Afro-brasileiros, Cotas e Ação Afirmativa: Razões Históricas*. Rio de Janeiro: Quartet; Niterói: PENESB-UFF.

Skidmore, Thomas. 1992. *Fact and Myth: Discovering a Racial Problem in Brazil*. São Paulo: Instituto de Estudos Avancados.

———. 1993. *Black into White: Race and Nationality in Brazilian Thought*. New York: Oxford University Press.

———. 1999. *Brazil: Five Centuries of Change*. New York: Oxford University Press.

Soong, Roland. 2004. "Evangelical Christians in Brazil: Demographics, Consumerism and Politics." <www.zonalatina.com/Zldata364.htm> (accessed July 7, 2004).

Souza, Laura de Mello e. 1986. *O Diabo e a Terra de Santa Cruz: Feitiçaria e Religiosidade Popular no Brasil Colonial*. São Paulo: Companhia das Letras.

Spivak, Gayatri. 1988. *In Other Worlds: Essays in Cultural Politics*. New York: Routledge.

Stewart, Charles, and Rosalind Shaw. 1994. *Syncretism/Anti-Syncretism: The Politics of Religious Synthesis*. London: Routledge.

Stewart-Gambino, Hannah W., and Everett Wilson. 1997. "Latin American Pentecostals: Old Stereotypes and New Challenges." In *Power, Politics, and Pentecostals in Latin America*, ed. Edward L. Cleary and Hannah Stewart-Gambino. 123–38. Boulder, Colo.: Westview Press.

Stoll, David. 1990. *Is Latin America Turning Protestant? The Politics of Evangelical Growth*. Berkeley: University of California Press.

Sturgeon, Noël. 1995. "Theorizing Movements: Direct Action and Direct Theory." In *Cultural Politics and Social Movements*, ed. Marcy Darnovsky and Barbara Epstein. 35–54. Philadelphia: Temple University Press.

Swartz, David. 1997. *Culture and Power: The Sociology of Pierre Bourdieu*. Chicago: University of Chicago Press.

Tavares, Luís Henrique Dias. 2001. *História Da Bahia*. São Paulo: Editora UNESP.

Taylor, Charles, and Amy Gutmann. 1994. *Multiculturalism: Examining the Politics of Recognition*. Princeton, N.J.: Princeton University Press.

Teles dos Santos, Jocélio. 1998. "A Mixed-Race Nation: Afro-Brazilians and Cultural Policy in Bahia, 1970–1990." In *Afro-Brazilian Culture and Politics: Bahia, 1790s to 1990s*, ed. Hendrik Kraay. 117–33. Armonk, N.Y.: M. E. Sharp.

Telles, Edward. 2004. *Race in Another America: The Significance of Skin Color in Brazil*. Princeton, N.J.: Princeton University Press.

Theodoro, Helena. 1999. "Mulher Negra, Dignidade e Identidade." In *Faraimará—O Caçador Traz Alegria: Mãe Stella, 60 Anos de Iniciação*, ed. Cléo Martins and Raul Lody. 281–92. Rio de Janeiro: Pallas.

Touraine, Alain. 1988. *Return of the Actor: Social Theory in Postindustrial Society*. Minneapolis: University of Minnesota Press.

Turner, Victor W. 1974. *The Ritual Process: Structure and Anti-Structure*. Hammondsworth: Penguin Books Ltd.

Urry, John. 2005. "The Complexity Turn." *Theory, Culture and Society* 22 (5): 1–14.

Vasquez, Manuel A. 1997. *The Brazilian Popular Church and the Crisis of Modernity*. New York: Cambridge University Press.

Verger, Pierre. 1992. *Os Libertos: Sete Caminhos No Liberdade de Escracos Da Bahia no Século XIX*. São Paulo: Corrupio.

Wagley, Charles. 1963. *An Introduction to Brazil*. New York: Columbia University Press.

Weber, Max. 1968. *The Sociology of Religion*. Boston: Beacon Press.

————. 1992. *The Protestant Ethic and the Spirit of Capitalism*. London: Routledge.

West, Cornel. 1994. "The New Cultural Politics of Difference." In *The Postmodern Turn: New Perspectives on Social Theory*, ed. Steven Seidman. 65–81. Cambridge, Mass.: Cambridge University Press.

Wilmsen, Edwin N., and Patrick McAllister, eds. 1996. *The Politics of Difference: Ethnic Premises in a World of Power*. Chicago: University of Chicago Press.

Winant, Howard. 1994. "Rethinking Race in Brazil." In *Essays on Mexico, Central and South America*, ed. Jorge Domínguez. 349–68. New York: Garland Publishing.

Yúdice, George. 2003. *The Expediency of Culture: The Uses of Culture in the Global Era*. Durham, N.C.: Duke University Press.

Index

Page numbers set in italics indicate illustrations.

Absolutism, *mestiçagem* versus, 3

Açao Social Proletária (Proletarian Social Action), 27

Activism, 5, 50; Afro-Brazilian, 26–28; from Catholic Church, 32–33, 34–35, 64–65; from CEBs, 33–34; culture and, 27–28

Affiliation, 106, 118

Affirmative action, 128, 154–55n1

Afoxés, 87

Africa, 4–5, 17–18, 86, *86. See also* Afro-Brazilians; Candomblé; Identity, Afro-Brazilian; Re-Africanization; Tradition; Yoruba

Afro-Brazilians, 10, 37, 148; activism of, 26–28; appropriation and, 137–38, 139; "consensus culture" for, 140; multiplicity for, 149. *See also* Identity, Afro-Brazilian; Religion(s); Tradition

Agentes de Pastoral Negro (APNs), 60

Agriculture, 48

Alberto, Luiz, 90

America, 4. *See also* United States

American Dream, 155n3

Anastácia, Escrava, 51, 52–53, *53,* 54

Anthropology, 5–6; conflict in, 155n4; on identity's multiplicity, 149–50; practice theory in, 6–7; on racism, 22–23, 104–5; on religion, 22–23

Antiracism, 1–2, 35; Candomblé as, 12–13, 41; from evangelicals, 151; post WWII, 12; Protestants and, 117, 154n2. See also *Festa*

Anti-syncretism, 79, 80; Iyalorixás versus, 77–78; practices and, 81, 154n2; re-Africanization and, 41, 74, 78

APNs. *See* Agentes de Pastoral Negro

Appiah, Anthony, 140–41, 144

Appropriation: of Afro-Brazilians' traditions, 137–38, 139; of Candomblé, 130; of Catholicism, 133; cultural, 40–41. *See also* Tourism

Apter, Andrew, 133

Asad, Talal, 15, 123

Atabaques (Afro-Brazilian hand drums), 37

Attacks, on *terreiros,* 1, 82, 112

Awareness, 90, 143–44

Bahia, 9–10, 116–17; agriculture in, 48; antiracism in, 1–2, 35; black consciousness in, 28–29; Candomblé's development in, 21; fieldwork in, 5–6, 104–5; identity in, 28–29, 75, *75,* 97–98; industrialization in, 48, 153n1; racialization in, 129–34; religions in, 28–29, 75, *75;* signifying practices in, 133. *See also* Tourism

Baptist Church, 108, 109

Baptist Church of the Ministry of Liberation, 114–16

Barracão, 37

Barracas (stalls), 55

Base ecclesial communities (CEBs): activism from, 33–34; gender in, 34; Pentecostalism and, 34

Bastide, Roger, 20, 23, 46

Bauman, Zygmunt, 144

Black Consciousness Day, 93–95

Black identity: essentialism and, 145, 146; festivals for, 93–95; for MEP, 112–13; *mestiçagem* and, 120–21

Black movement, 3, 30–31, 76, 148; classification in, 13, 132–33; emancipatory/life politics
in, 135–36; essentialism in, 145; evangelical
Christianity and, 117–19; identity for, 13,
134–35, 137, 146–47, 149; MNU for, 58–59;
mobilization for, 137; Pentecostalism versus,
46–47; solidarity within, 145. *See also* Agentes
de Pastoral Negro; *Blocos afros*; Centro Ar-
quidiocesano de Articulação da Pastoral Afro;
Festa; Grupo de União e Consciencia Negra;
King, Martin Luther, Jr.; Pastoral Afro
Black Soul, 30
Blocos afros, 87
Boa Morte, 5
Bourdieu, Pierre, 15, 128, 130, 131, 132
Brasil Para Cristo, 42
Brazil: antiracism in, 12; churches in, 26; race re-
lations in, 4; as "racial democracy," 16, 29–30,
147; racism in, 9, 29, 153n3; religion in, 2, 9,
26. *See also* Bahia; Cachoeira; Pelourinho;
Recôncavo; Salvador; São Paulo
Bruneau, Thomas, 16–17, 19
Burdick, John, 33, 35–36, 46–47, 124, 151
Butler, Judith, 125, 144
Butler, Kim, 18, 50

CAAPA. *See* Centro Arquidiocesano de Articulação da Pastoral Afro
Caboclos, 37
Cachoeira, 5, 10, *10*
Câmara, Hélder, 32
Candomblé, 2, 10, 22, 33–35, 92, 105; Afro-
Brazilian identity and, 111–12; as antiracism,
12–13, 41; appropriation of, 130; Black Consciousness Day and, 95; for black movement,
76; Catholicism and, 20–21, 40–41, 54–55, 57,
59–60, 68, 71–72, 78, 153–54n2; color in, 98,
131; consultations in, 39–40; folklorization of,
75–76, 77–78, 137–38; initiation in, 36, 39, *39,*
123–24; "nâgocentrism" in, 17–18, 153n1; openness of, 74, *75,* 75–76, 130; racial consciousness and, 145; racism and, 1, 22, 131; religions'
similarities with, 21; as religious syncretism,
40–41; repression of, 22; as resistance, 120; as
tourism, 74, 77, 78; women in, 20. *See also*
Communities: Candomblé; Felício, Gílio;
Obrigações

Candomblecistas, 70–72
Capoeira (Afro-Brazilian martial art), 10
Carnaval, 86, *86,* 87–88
Carneiro, Edison, 23
Catedral da Fé (Cathedral of Faith), 100, 101, *101*
Category, racial: mulatto as, 14. *See also* Clas-
sification
Catholic Action, class and, 32–33
Catholic Center for Social Study and Action
(CEAS), 64–65
Catholic Church, 19–20; activism from,
32–33, 34–35, 64–65; against African-derived
religions, 35; color in, 33–34, 55, 71, 78, 131;
against Protestantism, 23–24; racism and,
34–35, 65; tolerance of, 129–30
Catholicism, 11, 16, 17, 19; appropriation of, 133;
Candomblé and, 20–21, 40–41, 54–55, 57,
59–60, 68, 71–72, 78, 153–54n2; culture and,
62–64
CEAS. *See* Catholic Center for Social Study and
Action
CEBs. *See* Base ecclesial communities
Centro Arquidiocesano de Articulação da Pastoral Afro (Archdiocesan Coordinating Center
for the African Pastoral) (CAAPA), 34–35,
50–51, 60–61; and Afro-Brazilian identity,
62–64, 65, 66–70; and education, 66–67; and
self-esteem, 66–67, 68–70. *See also* Pastoral
Afro
Chesnut, R. Andrew, 47
Christianity, evangelical, 117–19; Afro-Brazilian
identity and, 108–10; mobilization within,
137; politics and, 108–10. *See also* Pentecostalism
Churches, 112, 114–16; in Brazil, 26; *obreiros*
in, 102; in Salvador, 49–50. *See also* Baptist
Church; Catedral da Fe; Catholic Church;
Igreja Universal Reina de Deus; Irmandade
da Nossa Senhora do Rosário dos Pretos do
Pelourinho; *Terreiros*
Class: Catholic Action and, 32–33; Catholic
Church and, 71; Catholicism and, 17, 19;
color and, 81, 154n2; mestiços and, 94; mobilization and, 145–46; NSMs and, 142; politics
and, 147, 155n3; Protestantism and, 24; racism
and, 29, 31
Classification, 13, 14, 132–33

Climbié, Victoria, 102
Clóvis, Padre, 64–66, 148
CN. *See* Consciência Negra
CNBB. *See* National Council of Brazilian
   Bishops
Coherence, 150–51
Color, 49, 69–70, 128, 146; in Candomblé, 98,
   131; in Catholic Church, 33–34, 55, 71, 78,
   131; class and, 81, 154n2; consciousness, 145;
   evangelicals and, 99; at inculturated Masses,
   55; *morena clara* as, 102; in Protestantism, 46;
   in race, 13–14; in racism, 143; of saints, 51, 53,
   53. See also *Embranquecimento*; *Indio*; *Negro*
Comaroff, Jean, 132–33
Comaroff, John, 129
Communities: Candomblé, 73–74; religious,
   123, 125–26. *See also* Base ecclesial communi-
   ties
Conflict: for anthropologists, 155n4; social, 132
Confraternities. See *Irmandades*
Consciência (black awareness), 90
Consciência Negra (CN). *See* Grupo de União e
   Consciencia Negra
Consciousness: black, 28–29, 30–31, 60, 67–68,
   90, 93–95; color, 145; racial, 145
Conservativism, 118
Consultations, in Candomblé, 39–40
Control (social), confraternities for, 18
Controversy, 13, 73–74; of religious syncretism,
   23, 153n2; over spirits, 100
Costa, Creuza, 107, 109, 110–12, 114
Covin, David, 138
Csordas, Thomas, 125
Culto de liberataço (worship for liberation), 100
Culturalism, 139
Culture, 61, 62–64, 77, 150; activism and, 27–28;
   in Afro-Brazilian identity, 4, 122, 140, 148;
   appropriation and, 40–41; "consensus," 140;
   politics versus, 95–96; as resource, 139–40;
   struggle in, 155n4. *See also* Exploitation,
   cultural; *Festa*; Religion(s)

Da Cunha, Euclides, 19
D'Adesky, Jacques, 145
Da Silva, Elizete, 45, 107, 108, 110, 112–13
De Certeau, Michel, 133
Degler, Carl, 29

Democracy: movements versus, 147–48, 49;
   racial, 16, 29–30, 147
Democratic Socialists (PDT), 91–92
Demographics, in Pentecostalism, 44–45
Descent, African, 4–5. *See also* Afro-Brazilians
Diaspora, identity versus, 149–50, 151
Diety, omniscient, 125–26
Discrimination, racial, 128, 154–55n1
Diversity, within black movement, 148
Durkheim, Emile, 122–23

Ecumenism, 65
Education, 28, 116–17; black movement and,
   146; CAAPA for, 66–67
Ekédis, 37
Embranquecimento (whitening), 69–70
Empowerment, 126
Encontro de Pastoral Afro-Americana (EPA), 68
EPA. *See* Encontro de Pastoral Afro-Americana
Essentialism, 143–44, 145, 146
Ethnicity: color and, 128; *índio* as, 114; and
   marginality, 127–28; race and, 126–29; religion
   and, 126–29. *See also* Color; Identity; *Nações*;
   Slavery; Whitening
Evangelicals: antiracism from, 151; color and, 99;
   conservativism of, 118; contemporary, 42–47;
   introspection for, 124; progressiveness of,
   118–19; racism and, 117–19. *See also* Christian-
   ity, evangelical
Exorcism, 102–3
Exploitation, cultural, 138–39

Farra, Robert, 25
Fazendas (plantations), 48
Felício, Gílio, 62–64
Ferdinando, Padre, 67–70
Fernandes, Florestan, 28
Festa (feast/festival), 5, 39, 40, 89–90, 94–95; for
   orixás, 37, 38, *38*; and politics, 92–93; posses-
   sion at, 37, 38; in Salvador, 86–90
Fidele, Padre, 66–67
Fields, as social spaces, 130
Filhos de Gandhy Carnival Association, 89–90
Filhos de santo (initiates), 36, 37, 38–39
FNB. *See* Frente Negra Brasileira
Folklorization, of Candomblé, 75–76, 77–78,
   137–38

Fotopoulos, Takis, 136–37
Foucault, Michel, 15, 123
Francison, Louis, 25
Frase, Ronald, 24–25
French, John D., 128
Frente Negra Brasileira (FNB), 27
Freyre, Gilberto, 15–16

Gender: in CEBs, 34; ITEBA and, 116–17. *See also* Women
Giddens, Anthony, 134–36, 144
Gilroy, Paul, 149, 151
Globalization, 135
Gods, 114, 115, 125–26; *orixás* as, 17–18, 71, 72, 75, 75. See also *Orixás*; Spirits
Government, military, 43, 88–89
"Governmentality": "pastorship" as, 124–25
Graça, 79–81
Gramsci, Antonio, 15, 139
Gramscian dilemma, 139
GRUCON. *See* Grupo de União e Consciencia Negra
Grupo de União e Consciencia Negra (Black Unity and Consciousness Group) (GRU-CON), 60, 67–68

Hanchard, Michael, 128, 139
Harding, Rachel E., 21, 22
Hasenbalg, Carlos Alfredo, 28–29
Healing: demystification of, 115–16; IURD for, 101–2; *terreiro* for, 81
Hess, David, 32

Identity, 120–21, 129, 135, 141; -based groups, 142–43; black, 93–95, 98, 112–13, 145, 146; coherence and, 150–51; diaspora versus, 149–50, 151; essentialism and, 144, 145, 146; ethnic, 18–19, 21–22, 119, 127–29; initiation and, 126; *irmandades* for, 64; within MEP, 142; mobilization and, 134, 151; movements, 136–37; multiplicity of, 149–50; *nações* and, 17–18; national, 2; politics and, 6–8, 135, 143, 144, 155n2; power and, 126–27; religion and, 14–15, 110–12, 121–26; social, 6–8; social mobilization and, 134. *See also* Bahia; Black identity; Black movement; Identity, Afro-Brazilian

Identity, Afro-Brazilian, 2–3, 18–19, 93–95, 120–21; in Bahia, 28–29, 75, 75, 97–98; CAA-PA for, 62–64, 65, 66–70; Candomblé and, 111–12; CENPAH for, 68–70; culture and, 4, 122, 140, 148; fieldwork on, 5–6; hybridity and, 7–8; Pentecostalism for, 25; religion and, 14–15, 110–12; tourism and, 129
Igreja Universal Reina de Deus (IURD) (Universal Church of the Kingdom of God), 45, 99, 101, 112; healing from, 101–2; intolerance from, 82, 83, 105; media for, 99–100, 101; money and, 103–4
Ilê Aiyê, 88–89
Imperialism, 128–29
Inculturation, of Masses, 54–55
Índio (native Brazilian), 114
Industrialization, 48, 153n1
Initiation: in Candomblé, 36, 39, 39, 74, 123–24; *filhos de santo* for, 36, 37, 38; for identity, 126
Intolerance, religious, 81–85, 105, 112
Introspection, 124
Irmandade da Nossa Senhora do Rosário dos Pretos do Pelourinho (Confraternity of Our Lady of the Rosary of the Blacks of Pelourinho), 50–51, 52, 52–53, 53, 54, 57–60
Irmandades (religious confraternities), 17–18, 64. *See also* Irmandade da Nossa Senhora do Rosário dos Pretos do Pelourinho
ITEBA. *See* O Instituto de Educação Teólogico da Bahia
IURD. *See* Igreja Universal Reina de Deus
Ivonei, 90–93
Iyalorixás, anti-syncretism versus, 77–78

Jeito (way of being or doing), 62–63
Jesus, 114, 115
Jogo de búzios, 39
Johnson, Paul, 131

King, Martin Luther, Jr., 47, 107, 108, 113

Langman, Lauren, 144
Lavegem do Bonfim, 92–93
Liberation, 114; theology, 116–17
Life politics, 135–36

Macro-ecumenism, 65
Mãi/pai de santo, 36
Marginality: and ethnicity, 127–28; and identity, 129; of practices, 81, 154n2
Marx, Karl, 15
Mass, inculturated, 54–57
Matory, J. Lorand, 2
Media, 99–100, 101
MEIM. *See* Multigroup Ethnic Identity Measure
MEP. *See* Movimento Evangélico Progressista
Merskovits, Melville, 23
Mestiçagem (hybridity): absolutism versus, 3; black identity and, 120–21; racism within, 7–8. *See also* Mestiços
Mestiços, 19, 94
Migration, urban, 43
MNU. *See* Movimento Negro Unificado
Mobilization, 145–46; for black movement, 137; identities for, 134, 151; social, 134, 140–43
Money, 103–4
Morena clara (light brown), 102
Movement(s), 26–28, 30–31, 84; democracy versus, 147–48, 148–49; identity, 136–37; NSMs as, 141–43; social, 144. *See also* Black movement; Movement Against Religious Intolerance; Movimento Evangélico Progressista; Movimento Negro Unificado
Movement Against Religious Intolerance, 84
Movimento Evangélico Progressista (MEP), 47, 106, 142; Afro-Brazilian identity in, 110–12; black identity for, 112–13; politics and, 106–10; racism and, 106–8; tolerance within, 111–12
Movimento Negro Unificado (MNU), 30–31, 58–59; politics for, 90–92, 136
Mulatto, 14
Multigroup Ethnic Identity Measure (MEIM), 6
Music, 55

Nações (nations/ethnic groups), 17–18
"Nâgocentrism," 17–18, 153n1
National Council of Brazilian Bishops (CNBB), 32, 65
Negro, 60, 128. *See also* Movimento Negro Unificado; Teatro Experimental do Negro
New social movements (NSMs), 141–43

NGOs. *See* Nongovernmental organizations
Nicholson, Linda, 144
Nishida, Mieko, 18
Nongovernmental organizations (NGOs), 44, 140
North America. *See* United States
Nossa Senhora do Rosário. *See* Irmandade da Nossa Senhora do Rosário dos Pretos do Pelourinho
November 20th, 93–95
NSMs. *See* New social movements

Obreiros (church assistants), 102
Obrigações (ritual obligations), 36–37
Ogã, 37
O Instituto de Educação Teólogico da Bahia (ITEBA), 116–17
Olodum, 88, 138
Opô Afonjá, 78, 79–80
Orixás (santos), 41, 45, 56–57, 77; festas for, 37, 38, *38;* as gods, 17–18, 71, 72, 75, *75;* and initiation, 36; Jesus versus, 73; saints and, 71, 72, 78, 79
Os Sertões ("Rebellion in the Backlands") (Da Cunha), 19
Oxum, as orixá, 38, *38*

Padê (offering), 37–38
Padre Heitor Pastoral Afro Center (CENPAH), 66–70
Palmares, 11
Partido da Frente Liberal (PFL), 118
Partido dos Trabalhadores (Workers' Party) (PT), 90, 106, 154n1
Pastoral Afro, 60–61, 62, 63, 64, 65, 70–72, 80
"Pastorship," as "governmentality," 124–25
PDT. *See* Democratic Socialists
Pelourinho, 49, 95. *See also* Tourism
Pentecostalism, 2, 33–34, 42, 43; and Afro-Brazilian identity, 25; black movement versus, 46–47; demographics in, 44–45; growth of, 11–12, 24–26, 43–44; racism in, 46, 47; from "theology of prosperity," 45; women in, 34. *See also* Movimento Evangélico Progressista
PFL. *See* Partido da Frente Liberal

Politics, 88–89, 90–93, 106–7, 118, 136, 138; affiliation in, 118; Afro-Brazilian movement for, 26–28; Baptist Church and, 108, 109; class and, 147, 155n3; culture versus, 95–96; emancipatory versus life, 135–36; ethnic, 127–29; evangelical Christianity and, 108–10; festas for, 92–93; identity and, 6–8, 135, 143, 144, 155n2; intolerance and, 84–85; liberation as, 114; life, 135–36; movements versus, 147–48; Pentecostalism in, 44; postmodern, 136; racial, 95–96; on racial discrimination, 128, 154–55n1; racism and, 26–28; of recognition, 141–42; religion in, 114–16; *terreiros* and, 76, 78, 154n1; in United States, 155n3. *See also* Carnaval; *Festa*
Possession, 37, 38
Power: appropriation as, 138; identity and, 126–27; pastoral, 125; relations, 139; among religions' groups, 129, 131; in religious communities, 123
Practice(s): anti-syncretism and, 81, 154n2; religious, 122–26; signifying, 132–33; theory, 6–7
Progressiveness, 118–19
Promessas, 103
Protestantism, 25–26, 42, 43–44; antiracism and, 117, 154n2; black identity within, 113; Catholic Church against, 23–24; Catholicism versus, 16; and class, 24; color in, 46; North American, 113; reforms from, 24
PT. *See* Partido dos Trabalhadores
Purity, of practices, 81, 154n2

Quilombos (communities of escaped slaves), 11, 94

Race: in America, 4; color in, 13–14; ethnicity and, 126–29; religion and, 126–29; in religions, 31–35
"Racial democracy," Brazil as, 16, 29–30, 147
Racialization, of religion, 129–34
Racism, 6, 7–8, 91, 94; anthropology on, 22–23, 104–5; in Brazil, 9, 29, 153n3; Candomblé and, 1, 22, 131; Catholic Church and, 34–35, 65; class and, 29, 31; color in, 143; evangelicals and, 117–19; within hybridity, 7–8; imperialism and, 128–29; MEP and, 106–8; mobilization against, 137; in Pentecostalism, 46, 47; politics and, 26–28; religious intolerance and,

82–85; in United States, 29. *See also* Antiracism; Attacks; Centro Arquidiocesano de Articulação da Pastoral Afro; Discrimination, racial; Identity, Afro-Brazilian; Intolerance, religious; Reparations
Racism and Life Experience Scales (RaLES), 6
RaLES. *See* Racism and Life Experience Scales
Ramos, Arthur, 23
Re-Africanization, as anti-syncretism, 41, 74, 78
Recôncavo, 10
Reforms, 24
Reichmann, Rebecca, 137
Religion(s), 20–21, 35, 40–41, 145; anthropology on, 22–23; in Bahia, 28–29, 75, *75*; in Brazil, 2, 9, 26; Candomblé's similarities with, 21; competition between, 130–31; ethnicity and, 126–29; identity and, 14–15, 110–12, 121–26; politics in, 114–16; power among, 129, 131; race and, 31–35, 126–29; racialization of, 129–34; racial politics and, 95–96; resistance and, 11, 153n2; in Salvador, 49–50. *See also* Candomblé; *Irmandades*; Mass, inculturated; *Orixás*; Santa Bárbara
Reparations, 94
Repression, 22, 32
Resistance, 11, 120, 143, 153n2
Resources: culture as, 139–40; money as, 103–4; scarcity of, 147
Rhythm of the Saints, 88
Rodrigues, Nina, 23

Saints, 55–56, 88; color of, 51, 53, *53*; *orixás* and, 71, 72, 78, 79
Salt, magic, 103
Salvador, 10, *10,* 73, 86–90; Black Consciousness Day for, 93–95; development of, 48–49; religions in, 49–50. See also *Festa*
Sansone, Livio, 138–39, 145, 146
Santa Bárbara, 55–56
São Paulo, 50
Scatamburlo, Valerie, 144
Second Vatican Council, 32–33
Second World Conference of the Traditions of the Orixás and Culture, 77
Seidman, Steven, 144
Self, transformation of, 123–24
Self-esteem, 66–67, 68–70

Self-representation, 148

Sertão (arid backlands), 114

Sewell, William, 150

Sisterhood of Our Lady of Good Death (Boa
Morte), 5

Slavery, 11, 15–16, 51, 94; Catholicism and, 16,
133; ethnic identity from, 18–19; irmandades
within, 17–18

Social movement, 27, 134, 140–43, 144; CEAS as,
64–65; PDT as, 91–92. See also Black movement; Irmandades

Solidarity, black, 145

South Africa, 12

Spirits, 100, 102–3, 126

Stella, Mãe, 76, 77, 78, 79, 80

Subjection, as empowerment, 126

Surveillance, 125–26

Syncretism, religious, 19, 57–58, 71, 72;
Candomblé as, 40–41; controversy of, 23,
153–54n2; practices' purity in, 81, 154n2;
re-Africanization versus, 74. See also Anti-
syncretism

Taylor, Charles, 141–42

Teatro Experimental do Negro (TEN), 27–28

Telles, Edward, 31

TEN. See Teatro Experimental do Negro

Terreiros (temples), 36–40, 73, 74; attacks on, 1,
82, 112; for healing, 81; obrigações for, 36–37;
politics and, 76, 78, 154n1. See also Churches;
Opô Afonjá

"Theology of prosperity," 42, 45

Tolerance, 111–12, 129–30. See also Intolerance,
religious

Toque (feast/festival), 37, 38, 38, 39

Tourism, 49; Candomblé as, 74, 77, 78; cultural,
97–98, 119; racial identity for, 129

Tradition, 74, 77, 137–38, 139

Transformation of Self, 123–24

Umbandistas, 41

UNESCO (United Nations Educational, Scientific and Cultural Organization), 28

United States, 12, 29, 113, 119, 155n3

Universal Church of the Kingdom of God. See
Igreja Universal Reina de Deus

Vargas, Getúlio, 19–20, 32

Verger, Pierre, 46

Wacquant, J.L.D., 128

Weber, Max, 15, 131

West, Cornel, 143

Whitening, 69–70

Wilmsen, Edwin, 127–28

Women, 20, 34; Da Silva as, 45, 107, 108, 110,
112–13; as ekédis, 37; Filhos de Gandhy and,
89–90; Stella as, 76, 77, 78, 79, 80; at toque,
38, 38. See also Graça; Iyalorixás

Yoruba, 17–18, 79, 153n1

Yúdice, George, 139–40

Stephen L. Selka is assistant professor of African American and African Diaspora Studies and American Studies at Indiana University. He is a contributor to *Journal of Latin American and Caribbean Anthropology*, *Latin American Perspectives*, and *Novio Religio*.

3 5282 00664 1586